PRETTY / FUNNY

Requests for permission to reproduce material from this work should be
sent to:
    Permissions
    University of Texas Press
    P.O. Box 7819
    Austin, TX 78713-7819
    http://utpress.utexas.edu/index.php/rp-form

 ∞ The paper used in this book meets the minimum requirements of
ANSI/NISO Z39.48-1992 (R1997) (Permanence of Paper).

LIBRARY OF CONGRESS CATALOGING-IN-PUBLICATION DATA
Mizejewski, Linda.
Pretty/funny : women comedians and body politics /
by Linda Mizejewski. — First edition.
        p.   cm.
Includes bibliographical references and index.
ISBN 978-0-292-75691-5 (cloth : alk. paper)
ISBN 978-1-4773-0760-1 (paperback)
1. Women comedians—United States.   2. Feminine beauty
(Aesthetics)—United States.   3. Racism—United States.   I. Title.
PN1590.W64M59   2014
792.702′8092—dc23

                                                    2013030223

doi:10.7560/756915

PRETTY / FUNNY

Women Comedians and Body Politics

BY LINDA MIZEJEWSKI

University of Texas Press ❧ Austin

For my parents,
EDWARD MIZEJEWSKI, 1910–2002,
AND ANN MIZEJEWSKI, 1914–2010

Contents

Acknowledgments

M ANY PEOPLE HELPED ME WITH *PRETTY/FUNNY* AND also made it a lot of fun to think about and write. Robyn Warhol and Kimberly Springer offered insightful readings of individual chapters and gave me excellent advice about revisions. Ann Kibbey and the anonymous reader at *Genders* made suggestions that much improved the Tina Fey essay that became a chapter in this book. I am particularly grateful to Kathleen Rowe Karlyn and Joanna Rapf, the reviewers assigned by the University of Texas Press, who put a great deal of time into careful and detailed recommendations that shaped the final version of the manuscript. Their input was simply invaluable. Jim Burr at UT Press was an ideal editor, enthusiastic and helpful from the start. In the final stages of this project, manuscript editor Lynne Chapman at UT Press and freelance editor Tana Silva were a joy to work with. I also appreciate the many enlightening discussions that I enjoyed with my Women's, Gender, and Sexuality Studies 620 seminar on women's comedy at Ohio State. My thanks also to Debra Moddelmog, Judith Mayne, Martha Nochimson, and Victoria Sturtevant for lively discussions on this topic and for friendship and support through the whole process.

In a wider sense, I am grateful for the inspiring scholarship on women and comedy by Lucy Fischer and Kathleen Rowe Karlyn, whose work had me thinking about this topic for many years. I felt I was in dialogue with Kathleen's "unruly woman" argument the entire time I was writing, and this was an immensely stimulating conversation.

I was able to write this book in a timely manner because of generous scheduling opportunities provided by Jill Bystydzienski, chair of Women's, Gender, and Sexuality Studies at Ohio State. Also, the College of Arts and Sciences there provided a Research Enhancement Grant for materials, research funds to cover illustrations, and a sabbatical that allowed me to focus on this project in its early stages.

Segments of Chapter Two appeared as "Feminism, Postfeminism, Liz Lemonism: Comedy and Gender Politics on 30 *Rock*" in *Genders* 55 (2012).

This book was most of all possible because of the patience and love of George Bauman, who made me laugh and fed the cats when I forgot. And I am grateful always for the raucous laughter of my brothers and sisters— Edward Vargas, Jer Mizejewski, Marian Pokrywka, and Patty Komar. We are lucky to have inherited our father's sense of humor and our mother's insistence on getting things finished; this book is dedicated to the memory of both of them.

PRETTY / FUNNY

Pretty/Funny Women and Comedy's Body Politics

FUNNINESS, PRETTINESS, AND FEMINISM

IN 2007, EMINENT JOURNALIST CHRISTOPHER HITCHENS published a widely circulated *Vanity Fair* essay called "Why Women Aren't Funny," making the provocative argument that humor is more natural, pervasive, and highly developed in men than in women. Women don't need to be funny, he claimed. It's not a trait men find attractive in women, while funniness is a trait women value in men. Funniness for Hitchens is like height or good teeth—advantages for natural selection. There are very funny women comedians, he conceded, but they tend to be "hefty or dykey or Jewish, or some combo of the three." He explained this remark by claiming that lesbian and Jewish humor, as well as the humor of large-bodied comics like Roseanne Barr, is "masculine" and thus does not actually fall into the category of women's comedy. But given his theory of attractiveness and natural selection, it is clear that he is drawing on the stereotypes of large/Jewish/lesbian women as unappealing to men.

The essay provoked the feminist outrage Hitchens no doubt intended, but the gist of his argument—that women are rewarded for what they look like and not for what they say—is one of feminism's most basic cultural critiques. Because of this bias, "pretty" versus "funny" is a rough but fairly accurate way to sum up the history of women in comedy. Attractive actors with good comic timing, from Claudette Colbert and Lucille Ball to Meg Ryan and Debra Messing, have had plum roles as the heroines of romantic comedies and sitcoms. These women weren't known for their own wit but for their performances of witty comic scripts. Most of all, they had to be pretty. In contrast, women who write and perform their own comedy have been far fewer as mainstream figures in modern popular culture, and most often they've gotten far because they were willing to be funny-looking: Fanny Brice, Phyllis Diller, Carol Burnett, Lily Tomlin. Or, like

Mae West, they were willing to camp up or otherwise make fun of traditional femininity. Stand-up comedy, meanwhile, which developed into the premier venue for comedians, was where the bad boys played—Lenny Bruce, George Carlin, Richard Pryor—and they didn't have to be pretty. As late as 2005, a *New Yorker* essay opined that "comedy is probably the last remaining branch of the arts whose suitability for women is still openly discussed" (Goodyear).

However, by 2005 comedy's "suitability for women" was a pertinent question because women were increasingly visible in the comedy scene—in clubs and comedy troupes like Second City but also on network and cable television. Women stand-up comics like Sarah Silverman, the topic of the *New Yorker* profile, were taking on the foul language, political incorrectness, and gross-out humor that had once been a boys-only zone—hence the issue of suitability. These women were expanding into other terrains as well. In 1999 Tina Fey became the first woman head writer on *Saturday Night Live* (1975–), which soon featured a number of talented women whose careers took off over the next decade—Amy Poehler, Maya Rudolph, Molly Shannon, Rachel Dratch. A 2003 *New York Times* article about this promising group was titled "It's the Revenge of the Ignorant Sluts," referring to an *SNL* skit from the 1970s, an era described by female cast members as singularly unfriendly to women comics and writers. The show may have been groundbreaking, but they complained it was also "a stinky boy's club" (Nussbaum).

In fact, a number of women comics who became mainstream stars between 2000 and 2010 were gritty survivors of similar "stinky" television experiences in the 1990s. Margaret Cho and Ellen DeGeneres made dramatic comebacks after failed network sitcoms in the previous decade. Kathy Griffin, declining the fate of the eternal sitcom sidekick, turned the tables by transforming the sidekick into the cranky D-list would-be star. Fey, meanwhile, skirted the dreaded sitcom wife/girlfriend roles by creating *30 Rock* (2006–2013), a metacomedy about mainstream television; and Silverman, her comedy famously unfit for network TV, was able to launch her own R-rated sitcom on cable, *The Sarah Silverman Program* (2007–2010). By the time Hitchens published his essay in 2007, Emmy awards had been picked up by *30 Rock*, *Kathy Griffin: My Life on the D List* (2005–2010), and the daytime talk show *The Ellen DeGeneres Show* (2003–); the roster of popular women comics included, in addition to the ones mentioned above, Wanda Sykes, Amy Sedaris, Mo'Nique (Imes), Kristen Wiig, Janeane Garofalo, Susie Essman, Lisa Lampanelli, Chelsea Handler, Sheryl Underwood, Joy Behar, Rita Rudner, and Cheryl Hines.

Citing this extensive history, *Vanity Fair* published a response to Hitchens the following year with a lushly illustrated cover story by Alessandra Stanley: "Who Says Women Aren't Funny? For the Defense: Sarah Silverman, Tina Fey, Amy Poehler, and Nine Other Queens of Comedy." Countering Hitchens's assertion that funny women aren't attractive, campy Annie Leibovitz photos pictured Fey, Poehler, Silverman, and the others as tarted-up vamps lounging in limousines, plunging necklines, and dimly lit hotel rooms. Stanley's essay refuted Hitchens's argument, but it also developed a feminist argument that for women comics, the issue of looks has always been crucial. Recently, as more women comics have entered a previously "masculine" field, she points out, a sexist dynamic has kicked in: because U.S. culture remains obsessed with image and looks, the better-looking comics have an advantage. "It used to be that women were not funny," she writes. "Then they couldn't be funny if they were pretty. Now a female comedian has to be pretty—even sexy—to get a laugh" (185). The latter part of this quotation refers to the booming careers of Chelsea Handler, Olivia Munn, and Whitney Cummings, for example, gorgeous women whose sex appeal is intrinsic to their commercial appeal as comics.

However, the dynamic of pretty versus funny, the default description of how women are usually perceived in the history of comedy, is richer and more nuanced than the Stanley summary suggests. In fact, notions of "pretty" are often what women's comedy exploits as funny. Mae West made an entire career of camping up all notions of femininity. The pseudo-fabulous Leibovitz photos in *Vanity Fair* exemplify the same point, parodying edgy clichés of femininity from the femme fatale to the scandalous female celebrity à la Paris Hilton. A similar comic strategy is evident in the cover photograph of Tina Fey's best-selling book *Bossypants* (2011), a collection of personal essays about show business and motherhood. The book's title as well as the photo refer to Fey's well-known position as "boss," first as *SNL*'s head writer and later as the creator, writer, producer, and star of *30 Rock*.

The medium-close-up photo spoofs the traditional author glamour shot. Fey poses serenely, wearing tasteful makeup and lipstick, her hair arranged in loose waves down to her shoulders, but her head sits on a male torso wearing a white dress shirt and a tie. More than that, the sleeves are rolled up to reveal huge, hairy, male forearms and hands—an unnerving way to picture the woman who "wears the pants" as secretly, monstrously male. More subtly, given Fey's reputation as a feminist, the photo alludes to and satirizes the popular T-shirt claiming "THIS IS WHAT A FEMINIST LOOKS LIKE." The photo is also a parody of Fey's magazine cover-girl images that have relentlessly emphasized her attractiveness, an ironic twist on her celebrity, given that she became famous for what she says rather than

Given Tina Fey's reputation as a feminist, the cover photo of her 2011 book, Bossypants, is a comic take on the T-shirt slogan "This is what a feminist looks like."

what she looks like. For both the Fey photo and the Leibovitz shoot, the joke turns on the high stakes of what these women look like—and that's a joke specific to the genre of women comics because funny-looking male comedians have never been an issue or problem. The pretty versus funny cliché about women comedians is so commonplace that Steve Martin used it in a joke introducing Fey as the winner of the 2010 Mark Twain Prize for American Humor. Spoofing her cover-girl status, he said, "Isn't it refreshing to find a female comic who's both really good and funny-looking? Excuse me—that should have read, 'Really funny and good-looking.'"

The major premise of *Pretty/Funny* is that in the historic binary of "pretty" versus "funny," women comics, no matter what they look like, have been located in opposition to "pretty," enabling them to engage in a transgressive comedy grounded in the female body—its looks, its race and sexuality, and its relationships to ideal versions of femininity. In this strand of comedy, "pretty" is the topic and target, the ideal that is exposed as funny. And although the pretty/funny tension is a way to characterize the comedy of a number of women past and present, I am particularly interested in a group of high-profile comics who emerged into mainstream stardom or made dramatic comebacks between 2000 and 2010, the decade when liberal political comedy also came into the foreground of a bitterly divided American politics. My topics in this book are Kathy Griffin, Tina Fey, Sarah Silverman, Margaret Cho, Wanda Sykes, and Ellen DeGeneres, comics who draw on the pretty/funny binary by targeting glamour, post-feminist girliness, the Hollywood A list, feminine whiteness, and romanticized motherhood as fodder for wit and biting satire. Except for Fey, who was trained in improvisation and usually performs as a fictional character, these women are stand-up comics who have also starred or co-starred in television sitcoms and occasionally in films, though my emphasis in the following chapters is on the work they wrote themselves in the first decade of the twenty-first century.

These women are successful performers, but they are most of all writers of their own material. They are comic auteurs whose work cuts across multiple media—television, film, theater, and books, including witty autobiographies by Griffin, Silverman, and Cho and collections of anecdotes and jokes by Sykes and DeGeneres. So while most of their writing is performed as scripts, some of it is also widely available as texts that can be read and reread; Fey's *Bossypants* was at the top of the *New York Times* best-seller list for five weeks when it was released and sold a million copies within six months. Following the cinematic meanings of auteurism as vision, we can see the style or signature of Fey's and Silverman's comedy even in the episodes of *30 Rock* and *The Sarah Silverman Program*, respectively, that they did not write. Likewise, *Kathy Griffin: My Life on the D List*, Griffin's reality television series about her scramble for stardom, bears her authorship through its choice of topics, its tone, and the editing of scenes, shots, and transitions. These comedians are stars and celebrities because, beyond having the acting chops and good comic timing of a Carole Lombard or Lucille Ball, they are exceptional writers of comedy.

My subsidiary claim in this book is that women's comedy has become a primary site in mainstream pop culture where feminism speaks, talks back, and is contested. I am not claiming that all the writer-performers covered in this book identify as feminists or should be seen as feminist spokespersons. Far from being politically correct, they often take political correctness as their target. And their articulations of gender politics cover a wide spectrum, from Cho, who openly embraces feminism as her politics, to Griffin, who is the most removed from feminist rhetoric even though she has openly campaigned for political causes—gay marriage and the end of the military's policy on homosexuality—that are aligned with contemporary strands of feminism. Overall, the political impetus of their work reflects the strategies, trends, and contradictions of the women's movement since the 1970s.

That is, their work reflects feminism as a diverse set of discourses that range from "women's lib" to the queer-friendly politics that veer away from acknowledging "women" as a category at all. We can hear the latter when Kathy Griffin jokes about identifying as a gay man or when Margaret Cho embraces the identity of a fag hag.[1] The comedians covered in this book were born between 1958 (DeGeneres) and 1970 (Fey and Silverman), the era when Second Wave feminism emerged primarily as a fight for legal equality. The division of feminism into three "waves" is a blunt and problematic way to historicize women's activism over the past five decades, so the following summary is offered not as a history but as a general guide to the ways feminism has been thought about and talked about as a context of these women's comedy. The Second Wave, named to acknowledge its follow-up to the first large-scale American feminist movement early in the twentieth century, was popularly associated with Betty Friedan's trapped housewife, Gloria Steinem's liberated career woman, and later, more radical figures like Shulamith Firestone and Robin Morgan who demanded full-scale institutional changes to marriage and the family. These "women's libbers" of the 1960s and 1970s campaigned not only for shifts in traditional gender roles such as child care provider but for equality in the workplace and for reproductive rights; they also targeted pornography as part of their larger attack on objectified images of women in culture. So the generation of women who came of age in the 1970s reaped many legal and social

PRETTY / FUNNY

benefits of Second Wave activism, including antidiscrimination laws (Title VII), the *Roe v. Wade* decision that legalized abortion, the wider availability of birth control, and a guarantee of equal athletic facilities for women and men in schools (Title IX).

This is the equality feminism often spoofed on *30 Rock*, with its flashbacks of a teenage Liz Lemon, who sued her school district to let girls play football. The episode "Luda Christmas" reveals that she played on the team for just one day. "But I did change everything forever," she rhapsodizes in happy self-delusion. As this suggests, one of the ongoing subtexts of *30 Rock* is that 1970s equal-rights feminism has remained uneven in its effects and benefits; Liz Lemon is able to rise into a powerful position as a network executive, but the networks persist in hopelessly sexist content, featuring series like *MILF Island* (Mothers I'd Like to Fuck Island). The popular status of feminism entails both its successes and the ongoing resistances to those successes. On the one hand, feminist-influenced legislation and institutional changes beginning in the 1970s made such an impact that feminism understood as gender equality became "Gramscian common sense," Angela McRobbie notes, even though feminism remained in some spheres of public life "fiercely repudiated, indeed almost hated" (28). The widespread circulation of Rush Limbaugh's term "feminazi" well into the second decade of the twenty-first century testifies to feminism's continued ability to trouble the status quo through its baseline resistance to traditional gender roles.

Even though women of color were active during this time in other liberation movements, Second Wave feminism was tethered to its popular image of liberating suburban housewives and was perceived as a white, middle-class phenomenon. This is the liberal, do-good feminism satirized by Wanda Sykes in a skit about performing for a feminist benefit event. In the version captured in an episode of her sitcom *Wanda at Large* (2003) titled "Clowns to the Left of Me," one of the WASPy feminist organizers gushes, "You're an African American woman, I'm a liberal. We're practically twins." Revolt against this myopic whiteness was a major dynamic in the formation in the 1990s of Third Wave feminism, which protested the racism and heterosexism of the earlier movement. Third Wave feminists like Rebecca Walker, Naomi R. Wolfe, and Donna Haraway advocated a more inclusive social critique—global, multicultural, media-savvy, and attuned to the needs of women of color and all varieties of sexual orientations.[2] Criticizing the Second Wave as "victim feminism," Third Wave feminism was aligned, although not entirely synonymous, with the girl power movement of the 1990s that found compelling role models of female clout in television series such as *Buffy the Vampire Slayer* (1997–2003) and *Xena:*

Warrior Princess (1995–2001). Third Wave feminism similarly drew on this model of female strength as opposed to male oppression as its axiom, but while girl power tended to reproduce middle-class whiteness as an ideal, Third Wave feminism prioritized difference and diversity—sexual, racial, class, ethnic, physical. The pro-sex stance of the Third Wave, including its embrace of popular culture and pornography, is evident in the gay male audience cultivated by Kathy Griffin, the gay visibility of Ellen DeGeneres and Wanda Sykes, the exuberant LGBTQ (lesbian, gay, bisexual, transgender, queer) rhetoric of Margaret Cho, and the bawdy irreverence of Sarah Silverman. And as I discuss in Chapter Two, feminists who identify along these lines attacked Tina Fey in 2011 for representing, on *30 Rock*, a feminism that was disengaged from queers, disability issues, and racial politics and that was conservatively aligned with the cisgender or "cis" (gender-normative) body that is unquestioned in 1960s-style equal-rights feminism.

However, contemporary feminism is far more complicated than this Second versus Third Wave schematic would suggest. In a 2009 retrospective, gender-studies scholar Carisa Showden summed up the current feminist mash-up as "postfeminism, power feminism, third-wave feminism, dome feminism, libertarian feminism, babe feminism, I'm not a feminist, but . . . 'feminism'" (166). To that list we can add what J. Jack Halberstam describes as "Gaga feminism," named after but not limited to the Lady Gaga persona, which disposes of stable gender identities, looks to "new forms of politics, social structures, and personhood," and is not about sisterhood but rather about "shifting, changing, morphing, extemporizing political positions quickly and effectively" (27–29). Analysis of this complicated picture is beyond the scope of this introduction.[3] Instead, I hope to map out in the next few paragraphs the various feminist issues in which the women comics in this book engage. The contradictions of their politics are the contradictions of contemporary feminism; when Wanda Sykes makes fun of feminism as white and bourgeois, she is taking a position popularized by the Third Wave, but when she incorporates abortion-rights advocacy into her stand-up acts, she draws on a legal-rights rhetoric associated with white, bourgeois, 1960s feminists.

The most salient feminist issue in *Pretty/Funny* is postfeminism, popular versions of which are widely derided in these comedians' satires of "pretty" femininity. McRobbie argues that postfeminism both appropriates and disregards feminism's successes; just as feminism became "common sense" or "taken into account" as an achievement, it became disposable as a past event. The empowerment rhetoric of feminism, originally directed toward social change, was instead easily funneled into an empowerment of the individual through sexuality, femininity, money, and cultural capital. In this line of thinking, sexualized images of women that the Second Wave had decried as degrading them can be recycled as proof of triumphant personal power; the woman in a sexist ad can be read as an assertion that feminism is no longer necessary, in that she "seems to be doing it out of choice and for her own enjoyment" (McRobbie, 33). In this logic, sexual attractiveness is an enabling choice despite cultural and consumerist pressure to purchase the clothes, cosmetics, and accessories necessary to produce it. The personal makeover — postfeminism's ubiquitous pièce de résistance — is extensively spoofed by the comics discussed in this book, from Ellen DeGeneres's queer renditions of being made over by her audience to Margaret Cho's funny but chilling account of how her sitcom-TV makeover nearly killed her.

Nevertheless, consumerist versions of postfeminism — the pressures to buy into the ideals and purchases of chic, forever-young femininity — to some extent overlap with strands of Third Wave feminism and certainly with Gaga feminism. Halberstam acknowledges this in the latter movement when she includes "a celebration of the joining of femininity to artifice" as one of its facets (xiii). A telling blind spot of Second Wave feminism, by some accounts, was its indifference to pleasure, not only the wide varieties of sexual pleasure but the pleasures of femininity, including fashion. In its condemnations of sexual objectification, Second Wave feminists often lost or overlooked the playfulness of dress-up and artifice, a dynamic joyfully enacted as high drag for Lady Gaga and seen in the elaborate self-Orientalization of Margaret Cho in some of her post-2000 performances. Rejecting the moralistic and often judgmental Second Wave rhetoric about attractiveness, feminism since the 1990s has been more likely to see women as co-creators rather than victims of fashion and consumerism. The result is feminists "giving workshops in high heels," as one young feminist describes it (Boris, 102).

The problem is that chic Third Wave or Gaga feminism may very well look exactly like the fluffy femininity or sleazy suggestiveness heralded by popular postfeminism as a return to traditional gender values — a luxury young women can well afford, advertisers imply, because the need for feminist activism is long gone. Or as Showden summarizes it, the typical postfeminist assumption is that "women today are confident in their bodies and with their sexuality and do not need a political movement to tell them what is demeaning and what is liberating" (171). When Liz Lemon protests this concept on the 30 Rock episode "TGS Hates Women," frantically pointing out the sexism of the "baby hooker" look of a young woman comic, Liz comes across as the frumpy Second Wave feminist who doesn't get it and who proves the old adage that feminists have no sense of humor. Overall,

30 *Rock* mines fizzy versions of postfeminism for comedy: in "Mazel Tov, Dummies!" Liz interprets the gushy every-bride-is-a-princess sentiment by getting married in her *Star Wars* Princess Leia costume, usually pulled out of her closet only to disqualify herself from jury duty. 30 *Rock* is a particularly rich example of women's comedy taking on the contradictions of the multiple feminisms registered in popular culture, and in Chapter Two I go into more detail on popular postfeminism as a dismissal of political feminism.

Given this complex field of gender politics, the comedians in this book nevertheless enact feminist assumptions in their challenges to cherished ideals about the appropriate behavior, race, and sexuality of the pretty—that is, appropriately feminine—female body. Prettiness is a tempting target for feminist comedy because it is a diminutive term associated with girlishness rather than womanly attractiveness. The title of the Roy Orbison song and the 1990 film starring Julia Roberts switch out the more colloquial phrase "pretty girl" for "pretty woman" exactly because of that connotation: the woman who is pretty is young and accessible. In the Orbison song she's approachable, and in the Roberts film she's available at an hourly rate. While the words "beautiful" and "glamourous" suggest power, "prettiness" implies delicacy and daintiness, the very qualities lampooned by Fey's boss photo and the comics-as-sluts photographed by Leibovitz. In mainstream culture, the pretty woman is not only slim and young but also and perhaps imperatively white or at least light-skinned—a fact brutally satirized by Margaret Cho and Wanda Sykes. It's not surprising, then, that feminist scholars have long found subversive pleasures in the power of female wit and waggery over feminine norms, from Fanny Brice's parodies of Ziegfeld Girls to Roseanne Barr's sardonic domestic goddess, and have traced the history of women in comedy as a feminist history.[4] When Lily Tomlin played Tina Fey's radical-feminist mother in the 2013 comedy *Admission*, many reviewers noted that the casting itself was a nod to the genealogy of women's comedy.

The women comics included in *Pretty/Funny* are the beneficiaries of this rich history, attaining a high-profile presence in mainstream culture despite—or because of—their association with queer and feminist politics and, in some cases, their legibility as queer, black, and ethnic bodies. Ellen DeGeneres's gay wedding, for example, was a large-scale media event that made the cover of *People* magazine. Wanda Sykes was the first lesbian comic to be invited to the White House Correspondents' Association Dinner. Griffin, who loudly proclaims her primary audience as her gays, is regularly asked to co-host CNN's New Year's Eve special, with the expectation that she can draw substantial ratings for her outrageous antics and language. Griffin and Cho base their comedy on an aggressive critique of Hollywood culture, Griffin with her D-list persona and Cho with her fierce outings of Hollywood racism. Both also take queer positions outside of a prevalent family-values politics. Sarah Silverman, meanwhile, mobilizes her Jewishness in a stunning and high-risk satire of bigotry and white privilege. And for highly visible political comedy, Tina Fey's 2008 impersonations of GOP vice presidential candidate Sarah Palin were singular in their impact. Never before has a comedian of either sex made such an imprint on national politics. An example of Fey's continuing clout, as well as her association with feminist public discourse, was her inclusion in a 2012 front-page *New York Times* article on a renewed debate about working mothers (Kantor, "Elite Women"). Fey was cited as an example of women "at the top of their fields" who have weighed in on the complications of motherhood and career, referencing a highly circulated chapter ("Confessions") from *Bossypants* on this topic. The inclusion of a comedy writer-performer as part of what the *New York Times* article calls a national "feminist conversation" sums up what's new about Fey's stardom: she is a comic who is being taken seriously. And what's very new is that she is a comic whose name often comes up in discussions of feminism.

This is not to say that all contemporary women comics or even most women comics participate in this kind of feminist conversation or edgy politics. Precisely because it is now a thriving field, women's comedy features brilliant stars such as Handler and Cummings whose work is less political. And the glamourous women comics are likely to be the moneymakers. Late-night host Handler was the only woman included in the top-ten lists of highest-grossing comedians in 2010 and 2011, and Cummings was television's cause célèbre in autumn 2011 when she created two network series and starred in one of them (2 *Broke Girls* and *Whitney*). Yet it's also the case that contemporary women's comedy includes far more feminists and feminist themes than discussed in the following chapters. In a May 2012 article in the *Washington Post*, Rebecca Traister cites Amy Poehler, Kristen Wiig, Samantha Bee, and Kristen Schaal along with Fey as evidence, the headline suggests, of "The End of the Hairy, Joyless Feminist." Her theme is that all these women comics challenge the concept of "what a feminist looks like."

In the bigger picture, women's comedy has become a space where feminist topics emerge not only in the stand-up comedy of performers such as Janeane Garofalo and Rachel Dratch but in films such as Mo'Nique's *Phat Girlz*, in Poehler's sitcom *Parks and Recreation* (2009–) and Mindy Kaling's sitcom *The Mindy Project* (2012–), in Lena Dunham's HBO dramedy *Girls* (2012–), and in debates around films such as *Bridesmaids* (2011) and *Juno*

(2007), both written by women and embroiled in controversies about representation. *Juno* was criticized for its take on teenage pregnancy and its snide portrayal of an abortion clinic, depictions defended by writer Diablo Cody, who claimed that her "feminist hat" is "permanently welded" to her head (in Wakeman). *Bridesmaids*, widely welcomed as a feminist perspective on wedding culture and class difference, nevertheless lit up blogs and websites with debates about its gross-out comedy scene and the jokes around Melissa McCarthy's large size: Could a feminist movie accommodate these elements? (Wallace). The arguments themselves are less important than the surprise that the dreaded "F" word—feminism—was being casually invoked as a pop-culture issue and, in the case of writers like Cody, an identification. Along the same lines, when the hit television series *New Girl* (2011–) was criticized in 2012 by comic Julie Klausner as "antifeminist," the show's creator, Liz Meriwether, responded by giving *Entertainment Weekly* an interview in which she explained herself as "a feminist who's actively trying to create interesting roles for women" (in Maerz). My point is that questions and debates about feminism and comedy are not limited to feminist blogs but show up in mainstream journalism and have become part of the public sphere.

BODY POLITICS

My argument so far has centered on women's comedy as a vehicle for feminism and as a site where the pretty/funny binary plays out in two ways: as the traditional organization of women's bodies in comedy and as a strategy women comics have used to resist and lampoon that dynamic. My more specific argument focuses on the latter—the strand of female comedy grounded in the body and its politics. The politics—that is, the power dynamics—is actually cited in Hitchens's notorious essay when he quotes author and wit Fran Lebowitz in support of his argument: "The cultural values are male," she says; "for a woman to say a man is funny is the equivalent of a man saying that a woman is pretty" (n.p.). Lebowitz reroutes Hitchens's argument from biology to culture to explain why a woman's looks get prioritized over what she says. A striking example is the unwanted media attention directed to Hillary Clinton's physical appearance during her run for the presidency in 2008. Commentary on her policy statements was often upstaged by remarks about her hair, clothing choices, and legs. Rush Limbaugh famously asked if, should she be elected, Americans will "want to watch a woman get older before their eyes on a daily basis" (in Nason). Significantly, one of the most scathing and high-profile feminist criticisms of this trend was an acclaimed *Saturday Night Live* skit by Amy Poehler and Tina Fey, who impersonated Clinton and Sarah Palin, respectively, being treated by the media in very different ways because of their looks. As this suggests, Hitchens's observation rearticulates "the male gaze," a theory that remains sadly relevant, especially in determining, for instance, which female bodies can become stars and what roles they can take.[5] Tom Hanks may get ever goofier-looking in middle age, but as of this date, he can still play any role in Hollywood, from dashing action hero hunting down the Da Vinci Code to romantic lead for Julia Roberts. A female star aging like Hanks would have no such range.

But she could have a shot at being funny. Joan Rivers, who has always identified as a feminist, made this point in her famous 1974 quip about the importance of looks in the making of a woman comedian: "There is not one female comic who was beautiful as a little girl" (in Shapiro, 638). The quip intimates a great deal about how a young girl might compensate for her failure to be what culture most desires in a girl, and many of the comics discussed in the book talk about their girlhoods in similar terms. In show business, the failure to be beautiful was, in the past, likewise compensated by comedy. Fanny Brice, Lily Tomlin, and Carol Burnett traded on their unglamourous looks to embody cartoonish characters, while women like Phyllis Diller and Joan Rivers herself felt obliged to make themselves funny-looking or to position themselves as grotesques. In the Stanley article in *Vanity Fair*, Amy Poehler remarks that while she and her comic cohort are considered good-looking, they are not the beautiful female bodies that dominate film and television. "For funny ladies, we're attractive. But when you open us up to real, professional attractive people — I do not want to run with those horses" (190). However, professional attractive people — stars, celebrities, models — continually proffer to female consumer-spectators endless images of impossibly perfect glamour and flawless femininity. As of 2010, a middle-aged Sarah Jessica Parker was still posing in frothy high school prom dresses to advertise perfume.

This is not to say that conventionally attractive women don't do transgressive comedy about gender but rather that the pretty versus funny dynamic is a rich source of humor for women because it is part of the larger social structure of how women are seen and judged. Consider the case of Jean Carroll (1911–2010), a lovely woman who shocked nightclub audiences in the 1950s by doing comic monologues "in a shimmering evening dress, dripping diamonds and mink. That in itself was subversive," her *New York Times* obituary notes, as were her jokes about "being driven crazy by spouse and children, a time-honored staple of male comics" (Fox). Carroll's shock tactic relied on the belief that a glamourous woman was supposed to show up in a nightclub as a showgirl or singer, not a joker. As this implies, the dynamic of stand-up performances by women often entails the male gaze even if the point is its subversion or elision. Nor does the gaze need to be literally male. John Berger's classic formulation about social power and women's internalization of male surveillance is especially relevant to the woman who, in stand-up comedy, literally stands up to be surveyed by the audience.[6]

Women comics are judged for their looks before they have a chance to speak, critic Danielle Russell asserts. She quotes comedian Abby Stein, who spoke of the anxiety about the audience "looking at your body instead of listening" to the jokes. Along the same lines, comedian Jenny Jones "estimated that she lost the first minute of her routine while people decided if a buxom blonde had anything to say" (n.p.). Male comedians are not subject to this judgmental gaze because, to use Berger's framework, their looks are not necessarily their source of power. Jim Carrey may look like a conventionally dashing leading man, but his power is his ability to contort his good looks into zany, absurd, or wacky faces. Conversely, the male comic who is not particularly attractive simply has another advantage; Louis C. K. can use his portliness and grubby looks as part of his bumbling schlep persona. Both cases prove the argument made by Laraine Porter that male comics don't need to deal with their status as visual objects to make themselves heard: "The male stand-up is much less likely to have his object/subject status determined by what he looks like" (80). Little wonder, then, that for many women comedy writers the cultural expectations about femininity and the female body have provided rich material for humor.

The body politics of this comedy resonates with ideological implications. Hitchens's argument hints at this larger picture: "Because humor is a sign of intelligence (and many women believe . . . they become threatening to men if they appear too bright), it could be that in some way men do not want women to be funny" (n.p.). Indeed, the pretty versus funny binary adheres to the traditional Western binary of body versus mind as well as the traditional gender alignment of that split, with women positioned as body, man as mind or intellect. When Hitchens gives credit to Jewish women comics as truly funny because of their "masculine" humor, he may be drawing on the stereotype of Jewish intellectualism that in the Western schema masculinizes a woman. The Judeo-Christian tradition strongly endorses the identification of women with their bodies rather than their minds: Adam was the rational one, but Eve seduced him into making a very bad decision—a theme Christian theologians elaborated with teachings that women are innately crasser and more tethered to their bodies than men. Women are "the devil's gateway," wrote the early Christian author Tertul-

PRETTY / FUNNY

lian, and Saint Augustine famously preached that a man is the image of God, but a woman can become part of this image only as a man's partner.

Even secular philosophies have positioned mind above body and relegated women to the lower term, along with darker-skinned races also considered socially and intellectually inferior. Elizabeth Grosz claims that, given this debasing identification of women with their bodies, early feminists sometimes aimed at "transcending" the body, with the unhappy result of reinforcing the body/mind dualism. Grosz points to more recent feminist thinking that embraces the body as "the political, social, and cultural object par excellence," irreducible to either biology or culture (18), and it is within this framework that I describe a female comedy grounded in the cultural body. The politics of this comedy centers on questions of race, sexuality, and power. What female bodies are valued? What bodies count as feminine? As sexy? As visible and legible? Feminist questions of long standing, they are now, for many women comics, the subtext and setups for punch lines.

THE POLITICS OF STAND-UP

Although the body politics of comedy can be traced back to this broad ideological heritage, a more specific and physical example is the practice of the stand-up monologue, which began in nineteenth-century vaudeville and music halls with humorists such as Mark Twain. It developed in the form we know it today mainly through post–World War II nightclub culture. Performing stand-up comedy, like piloting a plane or being a detective, was long considered an implicitly male undertaking. Lily Tomlin, commenting on this predominantly male history in the 2009 PBS documentary *Make 'em Laugh: The Funny Business of America*, explains the cultural logic: "A woman couldn't stand up and tell jokes because it was too powerful. To make an audience laugh meant you had control of them in some way." Joan Rivers has said, in the same vein, "Comedy is masculine. To stand up and take control of an audience verbally is very difficult" (in Horowitz, 107). Both comedians emphasize the authority of the physical positioning. The posture of standing up assumes status and power as well as qualities of aggression and authority, also considered innately masculine. As John Limon puts it in his eloquent theorization of the genre's posture, "What is stood up in stand-up comedy is abjection" (4). Limon focuses on subjectivity instead of masculinity in the power dynamic of this posturing, but his overview on stand-up as well as his cultural history of its masculinities generally supports the pretty versus funny paradigm I lay out here. Limon writes, for instance, that in the first decades of stand-up comedy a woman comic who added "sexual allure to her wit" would have been threatening instead of entertaining (55) and that a woman comic who was "not grotesque" would trigger a "vacillation . . . between pleasure and displeasure" (57).[7]

Given the anarchic thrust of comedy and the transgressive effect of the woman standing up to be heard rather than looked at, comedy is a rich site for queer performance. The entire rhetoric of female stand-up comedy, the confidence and antagonism of the woman comic "making" an audience laugh, is an undoing of gender, says Russell: "In 'doing' comedian the woman ceases to 'do' female; that is, the linguistic behavior of one contradicts the expected speech patterns of the other" (n.p.). The undoing of gender has profoundly disruptive results, as Judith Butler and queer theory have persuasively demonstrated. Certainly when female comics hijack male space and the authority to be funny, they are also hijacking the cultural organization of heterosexuality itself, the social order described by Berger in which female value resides in being pretty. The disruptive effect is reflected in the *New Yorker* comment about comedy's suitability for women and in Hitchens's remark that good women comics are masculine by virtue of their size, lesbianism, or Jewishness.

This suspicion about women comics as gender outlaws is summed up by cultural critic Rosie White in her remarks on the Stanley essay in *Vanity Fair*. She calls attention to a comment that Tina Fey and her cohort "don't look like comedians." Even if these comics "are said to be funny and sexy," White remarks, "they are still perceived as odd and unusual—as funny peculiar" (356). The expectation, she says, is that female comedians are butch lesbian, grotesque, ugly, or simply male—which is the expectation of Hitchens, too. Her conclusion about this is succinct: what's at stake is the issue of "appropriate femininity," a quality culturally opposed to "being intelligent, sharp-witted" (ibid.). But once appropriate femininity becomes the site of satire or outrageous flippancy, the most basic assumptions about sex and gender are hilariously imperiled, no matter how attractive or femme the performer. Marusya Bociurkiw makes this point when she links the physical slapstick of Lucille Ball and Ellen DeGeneres, both of whom have acted out a "silent rage" against feminine norms in their sitcoms, she claims. Because "the comic's body is structured as the site of dis-ordering and re-ordering of the symbolic order," their slapstick antics resulted in a "productive disequilibrium," undermining appropriate femininity (177). For DeGeneres, the disequilibrium is her queerness, but by linking her antics to those of Lucille Ball, Bociurkiw points to the queerness implicit in a comedy based on rage against gender norms. Of the women covered in this book, three identify as gay or queer—Cho, Sykes, and DeGeneres—but queer disequilibrium is also evident in Kathy Griffin's D-list persona, which eschews slapstick but embraces the abjection of failed glamour, flipping it into comedy.[8]

The gendered power dynamic of stand-up comedy—its presumed masculinity—is often associated with the raunchiness exemplified by high-profile comics Lenny Bruce (1925–1966), George Carlin (1937–2008), and Richard Pryor (1940–2005). For most of the twentieth century, suggestive jokes and off-color language were, for middle-class audiences, a male privilege. Freud's theorization of "smutty" humor, dated though some of its aspects may be, is spot-on about the aggressiveness and seductive intent of this humor, as seen in the comedy of bawds from Mae West to Lisa Lampanelli. Freud famously assumes that women can be only the targets (the pretty body), not the (funny) speakers, of dirty jokes. His argument is that "smut is directed to a particular person" for the purpose of sexually exciting that person. Freud can picture this scenario only in a Victorian gender arrangement: "Smut is thus originally directed towards women," he says, even if women's presence, "owing to social inhibitions cannot be realized, [but] is at the same time imagined" (*Jokes*, 97). In short, sexual jokes broadcast the desires of the male speaker, and the desired woman need not be actually present for the joke to be funny among men; in fact, owing to social inhibitions, the woman is likely not there at all. So, Freud's theory of sexual comedy imagines women only through their absence. Lucy Fischer, noting that the woman "is eventually eliminated from the scene entirely and replaced by the male auditor" in Freud's formulation, connects this "circumvention" to other notable absences of women in the history of comedy, such as the favoring of male cross-dressing as a comic staple (62).[9]

But Freud perceptively identified the roots of smut in sexual aggression and desire, and he was right about the social taboo of women publicly and assertively speaking about their own desires. In mainstream culture, this taboo remained in place until the sexual revolution of the 1960s, and we can see its tenacity in the shocked reactions Sarah Silverman garnered in 2005 for language that Lenny Bruce and other male comics had brought to mainstream attention four decades earlier.

A BRIEF HISTORY OF GENDER AND AMERICAN COMEDY

The pervasiveness of the pretty versus funny binary in comedy is evident in a toss-away remark by *New York Times* writer A. O. Scott ("The Lady or the Teddy"). Mocking the clichéd structure of a film he was reviewing, he says archly, "Mila Kunis is also in the movie, but she can't be funny because she's a girl, and her job is to be amused, tolerant and pretty." Pretty versus funny can easily describe the gendered history of American popular entertainment in the twentieth century, beginning with the theatrical revues that juxtaposed leggy showgirls with male comedians. The grand Broadway spectacles of Ziegfeld, the Shuberts, and others glorified the bodies of white women who were considered suitable for show, as I have demonstrated in my previous work (*Ziegfeld Girl*), and the silent choreographies of these bodies contrasted with the wit of the male comedians. The latter included African American comic Bert Williams (1874–1922) and a host of Jewish and ethnic comics, beginning the trend of Jewish and then black comics that would influence American comedy for the entire century and exploit comedy's richness as a site of minority unruliness and defiance. The few comic women in these early revue shows are striking for their transgressions of traditional femininity, as seen in the brash bawdiness of Sophie Tucker (1886–1966) and the insubordinate clowning of Fanny Brice (1891–1951)—both of them set up as the outrageous (and Jewish) contrast to the chorus girl. We can appreciate in Tucker's lewdness, her persona as the Red Hot Mama, how comedy provides a venue for lusty female sexuality even though it was positioned, for Tucker, as distinct from the pretty and more conventional appeal of the showgirl. Robert Allen points out about Tucker and other sexually assertive singers of this era, especially African American performers like Bessie Smith (1894–1937) and Ethel Waters (1896–1977), that their sexuality was linked to qualities considered inappropriate for bourgeois audiences—their age, excess, and nonwhiteness (272–273).

In her history of the liminal spaces of vaudeville and burlesque, M. Alison Kibler documents how bawdy women comics and singers of the early twentieth century operated under the radar of bourgeois culture. These women could be raunchy-funny, Kibler tells us, because they "were often outside of the ideals of feminine beauty—they were fat, dark-skinned, or 'too mannish,'" and their comedy often consisted of parodies or "battles" with middlebrow feminine icons such as ballerinas (14). Predictably, this counterhistory of bawdy female comedy is also predominantly Jewish and African American, composed of women whose color, ethnicity, or immigrant status marked them as not feminine, giving them license to participate in the male world of smut. Late in their careers, black comics Jackie "Moms" Mabley (1894–1975) and Pearl Bailey (1918–1990) went mainstream with cleaned-up versions of their personas for the stage and screen, but their work in clubs and on the Chitlin Circuit—the entertainment venues for black performers up until the 1960s—was renowned for its raciness (Haggins, 147–150, 157–160). And, Kibler recounts, white women who performed in blackface in vaudeville could appropriate this "low" cultural standing, giving them "space for rebellious and sexually aggressive performances" that were comic but also provocative (130).

For much of the twentieth century the raunchy comedy of many of these women, including Jean Carroll, was circulated in under-the-counter "party records," 78 rpm recordings of adult comedy that flourished from the 1930s through the 1970s, featuring risqué songs and monologues by comics such as Rusty Warren and Bea Bea Benson. One of the best known of these, Jewish bawd Belle Barth, recorded albums with titles like *My Next Story Is a Little Risque* (1961), *I Don't Mean to Be Vulgar, but It's Profitable* (1961), and *If I Embarrass You, Tell Your Friends* (1960) and ditties about female sexual prowess: "I'm gonna line a hundred men up against the wall. / I bet a hundred bucks I can bang them all." Given the ways female sexuality was silenced, euphemized, or neglected in mainstream pop culture in the early 1960s—the era of Doris Day virginity and twin beds for Mr. and Mrs. Cleaver—the work of Barth and others in party albums and clubs suggests the value of comedy as a venue for female sexual expression and insolence. However, Joanne Gilbert claims, in this tradition of the raunchy female (heterosexual) comic, no matter how threatening her sexual power might be, she can be "palliative" in her suggestion that she is sexually available so that her overall effect may be "What you see is what you get—are you sure you can handle it?" (108). Again, the status of the female body itself—its visibility, availability, and presumed heterosexuality—is intrinsic to women's comedy even at its most transgressive.

Certainly the most high-profile comic bawd of the twentieth century was Mae West, who by 1932 was "the most famous woman in America," according to biographer Marybeth Hamilton, "her persona a hot topic of controversy, her name a byword for sex" (193). West's comedy was grounded in her curvaceous body, its lush size implicit to its appeal and threat; in *I'm No Angel* (1933) she eyes her slim, young co-star Cary Grant as she would an hors d'oeuvre. Her scholars have shown that West's hourglass plumpness was a throwback to the burlesque heyday of the 1890s; its sheer excessiveness in the 1920s and later was part of its meaning as insatiable and lewd. Its excesses were also part of West's affront to traditional meanings of gender. Her over-the-top, camped-up performances of feminine wiles, combined with her husky, masculine mannerisms and walk, suggested that femininity is a performance that can be pulled off by men or women alike, as she had learned in the gay subculture of New York City's theater world. Her subversive sexiness also had distinct racial implications, as Pamela Robertson Wojcik has demonstrated. On the one hand, West positioned her "glowing whiteness" as part of her sexual value, carefully surrounding herself with darker women; on the other hand, her film roles and songs affiliated her with black working-class and black lesbian cultures—that is, with abject sexualities certainly not considered pretty (290–292).

West's career in Hollywood peaked in the early 1930s before a new kind of comedy appeared that quickly surpassed in popularity West's gold-digger narratives. Romantic comedy featured far less edgy women wholly distanced from West's campiness and grotesquery. For the rest of the century the idea of women and comedy was tethered to this type of film and to beautiful white stars such as Katharine Hepburn, Carole Lombard, Doris Day, Meg Ryan, and Drew Barrymore—that is, to women acting in comedies rather than to women comics. Kathleen Rowe has eloquently argued that romantic comedy is the film narrative where the comic, unruly woman has historically done best, her feistiness and insubordination given free rein but in the end safely contained through coupling or marriage (95–106). But throughout the twentieth century, Hollywood also popularized what Steve Seidman has dubbed "comedian comedy," the type of film that centers on the antics and persona of the comic star—as Mae West's films had done. This type of film became a vehicle for comic teams such as Laurel and Hardy and solo stars from Jerry Lewis to Adam Sandler. Rowe sums it up succinctly as "male-centered comedy" (104).

While cinema favored pretty women who were good with comic scripts, funny women who wrote their own material were scarce until the late 1950s and early 1960s, when Elaine May, Phyllis Diller, and Lily Tomlin emerged as the first mainstream postwar female comedians.[10] All three began with work onstage and became household names through their appearances on television. Generally, women comics have fared better in television than in cinema because glamourizing close-ups are fewer on the small screen and niche marketing can target female audiences. Writer-performers like Carol Burnett, Roseanne Barr, Brett Butler, Julia Louis-Dreyfus, and Mindy Kaling have had their own sitcoms, and Joan Rivers became the first woman to host a late-night talk show. But despite the importance of television as a venue for women comedians, women seen in television comedy are still mainly attractive actors in the vein of Lucille Ball, Mary Tyler Moore, and Debra Messing rather than comedy writers. The standard casting for most sitcoms, from *The Honeymooners* (1951–1955) to *Modern Family* (2009–), continues to be the funny-looking husband and his requisitely lovely wife. In films the same dynamic allows comical bodies Seth Rogen and Jack Black to be coupled with the likes of Katherine Heigl (*Knocked Up*, 2007) and Kate Winslet (*The Holiday*, 2006), respectively.

This minihistory gets to the pivot of the pretty versus funny binary: because their looks are less important, men have been more likely to take on the physical grotesqueries of comedy, where the funny-looking body and face are assets, which is rarely the case for women in popular entertainment and more generally in culture. From Harold Lloyd and the Marx Brothers to Bob Hope, Seth Rogen, and Zach Galifianakis, men with far-from-handsome bodies and faces have been prime for stardom as performers in stand-up, television, and film comedy, as less-than-pretty women have not. Two traditions of comedy, both of them charged with gendered implications, account for this discrepancy.

First is the convention of the uncomely comic or clown who is the sympathetic outsider. Frank Krutnik describes how this "outsider or misfit . . . presents a spectacle of otherness by serving as a conduit for energies that are marginal, non-normative or antisocial" (3). The liminality of this figure has traditionally given the fool, court jester, or sidekick character the power to buck authority and cause chaos because he has nothing to lose. However, my stress here is on the physical appearance of this character as a spectacle of otherness—Buster Keaton's sad sack, Steve Carell's hapless loser, Jack Black's slob. This comic misfit can be a sympathetic character who assumes comedy's most common narrative—and certainly a cultural favorite—the romance. Keaton's homely clown, Charlie Chaplin's Little Tramp, and Billy Crystal's nerd can pursue and get the girl at the end, as can the characters played by Carell and Black. Woody Allen as the skinny, bespectacled nebbish can woo lovely Diane Keaton not only with the power of his wit but with the cultural cachet of the underdog and the loner. But there is no female equivalent of Allen's nebbish—a lovable, funny-looking female outsider who can also carry a romantic storyline. The female outsider is a trickier position to negotiate; in cultural iconography, the "lone woman" connotes the witch, spinster, or hag.

My point here is not simply that funny-looking male comics can get romantic roles, though that's a huge advantage given that most film comedies include romance and films can launch a comedian to mainstream stardom. My emphasis is rather about the cultural roles one might imagine for a funny-looking man as opposed to a funny-looking woman. Those cultural roles and bodies animate popular fictions and narratives. The male comic whose odd-looking appearance signals the misfit and outsider has traditionally had more—and more sympathetic—narrative options. But this tradition is neither inevitable nor fixed, as demonstrated by the popularity of Melissa McCarthy's sitcom *Mike and Molly* (2010–) and McCarthy's award-winning role in *Bridesmaids*. Victoria Sturtevant makes a similar point in her study of Marie Dressler (1868–1934), who was MGM's most profitable star in the early 1930s. Because of her looks and size (five feet seven, two hundred pounds), Dressler was limited to roles as dowagers, matrons, ugly ducklings, and rowdy drunks, although that didn't prevent her from "hijacking the camera's gaze from her costars" and achieving widespread popularity during the Depression (2–3). But Dressler is the exception. Film comedy includes no long, ongoing line of Marie Dressler types, as opposed to the long line of Buster Keaton types extending to Steve Carell and Jonah Hill. Instead, a large-bodied woman like McCarthy or Rebel Wilson occasionally does well against the odds. Sturtevant notes that the uncomely or excessive woman comic can be appealing to female spectators "as a model of feminine energy and transgression" but is profoundly at odds with the way women need to look and act in patriarchal culture, where they "rely on men for economic and familial security" (34). The crux of female value in that system is femininity—being pretty.

The second convention of comedy that treats funny-looking male and female bodies differently is the tradition of the grotesque carnivalesque. Theories of the carnivalesque are about the ways bodies are mapped in culture rather than the ways they are imagined in stories, though there are obvious connections. Mikhail Bakhtin was the first to point out that instead of the "classic," well-proportioned body idealized in Western culture, the grotesque body—disproportionate, ludicrous, misshapen—is the one celebrated in comedy. Bakhtin's topic is the Medieval carnival, the festival where order and hierarchy could be turned inside out and upside down, with the pauper crowned as king and the "lower body"—guts, sex organs, buttocks—idealized instead of the head and heart. As opposed to the self-contained classic body, the grotesque body is open and leaky, so that "the emphasis is on the apertures or the convexities . . . the open mouth, the genital organs, the breasts, the phallus, the potbelly, the nose" (26). This is the voracious, out-of-bounds comic body of Falstaff and John Belushi, Chris Farley and Cedric the Entertainer. Sturtevant claims it is the excessive body of Marie Dressler as well, who often performs as "the unruly woman," breaking physical and social boundaries of femininity with her size, behavior, and appropriations of male prerogatives such as being drunk. But Sturtevant warns about the considerable penalties for women who embody carnivalesque grotesquery in that women's bodies are always already under suspicion as contemptible; most likely this body is "mocked because it does not comply with cultural codes of female beauty," even if women audience members admire its indiscretions (33–34).

In characterizing Dressler as an "unruly woman," Sturtevant uses

Kathleen Rowe's influential moniker and model of the insubordinate woman in comedy, which in turn draws on Bakhtin's theory of the carnivalesque. Rowe traces the unruly woman as a comic character dating at least from Medieval mystery plays. This figure is characterized by her excessive body, speech, and laughter and her associations with dirt, disorder, looseness, and liminality; she "may be androgynous or hermaphroditic," the crone or the hag, and "excessive or fat, suggesting her unwillingness or inability to control her physical appetites." Because the unruly woman is impervious to patriarchal claims on her, she is ultimately the "prototype of woman as subject—above all when she lays claims to her own desire" (31). Rowe finds this robust persona in the character of Miss Piggy, whose ferocious appetites match her aggressiveness, a combination Rowe also finds in Mae West and Roseanne Barr. But Rowe, along with other feminist scholars who have drawn on Bakhtin, foregrounds the cultural uneasiness about the female grotesque in Western culture. The unruly woman is an ambivalent rather than wholly positive figure because of misogynist suspicion and contempt for the female body's leakiness and openness, a body that "through menstruation, pregnancy, childbirth, and lactation, participates uniquely in the carnivalesque drama of 'becoming'" (33). This is the female grotesquery Sarah Silverman uses as the basis for much of her comedy, as described in Chapter Three. Generally, however, because of the cultural mistrust and even abhorrence of the female grotesquery incarnated by the likes of Miss Piggy, Rowe finds that the more socially acceptable version of comic female unruliness is romantic comedy, as mentioned above, where funny women are pretty, heterosexual, and eventually positioned in stable, conventional relationships if not marriage.

They are also mostly white. "Pretty," after all, is a loaded term signifying whiteness as well as heterosexuality. If the leading ladies of romantic comedy are not white, they are slender women of color with Caucasian features and light skin—Jennifer Lopez, Paula Patton, Robin Givens, Halle Berry, Sanaa Lathan, Gabrielle Union, Nia Long, Vivica A. Fox—and, except for Lopez, in films targeted at African American audiences. In my previous work on this issue ("Queen Latifah"), my argument is that the ideal bodies of romantic comedy are white because the ideals, tropes, and images of heterosexual romance are white. I note that femininity itself is racialized, and its idealized versions are white, a crucial element in the pretty/funny dynamic of women's comedy. In his book-length study of whiteness in visual culture, Richard Dyer documents the cultural associations of whiteness with the ideal woman ("the fair sex") as well as the standard cinematic lighting techniques that privilege whiteness and produce, for white women, beauty that literally "glows" (White, 122–142).

Assumptions about femininity are not only racial but race-specific; Margaret Cho satirizes the clichés of the fetishized China doll and geisha girl, while Wanda Sykes works against the stereotypes of the Jezebel and the Sapphire, dangerous and undesirable versions of black womanhood. As Sykes's work suggests, prettiness is an especially prickly issue for African American women, whose femininity has been consistently denied and erased in the historical trajectory impelled by slavery. The disavowal of attractive black womanhood was a disavowal of the white rape of slave women; in this logic, interracial sex could be blamed on the primitive Jezebel who was the seductress. Scholars have amply demonstrated how black women have been portrayed "as the antithesis of the American conception of beauty, femininity and womanhood" (Jewell, 36), often masculinized through attributes of aggression, size, and independence (42). At the same time, Patricia Hill Collins asserts, femininity was consistently associated with "milky White skin, long blond hair, and slim figures," standards by which black women were deemed "less beautiful, and at worst, ugly" (*Black Sexual Politics*, 194). The upshot of this, she argues, is that disparaging images of black femininity are necessary to uphold the white ideal (199). This troubled cultural history gives a decidedly political spin to the comedy of Mo'Nique, for example, who defiantly celebrates the large-bodied black woman as desirable in her 2006 film *Phat Girlz*, her miniseries *Fat Chance* (2005–2007), and her exuberant self-promotions as a bona fide sex symbol. As scholars have noted, comedy's anti-authoritarianism and outlaw stance have long provided a site of defiance and identification for minorities. The liminality of comedy itself—its "safety" as a form of speech that doesn't have to be taken seriously—has allowed comic venues to air and popularize debates about sensitive topics, as seen in pop-culture phenomena such as *Guess Who's Coming to Dinner* (1967) and *Glee* (2009–).

WHY NOW?

Even given this longer history of women comics, the more prominent place of women's politicized comedy after 2000 begs the question "Why now?" Why would an admittedly polarizing comedy of gender and race emerge in mainstream entertainment in the era of the tea party, Fox News, and *Sex in the City*–style postfeminism? The popularity of this progressive women's comedy occurs at a particularly conservative moment in American culture, when traditional notions of appropriate femininity are being lionized. In 2011–2012, one of the top two contenders for the GOP presidential nomination was Rick Santorum, who espoused a position that

FEMINISM
The Ugly Truth

mike buchanan

Kindle book published Feb. 12, 2012

The rise of politically oriented women comedians comes at a time when feminism is more visible but also more visibly reviled. The cover of this 2012 book suggests that feminists are neither pretty nor funny.

a woman's place is in the home, a clue that in a contentious U.S. political scene the comedy of these women is outright offensive to some segments of the American public. While motherhood is being romanticized and even fetishized in pop culture and politics, with reality shows hovering over teenage moms and with state legislators at war on reproductive rights, Kathy Griffin on her 2012 stand-up tour told audiences about her contempt for fertility: "If I have one egg left, I'll fry it tonight."

And precisely because feminism has regained visibility, it has also gained renewed loathing as a source of social and economic problems. Tina Fey's clever takes on what a feminist looks like are contemporaneous with books such as Mike Buchanan's *Feminism: The Ugly Truth* (2012), featuring a cover photo of a repulsive female zombie, her mouth red with blood and jagged with fangs. So the politicized women's comedy discussed in *Pretty/Funny* emerged not from a growing liberal consensus but as resistance to the rising power of American conservatism and mounting anxieties about race and difference.

As it turns out, contemporary women comics with progressive politics have benefited from a convergence of historical and political developments. As taboos about women using risqué language relaxed in the 1970s and 1980s, women comics began to infiltrate the bad-boy space of stand-up comedy. By the end of the 1980s, videos and cable television enabled more stand-up performers previously limited to club audiences to become more accessible. Because of technology it was no longer the case that comedians had to rely on a spot on late-night television or *Saturday Night Live* to make a breakthrough. In the 1990s, women who wrote and performed their own comedy began to appear as stars of their own sitcoms (Roseanne Barr, Ellen DeGeneres, Margaret Cho, Brett Butler), and women comedy writers became a more common presence in both film and television. In the following decade, just as women comics became more established and visible, bitter ideological divides in the United States pushed political satire into the national spotlight, with Jon Stewart and Stephen Colbert becoming household names for comedy that targeted the country's growing nationalism and anxieties about race and immigration following the events of 9/11. The merger of comedy and liberal politics was perhaps most visible during the 2008 presidential campaign with Fey's impersonations of Sarah Palin. But this is part of the larger dynamics of comedy, which are inclined toward disruption and subordination. As a result, right-wing politics has no equivalent of *The Daily Show with Jon Stewart* (1999–) or *The Colbert Report* (2005–). Comedians rarely show up in support of rallies for stronger immigration laws, shutdowns of abortion clinics, or oil drilling in national parks. But Kathy Griffin and Wanda Sykes have campaigned for gay marriage; Sarah Silverman launched a get-out-the-Jewish-grandparents-vote movement for Obama in 2008; and Margaret Cho has made fierce critiques of Republican policies a regular part of her routines.

Pretty/Funny begins with a chapter on Kathy Griffin because her gimmick of the "D list" is central to the pretty/funny binary and its defiance by women comics. For Griffin, the D List is the fate of the abjected female body, the star who fails at glamour and femininity. Describing herself and her stardom as "the anti–Julia Roberts," "the anti–Nicole Kidman," Griffin appropriates her D-list liminality as a space of play and subversion. This chapter focuses on the camp and queer foundations of Griffin's comedy, particularly her assumption of the queer sidekick role, the pal of the pretty star, a position that undermines the status quo by calling attention to a body and narrative — the narrative outside of romance — that is compelling and powerful. It explores the political impact and potential of liminality, the position of the insider/outsider, as a comic strategy with potential for social change.

Chapter Two, on Tina Fey, focuses on Fey's award-winning sitcom *30 Rock*, which similarly uses failed femininity as a touchstone of her character Liz Lemon, who, as the idealistic feminist comedy writer in a male milieu, is Fey's alter ego. This chapter investigates questions of feminism and postfeminism, given Fey's associations with both monikers and *30 Rock*'s inclination to centralize topics such as the nature and limits of feminist comedy. My claim is that *30 Rock* is not a feminist text but rather one that explores the unruly ways feminist ideals actually play out in institutions and in popular culture. Ironically, one example of how the new pretty and funny dynamic works is the backstory of the show's casting; Fey had wanted Rachel Dratch as her co-star, but the network insisted on the more conventionally attractive Jane Krakowski as Jenna Maroney. As it turns out, Krakowski enables 30 Rock to skewer the "pretty" ideals of certain popular postfeminist trends that glorify the girly, white, heterosexual woman as proof that feminism is no longer needed. This chapter emphasizes Fey's stardom as well, including her work on Saturday Night Live, her embroilment in feminist controversy over her Liz Lemon character, and her celebrity image, all of which revolve around the question of What a Feminist Looks Like.

Chapter Three covers Sarah Silverman, whose engagement with the abjected body is far edgier than Griffin's D list or Liz Lemon's well-meaning social clumsiness. Silverman exploits the pretty/funny dynamic by playing her feminine, Jewish-princess persona against her gross-out comedy and the comedy of political incorrectness, both of which have been traditionally male territory. Silverman herself links these domains of body and ethnicity through her frequent self-identifications as "dirty Jew," or "hairy Jew," or, as she sings in one of her sitcom episodes, "half monkey, half Jew." This chapter explores the connections in these topics—the abjected female body and the abjections involved in racial/ethnic identities and hierarchies—through Bakhtin's theories of the carnivalesque, the feminist critique and expansion of that theory, and Mary Douglas's work on pollution and dirt.

Margaret Cho's comedy, the topic of Chapter Four, centers on the politicized celebration of the queer Asian body. Brazenly self-identified as feminist and queer, Cho is similar to Silverman in her embrace of taboo topics about sex and the body, but her comedy springs from a far more emotional engagement with the pretty/funny paradigm because of her disastrous experience with her 1994–1995 ABC sitcom All-American Girl. Network and media criticism of her face and body, combined with the eventual failure of the sitcom, nearly destroyed her health, sanity, and career. Cho's 1999–2000 comeback tour, DVD, and memoir, all titled I'm the One That I Want, interpret her story of the failed sitcom in the context of American racism and the tyranny of unrealistic body ideals for women. While much stand-up comedy is autobiographical, my argument is that Cho's comedy is unique in its two passionate forms of autobiography, both of them rhetorically charged with life-or-death urgency and both focused on the body: the addicted body in recovery and the queer body positioned as the basis of a feminist, queer, Asian American manifesto about body politics.

For Chapter 5, on Wanda Sykes, I am indebted to bell hooks's writings on "black looks," which develop the raced implications of the male gaze and more generally the way black female bodies are seen in American culture. Sykes is one of the contemporary black women comics who target white assumptions about what kinds of female bodies are considered sexy or pretty, and like Cho, she performs devastating impersonations of how the raced body looks to that audience. Sykes has been praised as the "diva in training," the promising heir-apparent to crossover diva Whoopi Goldberg, and Sykes made history as the first mainstream black woman comic to come out as a lesbian. My interest here is how Sykes's comedy successfully manages two aspects of black womanhood that have taken on troubling "looks," or more precisely, that look threatening to white culture: the "angry black woman" and the sexualized black female body. This chapter focuses on how Sykes resists the restraints and stereotypes of the white gaze and successfully expresses both anger and sexuality—her own pleasure and later, her lesbian identity—under the scrutiny of a spectatorship keyed to specific expectations and preconceptions about African American women.

Pretty/Funny concludes with a chapter on Ellen DeGeneres, whose comedy is profoundly grounded in the body—the legibility of the lesbian body, its mobility through multiple contexts, its resistance to social and sexual categories, and its blond whiteness that enables this versatility. The structure of this chapter is different from that of the other chapters because it serves as a coda on affect, comedy, and "the way bodies speak to us," to use Susan Bordo's term. The other chapters analyze the women comics' performances, routines, and television shows as texts that illustrate the pretty/funny dynamic and tension. But my argument about DeGeneres is that even though her sitcom outing in the 1990s made television and pop-culture history, she has had a far greater impact as a daytime talk-show host, moving away from narrative entirely. The transgression and power of her comedy is less in what she says than in the body she so comfortably inhabits—in the process, remarkably, making mainstream audiences comfortable with it, too. DeGeneres, after all, has taken the public image of pretty to a startling place as a model and spokesperson for CoverGirl makeup. Her CoverGirl status is an ongoing joke on her show, but the joke is exuberantly joyful: the all-American girl next door is a soft butch dyke—pretty, funny, and queer. The chapter concludes with a preliminary exploration of Deleuzian thought as a way to consider the importance of comedy and the social impact of the comedian's body and presence, as seen in DeGeneres's popularity.

Because this introduction begins with Christopher Hitchens's contention that women aren't funny, let me end with Tina Fey's comment on this idea in her book *Bossypants*. She tells the story of what happened when Amy Poehler started work at *Saturday Night Live* and at a writing session made a joke that one of the male stars didn't like because it wasn't "cute." Poehler said, "'I don't fucking care if you like it,'" and Fey describes this as a "cosmic shift" in atmosphere. "Amy made it clear," she writes, "that she wasn't there to be cute. She wasn't there to play wives and girlfriends in the boys' scenes" (144). Fey then connects this to the women and comedy question. "I think of this whenever someone says to me, 'Jerry Lewis says women aren't funny' or 'Christopher Hitchens says women aren't funny. . . . Do you have anything to say to that?' Yes," says Fey. "We don't fucking care if you like it. . . . I don't like Chinese food, but I don't write articles trying to prove it doesn't exist."

CHAPTER ONE

Kathy Griffin and the Comedy of the D List

QUEERING A SPACE

KATHY GRIFFIN OFTEN BEGINS HER STAND-UP PERFOR-
mances by asking fans in the audience to identify themselves,
but it's a strategy that identifies Griffin herself as a performer with a queer
twist on the dynamic of pretty versus funny. In a clip in the "Extras" on
She'll Cut a Bitch (2009), she makes her usual call for her gays. "Where are
my gays at?" she yells to the crowd, and a roar goes up. "Thank you, boys
and lesbians! Where are my women, lesbians and otherwise?" Another roar
from the crowd. She does a girlie imitation of fashionably dressed, presumably straight women she saw walking in. "You're SO not getting laid at this
show," she warns them.

Then Griffin turns her attention to the other men in the audience. "And
I know there are a few straight guys who were dragged here by a wife or girlfriend," she says. "Where are my straight guys?" When she gets another roar
from the crowd in response, she says, "Oh bullshit. You're so fucking full
of shit. I've never had that many straight guys [in an audience] in my life.
Half of that was gay guys who felt sorry for me." She does a slightly different
girlie imitation: "Just clap, girl, this is pitiful" ("Maggie Griffin Update").
Discounting straight men, Griffin queers the performance space because
she dismisses not the heterosexual male bodies—we do hear applause from
those men—but a dominant, heteronormative point of view, one in which
her appropriate role would be performing as pretty for male appreciation.

The culling out of "straight guys" in a stand-up audience is the kind of
joke we would expect to find from openly gay performers such as Suzanne
Westenhoefer or Kate Clinton or at alternative clubs thronged by a queer
crowd. But it would be difficult to characterize Griffin's venues as alterna-

tive or to describe her audiences as exclusively LGBTQ. By 2010 Griffin was selling out at 2,500-seat theaters across the country. A 2011 *New York Times* review characterized her fans as "mostly gay men, and women who like the same things gay men like" (Isherwood).

Griffin's alignment with marginalized groups is part of her persona as a marginal or D-list celebrity. Because the D-list gimmick is central to Griffin's comedy, I often refer here to the Bravo channel award-winning reality show in which Griffin launched this outsider persona, *Kathy Griffin: My Life on the D List*. Her character draws from comedy's long history of the loser or the outsider, from the Little Tramp to Mr. Bean. However, Griffin's stake in this dynamic is specifically gendered, as suggested by her exclusion of straight guys from her target audience. In this particular joke, the dynamic entails gender failure—the failure of a heterosexual woman to attract and relate to heterosexual men—and a mockery of that failure, channeled from the perspective of the imaginary gay male spectator whose comment "This is pitiful" is also a knowing wink. The failure at heterosexuality, like the failure at mainstream stardom, is funnier and more interesting than success.

Even though there is technically no D list in the official Ulmer Scale of the "bankability" of stars, the D list has become, in the first decade of the twenty-first century, an informal way to describe minor celebrities, particularly those who originated in reality television shows.[1] As the loathsome sludge of the entertainment world, the D list is also its base of value: stardom requires this abjected space below, outside, or at its edges to distinguish itself as a coherent identity, to paraphrase Julia Kristeva.[2] Griffin's D list is both a real and imaginary self-location, the dregs of celebrity culture but also her comic appropriation of that site as a space of play and subversion.

The primary subversion is heterosexuality itself. In her comedy, Griffin's failure at glamour translates into her comic self-alienation from the world of dating and romantic relationships with men. "I'm a crappy girlfriend," she says in an interview. "I'm a barrel of monkeys in the sack but I can't be there for your office party and I can't cook" (in Jones). Failure at domesticity has been a theme of women's comedy since Phyllis Diller, and being the bad girlfriend is likewise a standard female stand-up routine. But Griffin's status as a gender misfit is far more radical because she does not in fact fit into conventional structures of partnership or family. She occasionally refers to her five-year marriage, her divorce, and her sexual history with a number of men in Hollywood, but these are not the basis of her comedy. In her 2009 *Official Book Club Selection: A Memoir According to Kathy Griffin*, her marriage is so underplayed that she doesn't mention it until two-thirds of the way through the book. Then she refers to her husband as someone who would be affected by the production of *My Life on the D List*. "Wait, I'm married?" she writes. "I'll get to that story in the next chapter. Stay focused, people" (204). Griffin's husband, an IT specialist, was a quiet, amiable background presence in the first two years of *D List*. After their divorce, the reality show documented her staged dates with straight men for publicity or gags, but serious heterosexual romance was never in the picture. Since then Griffin has occasionally been seen with men she is dating, while her comic persona relentlessly skews her alignment with heterosexuality. She writes in a 2012 essay, "Heterosexual men are like Martians to me—they may as well have antennae and arrive on a spaceship instead of picking me up in a Prius" ("When to Try").

Griffin skews the standard stardom profile in other ways as well. Wholly outside the Hollywood party crowd, she has never had an alcoholic drink in her life and is a devoted daughter whose parents figured prominently in her life and in her work. Born in 1960 into a Catholic Irish American family in Oak Park, Illinois, Griffin moved to Los Angeles when she was eighteen so she could pursue a career in comedy. After nearly twenty years of stand-up work and occasional guest roles on television, she made a breakthrough in a co-starring role in the network sitcom *Suddenly Susan* (1996–2000). The internationally acclaimed beauty Brooke Shields played the lead, but Griffin often stole the show as her rowdy, less-gorgeous co-worker and friend. Griffin had found her niche as the raucous minor star who doesn't quite fit the leading-lady ideal. When the series ended, Griffin continued her persona as the comic second: not the star, not the glamourous one, but the one who is in proximity to stardom and glamour. Judith Roof has argued for the subversive queerness of the female sidekick character, a role Griffin has never entirely abandoned in the years since *Suddenly Susan*.

In this sense, *My Life on the D List*, which debuted five years after *Suddenly Susan* ended, served as a metanarrative about that secondary status, playing up Griffin's hapless identification against a flawless feminine ideal. "My life is the anti–Nicole Kidman," she says in the first episode of *My Life on the D List*. "My celebrity is the anti–Julia Roberts." Her reality show was a behind-the-scenes look at the life of a second-tier comedian, someone who was scrambling for publicity, gigs, and recognition. Griffin reports in her memoir that agents and producers balked at the concept of this show because she wasn't what they called "an earner" (203), and when Bravo launched *D List* in 2005, it indeed got low ratings its first season. But the series gradually generated attention and larger audiences, and its back-to-back Emmy awards for seasons 2 and 3 boosted its status and Griffin's visibility. In its first years, the show documented Griffin's D-list status through

Fans rely on Kathy Griffin to show up at red-carpet events as the tattletale and spy eager to bring back tales about the follies and pretensions of the A-list crowd. Photo courtesy of Photofest.

such humiliating situations as in the episode "Adjusted Gross" of having her parents pose as customers for her CD sales. Insulted by a fan who points out that she has a frontal wedgie in season 2 ("Puppy Chaos"), she comments that her dream is to have "[Jennifer] Aniston live not even a day in my life, but ten minutes. She's crying by minute three." But even after Griffin gained visibility and power several years into the show, she continued the D-list gimmick as her stake outside the ideals of glamourous stardom and as her comic perspective on mainstream celebrity culture, the gist of her stand-up comedy performances. Fans depend on her insider/outsider status for gossip and snarky commentary on uppity A-list stars. Her stage persona remains the would-be star who gets invited to red-carpet events but is never entirely welcome there, making her the ideal tattletale and spy.

Griffin can occupy this liminal space because of her ambiguous status in the entertainment world despite her mainstream success. In many ways she manifests the marks of genuine stardom: two Emmy awards as of 2013, headliner appearances at venues such as Carnegie Hall and Madison Square Garden, and the co-host spot on CNN's New Year's Eve specials. These are not the haunts of B- or C-list celebrities, the formerly posh or forever second-rate citizens of *Hollywood Squares* (1966–) and disease dramas on Lifetime television. She is not, in fact, a celebrity comic on the level of the ones she invokes as "real" stars, some of whom are her friends who appeared on *My Life on the D List*—Rosie O'Donnell, Lily Tomlin, Ray Romano. As Griffin often points out, she is repeatedly confused with television personality Kathie Lee Gifford, and she can easily walk through an airport or crowded street without being recognized. When *Rolling Stone* and *Vanity Fair* published cover stories on current comedy stars in 2008, Griffin was not included. "Too old, too unfunny," she told a journalist, admitting she was "crushed" (Stadtmiller, 39). In the same interview she pinpointed the markers of her subordinate status as her lack of a major movie role and not being asked to host *Saturday Night Live*, suggesting a reluctance on the part of producers and sponsors to make an investment in Griffin as a central draw for the box office or network television. This reluctance points, in turn, to her reputation in some quarters as "the ultimate showbiz bottom-feeder, an unfunny has-been," a nonstar who "shamelessly screeched her way back to hog a spotlight that was never hers to begin with," an assessment with which Griffin readily agrees in an interview labeling her, among other epithets, "the most polarizing woman in Hollywood" (Fonseca, 34). The uneven nature of Griffin's success also illustrates the fragmentation of popular taste and the niche nature of contemporary entertainment markets. For example, in a season 3 episode of *My Life on the D List* ("Suddenly Single"), Griffin's concert in Manhattan is sold out, yet she is unrecognized and unacknowledged on the street even when she stands beneath the poster of her own show at Carnegie Hall. "It's what's-her-face!" cries a young New Yorker.[3]

Griffin can be a polarizing figure not only because of her queer politics and aggressive style but because of her caustic gossip about other stars. Griffin sometimes targets male celebrities in her routines, but playing on her own double "failures" as a woman and a star, Griffin has more to say about female celebrity in the excessive public behaviors and quirks of A-list stars and tabloid favorites. Diane Negra and Su Holmes note that celebrity culture since 2000 has obsessively focused on and sensationalized female gender issues as melodramatic clichés: bad motherhood, the good girl versus the bad girl, rivalry for the man, tortured marriages, the impossible quest to have it all.[4] Generally, female celebrity functions as a minefield of gender performance for women, and this minefield is Griffin's mise en scène. In her stand-up acts she punctures pretensions, spotlights absurdities and excesses, and turns melodrama into comedy in the inversion Kathleen Rowe has described as central to women's comic unruliness (110–111).

In one sense, Griffin's mean-girl celebrity gossip continues the bitchy stance of her friend and mentor Joan Rivers, with whom she shares a brash comic style and humor about failing to live up to glamourous feminine ideals. And while the difference between Griffin and Rivers could be described as generational—Rivers hailing from a much earlier era of women in comedy—the more important difference between these two comics is their relationship to a heterosexual framework. Rivers's approach to sex, glamour, men, and relationships is grounded in anger against men and male power structures. Rivers became famous with comedy focused on inequities in marriage and women's need to manipulate their way to power and money in a man's world. One of her key moves was to point out diamond rings on the fingers of women audience members, urging them to use their sexual power to cash in for more. "Don't give me all this liberation shit—men like 'em stupid," Rivers would say. "All you need is a pretty face and a trick pelvis and you're home free" (in J. Gilbert, 108). In contrast, Griffin's comedy is not fueled by anger toward men because the heterosexual male versus female axis is not her main point of reference. Her perspective on the power of the pretty face is often as embittered as that of Rivers, but Griffin's line of defense about that power is camp humor and its concomitant alignment with gay men, who share with her the marginality of the insider/outsider.

By the time Griffin moved from the *Suddenly Susan* sitcom to the reality show, she had found her ideal audience in the gay L.A. nightclubs where her celebrity gossip was appreciated for its campy elan. This campy perspective roils against but can never entirely vanquish the ideals of femininity that camp adores as much as it satirizes. Given the tension about glamour and femininity in camp, my argument is that Griffin's D list is a highly conflicted space where mainstream gender norms are endorsed as often as they are contended. The conflicts are evident, for instance, in Griffin's transparent investments in plastic surgery and dieting as routes to a glamourous body she mocks as much as she affirms. This ambiguity does not diminish the queer impact of Griffin's comedy. It does, however, signal the enormous social and emotional stakes, for a woman, of being pretty, even in comedy that demonstrates the charm and power of being the funny insider/outsider instead.

MARGINAL IDENTITY AND THE D LIST

In her stage performances, Kathy Griffin often makes an exuberant announcement about ticket sales: "Sold out, motherfuckers! Sold out!" Vulgar language, especially in contexts that she herself would describe as "inappropriate," is Griffin's trademark. Her language is hardly shocking in the world of stand-up comedy, but it is part of the larger comic dynamic of the D list, a site of category and boundary violation. Her foul language and in particular her rude signature phrase "Suck it!" work as an affront to class and gender codes, emphasizing the contrast between Griffin's innocuous appearance—white, middle class, neatly dressed and coiffed—and what she calls her "potty mouth." Given Bakhtin's descriptions of how the body is mapped, with the rational "upper body" in contrast to the "lower" body of belly and sex, the potty mouth is a violation of this map, a sullying of the upper body by the lower. Her foul language and trash talk have resulted in bans from several network talk shows, so she appears most often as a guest on late-night shows on cable. In one of the most controversial moments of her career, Griffin parodied the pious, Jesus-thanking acceptance speeches of celebrities by saying, when she won her 2007 Emmy, that Jesus had "nothing to do with this" and that Jesus could "suck it," too. On the 2008 and 2009 CNN New Year's Eve specials that she co-hosted with Anderson Cooper, she "accidentally" said "fuck" on the air, and in *My Life on the D List* she repeatedly uses the word at convention gigs and local performances where it surprises and offends the audiences. Jeff Zucker, president and chief executive of NBC Universal, says Griffin "does not have a seven-second delay in her head, which is part of Kathy's charm and also what's dangerous about her" (in Hart, 18).

Far more dangerous and interesting is Griffin's willingness to describe herself as gay. While Griffin often addresses gays and assumes they're the ones who fill her audiences, she is usually much more specific about her affiliation and identification with gay men.[5] In season 2 of *My Life on the D List* Griffin describes herself as "a gay guy who wants everything perfect" ("Going, Going, Gone"), and in season 4 she confesses, "I've always wanted to meet Cher. I know I'm just like any other gay guy on the block" ("Speak Now or Forever Hold Your Peace"). When she talks about meeting Cher in *She'll Cut a Bitch*, Griffin describes herself as having "queened out" on her. In a season 6 episode of *My Life on the D List* ("Getting My House in Order"), she characterizes her new home decor theme as "middle-aged gay man, which is what I am." The gay male identification is, on one level, a tongue-in-cheek refraction of Madonna's statements along those lines in the 1980s and 1990s that culminated in her usage of queer bodies and scenarios in the documentary *Truth or Dare* (1991) and in the 1992 photobook *Sex*. Thus in Griffin's memoir a chapter titled "Reinventing Myself: I'm Just Like Madonna!" sets up the camp glamour queen, herself a gay icon, as another impossible benchmark and satirizes the reinvention trope with a skeptical roll of the eyes.

However, while Madonna in her gay male days could play with identities from the position of sexual power and value, Griffin's alliance with gay men is grounded in shared marginality rather than shared glamour.[6] In a 2006 interview with *Newsweek*, Griffin specifies the outsider status that led her to queer affiliations: "I just always related to gay people, that sense of being outside. In high school I made fun of the cheerleaders, but then I'd have that moment where I wished I was a cheerleader. . . . So the cheerleaders went to the prom, and I hung out at the doughnut shop with the gays" (in S. Smith, 70). This is a key commentary to which I'll return because it encapsulates the pain and defiance of the queer outsider identity while it also indicates the vast difference in the stakes between this emotional queer identification and the sexy one made by Madonna.

Also, Griffin can make this claim because of an entire body of work, from *Suddenly Susan* through *My Life on the D List*, that positions her outside the narratives of heterosexuality and romance with men. She can comically claim to be "really" a gay man because she has obviously failed at being a "real" woman, lampooning both of these essentialist identities. For these reasons, Griffin's play with gay male identity can be read as a "performative disidentification," to use José Esteban Muñoz's term, the "dissing" of identity as a fixed entity. Disidentification involves the enactment of a self "at precisely the point where the discourses of essentialism and constructivism short-circuit" (6). It is true that Griffin's casual self-identity as a gay man risks the trivialization of groups and individuals who are disenfranchised or actually endangered by their gay identity. But the de-essentializing of gay identity moves it out of stigma and, in the discourse generated by Griffin's world, privileges it as the desirable site of insider knowledge and comic perspective.

This queer D-list perspective gives Griffin's comedy its edge because it dismisses the straight male gaze, asking us to reimagine bodies, genders, and sexualities by reframing how and what we see. "Have you ever looked at the online photos of Britney's peesh?" she asks in the first sentence of her memoir (3). This is a reference to the 2007 flashing fad, when Britney Spears, Paris Hilton, Lindsay Lohan, and other bad-girl celebrities appeared in public places conspicuously wearing miniskirts without underpants, providing opportunities for X-rated photography as they exited their limousines. Margaret Schwarz has argued that this fad and its aftermath strikingly illustrate how female sexuality is defined and policed through the visibility of female celebrity and how celebrity culture posits "a (famous) woman's body as the source of her subjectivity." But when Griffin invites readers to join her perspective on Britney's peesh, she resituates the scandalous photos by writing off an audience of straight men—the supposed ideal viewers of these crotch shots—and suggesting alternative views as the ones that are more entertaining. "I find it nearly impossible to turn away from an online snapshot of any celebrity's peesh," she gushes (3). This comment, which I'll characterize as campy in its breathiness and pseudodrama, rebuffs the male gaze but also the solid, middle-class standard-bearers of decency who would not look at—or would not admit to looking at—the online photos. Instead, the comment mobilizes the transgressive D-list point of view, defiant and shameless because there's nothing to lose.

As perpetually D-listed, Griffin falls into the comic tradition of the clown as "a liminal figure, an outsider, a social vagrant or conversely, a representative of the lowest orders of the social hierarchy," as Henry Jenkins puts it in his study of the "anarchistic comedy" of early Hollywood sound films. This clown is the figure who speaks for the underclass even though "this stance masks his or her economic ties to consumer capitalism" (224). Constantly highlighting her efforts to get publicity, sell tickets, and "move the merch" (merchandise), as she puts it, Griffin hardly masks her ties to consumer culture. However, her emphasis on labor rather than privilege aligns her with the populist thrust of the tradition Jenkins describes as the comedy of disorder, a comedy that speaks against hierarchy and points to ruptures in powerful discourses such as gender and sexuality.[7]

Because the larger question of *Pretty/Funny* involves the long-term stakes of comedy's body politics, it is worth exploring the question about the social impact of insider/outsider comedy in regard to Griffin. Jenkins

The logo for Kathy Griffin: My Life on the D List *pictures Griffin as a liminal figure clinging to the famous "Hollywood" sign as an imperiled insider/outsider to the world of fame and celebrity.*

cautions against interpreting anarchistic comedy of the late 1920s and early 1930s as progressive, as the upper class could benefit from the portrayal of the subversive clown as crazy and absurd (243–244). However, Jenkins acknowledges the "vitality and exuberance" of the comic insider/outsider who enjoys "a freedom from fixed categories" as well as the ability to disrupt the status quo (226). For Jenkins, the key element in the clown's oppositional voice is liminality, a quality that Kathleen Rowe likewise cites in her study of the social and political dimensions of comedy. Both theorists draw on Victor Turner's use of the term "liminality" in his anthropological treatises on the marginal figure in folk performances, rituals, and festivals, the joker who is given special powers of critique or satire. Turner notes that these individuals are found on the margins or "lowest rungs" of society or fall between categories (125). Their importance is their role in the resistance of power; they signify community values in opposition to top-down power (110).[8] Griffin fits this profile as an entertainer with an ambiguous status, a fan base in the gay community, and a persona located on the lowest rung of the celebrity ladder of prestige. Her relationship to power is complicated by her ambivalence about glamour, yet she positions herself against mainstream power in her campaigns for gay rights, for example, an issue to which she has lent her support as an activist.

So for Jenkins and Rowe, the cultural dynamic of liminality explains the freedom of the comedian to question and disrupt the status quo. Jenkins foregrounds the narrative function of the clown, the slippery mobility that disrupts and displaces order, identity, and coherent narrative (224–245), a description relevant to Griffin's role as sidekick in *Suddenly Susan* and as unpredictable loudmouth in *My Life on the D List*. But while Jenkins views the liminal figure in comedy as a register rather than a catalyst of social change, Rowe argues for a more dynamic, transformative role for this figure as gender outlaw—the unruly woman. Her profile of the comic unruly woman matches Griffin's persona: foul-mouthed, disruptive, associated with taboos and borderline locations (31). Rowe is interested in liminality as the enabling space for transgressive gender behavior not so much in particular fictional narratives as in the much larger cultural narratives of gender and power. Following Natalie Zemon Davis on the subversive power of the "woman on top," Rowe argues that liminality provides the space for women to appropriate masculine privileges and utilize "visibility as power," a means of changing "the terms on which she is seen" (11).

One of my key arguments about Griffin's comedy is that she enables that shift in perspective. She identifies as the anti–Julia Roberts, loser, and tattletale, exiled from endless talk shows, red carpets, and respectability. However, her markers of mainstream success—the sold-out Carnegie Hall,

CNN's New Year's Eve specials—demand that this "anti–Julia Roberts" be seen differently, which entails seeing Julia Roberts differently, too. From the D-list perspective, the glamourous A-list star is less inevitable as the glossy ideal, and the raucous sidekick is equally pleasurable as the object of our attention. On *Suddenly Susan*, Brooke Shields was drop-dead gorgeous, but Griffin's character was far more interesting. In her memoir Griffin claims Shields was often jealous of how Griffin's character got more laughs and better lines (122). The purported jealousy suggests the power of comic marginality, illustrating Rowe's argument that the comic woman on top can mobilize a shift in perspective on gender relations and ideals.

Griffin's D-list gimmick ridicules Hollywood hierarchy without contesting its weight and authority. As Griffin herself puts it, "My whole career is knowing your place" (in Stadtmiller, 39). Her jokes about Nicole Kidman and Julia Roberts indicate that Griffin knows her place in the pecking order of celebrity beauty and most forcefully reveal how the D-list attitude straddles defiance and compliance regarding conventional gender roles. Even though her supposedly average looks are the basis of her comedy, Griffin writes in her memoir that she began having cosmetic surgeries when she was twenty-six as a standard show-biz procedure (171–183). And while the first few seasons of *My Life on the D List* documented her efforts at dieting and fitness training as comedy, she gradually became slimmer and more toned, so that she received considerable media attention for flaunting a "bangin' bikini bod" during her 2009 Paris Hilton episode. During the following season of the show Griffin showcased her fit bikini body on every possible occasion: at a kiddie beauty pageant ("Toddlers and Remodelers"), at a public pap smear ("Kathy's Smear Campaign"), and in backroom scenes in which she walks around in her underwear or less.

The entire final chapter of her memoir focuses on the adoring publicity she got for the 2009 bikini shoot, and her tone flip-flops between ecstatic triumph and comic self-deprecation. She jokes that she's thrilled to be considered attractive—"a few extra straight guys turning on my show to jerk off to me would be so great" (326). But she also grimly acknowledges that she still struggles with her weight and body image. When someone asks her to autograph a copy of the bikini photo, she says her first impulse is to explain it was from "five pounds ago," taken during a week when she didn't have time to work out (327–328). Even among bangin' bikini bods there is a ranked hierarchy in which she knows her place. My point here is that Griffin's liminality is constituted by contradiction rather than coherence; the interface of identification and defiance of gender roles is particularly relevant to the insider/outsider comedy of camp that I find central to Griffin's overall agenda.

The best example of the profound ambivalence of the D-list perspective about gender norms is Griffin's treatment of a joke about her by Jay Leno. In the "Adjusted Gross" episode in season 1 of *My Life on the D List* Griffin documents her appearance on *The Tonight Show* during which Leno quips that she looks like the "before" shot of before-and-after makeover photos. Griffin laughs with Leno on stage, then weeps with humiliation when she's off the set, revealing her stake in traditional feminine attractiveness. Griffin is still at the mercy of the gender norms she sometimes scoffs at; the double standard about attractiveness allows a man who looks like Jay Leno to make a crack about Griffin's looks and enables his joke to hurt. Because her looks are part of her gimmick of failed glamour, Griffin uses the exact same line about herself—that she looks like the "before" photo—when she appears on the Home Shopping Network as part of a skin-care pitch in season 3 of *My Life on the D List* ("What I Won't Do for a Buck"). When the conventionally beautiful model next to her "laughs too hard" at the joke, Griffin says suspiciously in her voice-over, Griffin admits she's "bitter," especially when the model then gives her a hug "in that mean high school girl way." The voice-over about her bitterness and the pernicious return of the beautiful high school mean girl is funny, but there's an edge to the humor, a concession to what's not very funny about knowing one's place in the hierarchy of looks in Hollywood or in high school.

CUTE BUT NEVER PRETTY

Griffin's role as the comic pal in the 1990s sitcom *Suddenly Susan* is a fascinating origin story for *My Life on the D List* because it demonstrates Griffin's shrewd exploitation of the pretty versus funny stereotypes embedded in the star versus the comic second who knows her place. At the same time the role demonstrates the racial blind spot of both shows in their assumption of whiteness as implicit to glamour and real stardom. On *Suddenly Susan* Griffin played the sidekick, familiar from film and television as the wise-cracking foil to the more conventionally attractive female lead. The sidekick role was one Griffin had aimed for all her life, she explains in her memoir, pointing to the Rhoda character on *The Mary Tyler Moore Show* (1970–1977): "That's who I wanted to be. She had all the jokes. I knew I could never be Mary." In the same passage Griffin acknowledges the key factor of looks in this self-placement, remembering her mother's frequent remark to her: "You'll always be cute, but you'll never be pretty" (29). *Suddenly Susan* starkly lays out the alternative narratives possible for the pretty heroine in contrast to the cute or funny sidekick who, by mimicking the main narrative, transforms it and tells a different story.

The female comic sidekick is inherently queer, according to Judith Roof, whose extensive study of this character in Hollywood cinema argues for her subversive power in turning attention away from heterosexuality and its narratives. This was the dynamic of *Suddenly Susan*, in which Griffin plays Vicki Groener, the loud, outlandishly dressed, Jewish pal of the eponymous Susan, played by Brooke Shields, the film star and model famously labeled by Eddie Murphy as "the whitest woman in America" in *Eddie Murphy Raw* (1987). As even this much suggests, Vicki's Jewishness conflated the racial, class, and gender failures by which Susan's WASPy glamour was all the more powerful. Roof emphasizes that the sidekick is less feminine and attractive than the star, and in the case of Shields, the star was an iconic, internationally known beauty, the essence of the all-American girl, as satirized by Murphy: "Miss America every year is Brooke. Fuck who you see with the crown. You look up 'white woman' in the dictionary, be a picture of Brooke." *Suddenly Susan* blatantly invoked Shields's star image and her well-known upper-class background, portraying Susan as a swank runaway bride whose bolt from the altar is her first grown-up act of independence. The four seasons of the show were bookended by the "wrong" wedding and the "right" wedding, a formula familiar from cinematic romantic comedies.

Vicki's story, a series of misadventures and disruptions, works as a queer, parodic version of Susan's. The Vicki character is a single, casually promiscuous woman who implausibly becomes involved with a rabbi and then marries him in a double wedding with two gay men. In her nuptial episode ("How They Danced"), Vicki sports a bridal crown that looks alarmingly like a bird cage, no doubt a reference to the campy 1996 film *La Cage aux Folles*. In a brilliant cameo, Joan Rivers appears for the wedding as Vicki's overwhelming Jewish mother dressed like a drag-queen version of Marie Antoinette. Several episodes later Vicki's husband drops dead of a heart attack while making love with her, and even though much is made of his secret heart condition, the implication is that sex with Vicki is lethal. By the middle of season 4 Vicki has moved upstairs from Susan, nodding to Rhoda's narrative and spatial location in *The Mary Tyler Moore Show*. Unlike Rhoda, though, Vicki openly plays out the dangers and monstrosity of the unattached, unnatural woman: she kills men and was apparently mothered by a drag queen.[9]

For the two sitcoms, the flamboyant Jewish pals are the racial and ethnic contrast to the all-American-girl heroines Susan and Mary. However, Vicki's Jewishness is often used as shorthand for bad taste and obnoxious manners, which in turn suggests a lack of femininity, a trait WASPy Susan comes by naturally. Because Jewish identity is passed along through the mother, Joan Rivers's role as the monstrous Mother underscores the contrast. At their initial meeting, Rivers as Mother admires Susan's nose and is not convinced it wasn't done by a surgeon; this is followed by a series of gags about Mother's own multiple plastic surgeries, pointedly contrasting Susan's "natural" femininity with its Jewish, comically counterfeit versions.

Nearly a decade after Eddie Murphy's well-known riff on Shields's whiteness, *Suddenly Susan* never satirized whiteness as part of Susan's appeal. Instead, Vicki's Jewish loudness and vulgarity demonstrated by contrast the value of Susan's racial pedigree. Vicki's Jewishness thus becomes a class marker as well; her attempts at upscale glamour always fall flat. Conniving her way into a swanky hair salon, she admires the stylist's chic leather pants and asks, "Do they make your ass sweat or what?" ("Wedding Bell Blues"). The jokes reflecting Vicki's bad taste, her lack of class, also reflect her lack of femininity. Roof comments on the comic sidekick that the class difference is "expressed through a gender difference where female comic secondary characters are less traditionally feminine" (16).

When Griffin went from secondary character to star of her own show she amped up the queer qualities associated with the sidekick by basing the new show on the premise of always being the second, the loser, the outsider to "real" glamour and stardom.[10] One of the themes of *Suddenly Susan* that Griffin carried over to *My Life on the D List* is the privilege afforded to female beauty as opposed to the harder realities for women considered less attractive. "For some of us," Vicki tells Susan, "attracting a man is more than just a matter of showing up" ("The Ways and Means"), a line she repeated with some variation on her reality show years later. On the first season of *Suddenly Susan*, this was the premise of an entire episode ("The Me Nobody Nose"): Susan refuses to believe that life is easier for her because she's beautiful, so she wears a large, Karl Malden–style prosthetic nose to make her point. The experiment teaches her that she in fact has none of the power she did when she was gorgeous. Vicki shakes her head at Susan's frustrations and says, "You have the nose of an ugly woman, but you don't have the spine."

Griffin's voice-over on *My Life on the D List* often insists on acknowledging the privileges of beauty as opposed to the extra effort—the spine—required of those not considered attractive. Echoing the *Suddenly Susan* line about attracting men, Griffin makes a comment about work and labor that encapsulates the D-list dynamic: "A-listers like Julia Roberts make millions by just showing up on the set and smiling. Smiling doesn't work for me. I have to work for a living" ("Puppy Chaos"). This quip seems to deny the labor of acting and stardom, furthering the illusion of moviemaking as glamourous, as just showing up, but it would be difficult to take this denial at face value in the context of *My Life on the D List*. The premise of the show is the deflation of glamour and painstaking exposure of the labor of the entertainment business. Yet this remark zeroes in on the physical realities of a system in which a woman's value can indeed reside in her ability to smile and show up, her ability to take the role of pretty.

Suddenly Susan, like many sitcoms, replicated the ideology of romantic comedy, the genre of *Pretty Woman*, which posits that marriage is the answer to a woman's life and problems. The romantic comedy sitcom builds in a linear way toward the coupling of the leads. But as a reality show, *My Life on the D List* dropped the linear narrative and more importantly was wholly untethered from all narratives about romance, marriage, or the nuclear family. Instead, each episode was built around an upcoming performance or gig or publicity stunt, all based on the larger cultural narrative of scrambling for A-list status. Reality television enabled Griffin to exploit her position as a Hollywood outsider, someone not in the league of Brooke Shields, a pretty star who could carry her own network show.

Roof describes the female sidekick as "degendered, masculinized, or queered" and associated with "perverse alternatives of nonmarriage, independence, and business success" (10). The description uncannily fits Griffin in *My Life on the D List*, where we see her first in an affectionate but nonromantic marriage and then associated with a series of men in quasi-business relationships. Following the divorce, her schemes to date for publicity result in wildly incompatible match-ups to satirize the inappropriate choices made by D-listers for media attention. Thus she dates a porn star and one of the Backstreet Boys who is half her age. In season 6 she dates Levi Johnston, the teenager who fathered the child of Sarah Palin's teenage daughter Bristol. Similarly, the season 4 escapades with "our new [sugar] daddy" Steve Wozniak, the computer genius and Apple CEO, emphasize comedy rather than romance. In the episode "Woz Love Got to Do with It," Griffin remarks, "I have no idea what he's talking about. Ever," and adds, "Let's just say he doesn't click my mouse." In the same episode she comments that she has no plans to remarry, thus shutting down the primary tension and dynamic of popular female narratives.

Far from aiming toward marriage as a goal on *My Life on the D List*, Griffin often articulates her cynicism about it. In season 4, faced with the grim prospects of entertaining heterosexual couples at a resort, she comments that she's against marriage, all marriages ("Busted in Bora Bora"). But in season 5, when Proposition 8 in California rescinds the right to gay marriage, she takes it personally: "You mess with my gays, you mess with me." She enlists as an activist, canvassing neighborhoods and speaking at a rally ("Norma Gay"). That is, she is pro-marriage only for a queer cause. Yet her relationship with her own heteronormative family is represented in wholly favorable ways in her stage performances and on *D List*. Griffin included her often tipsy, elderly parents on her reality television show from the start, and in her memoir she emphasizes their support of nontraditional roles for women. "Dad never had a sexist bone in his body," she writes, "[and] never subscribed to the belief that there was woman's work and man's work" (217–218).

Despite this supportive model of parenting, Griffin refuses to reproduce a traditional family structure. When she was still living with her husband in season 1 of *D List*, her household included a handsome young man identified as her "live-in gay visionary," and following her divorce, her tour manager, Tom, usually identified as heterosexual, became her nonromantic housemate. Griffin's domestic scene also included her assistants who worked at her house all day and her mother, Maggie, who lived with her for a while and was often on site. The frequent changes and reformulations of Griffin's household resist not just the traditional family structure but any stable structure at all. A redefined "queer family" has become a standard device for television shows, as seen in popular series such as *Sex in the City* (1998–2004) and *Will and Grace* (1998–2006). But *My Life on the D List* never settled around a permanent group. Griffin's husband moves out, Tom moves in, the assistant Jessica disappears, and her mother moves in and then moves out again. The stable family, like romance, is simply not the point of the show.

Griffin's resistance to family and especially to children is striking given the wholesale romanticization of motherhood in post-2000 pop culture as well as melodramatic anxieties about single women's ticking clock.[11] Griffin often talks about her dislike of children, joking that her lack of maternal instinct is what makes her different from lesbians. She seems to be referring here to her friends Rosie O'Donnell and Melissa Etheridge, often seen on *My Life in the D List*, celebrities known for their family lives that include children. In season 5 Griffin goes to Etheridge's house to bake "lesbian cookies" with the kids, and in season 3 she is getting ready to perform on a lesbian family cruise organized by O'Donnell. "I hate kids. Don't tell Rosie," she confides in an interview (S. Smith, 70). But by insisting that she can't identify with lesbians because they are "too much into motherhood, nurturing, and nesting" ("Fly the Super Gay Skies")—that is, too conventionally feminine—she participates in what Steven Cohan identifies as delight in the "incongruity of cultural dualisms like 'masculinity' and 'femininity,' 'straight' and 'queer,' 'normal' and 'deviant'" typical of a camp perspective (339).

As a reality show, *My Life on the D List* was also freed of the constraints of traditional narratives with neat closures; most often the episodes show madcap adventures rendered in the tradition of Lucy Ricardo's doomed attempts on *I Love Lucy* to break into show business but without the house-wife motif. In the "Puppy Chaos" episode Griffin agrees to appear on a Paws for Fashion benefit and finds the dogs are better dressed than she is. In London she pretends to fall drunkenly out of a taxi to get tabloid attention ("Kathy Goes to London"). When she plots to become an A-lister by buying a second home in a fabulous celebrity neighborhood, she's shocked to have her $1.5 million offer turned down in a neighborhood where house prices begin at $20 million ("Rosie and Gloria and Griffin, Oh My"). Even in season 6, when Griffin's reputation and star power were clearly much stronger than they were six years previously, she agrees to a gig in Alaska because, she says, "I'll book a gig anywhere. East Bumfuck. South Bumfuck. Any of the Bumfucks" ("Freezing My A-List Off"). Generally, as the show progressed, the D-list theme was less literally about star ranking and more emphatically about playing the outsider.

Most of all, *My Life on the D List* focused on the labor of being in the entertainment business without glamour as the fallback appeal and money-maker. The show's theme song expresses a defiant address to A-listers: "I work twice as hard to get half as far as you." Zooming in on the hard work, Griffin's reality show documents her plotting for publicity and gigs, sitting at shopping malls to sell her CDs, and driving herself to local appearances. She deals with financial details and budget decisions. After winning her first Emmy, Griffin began her *D List* episode with a warning: "The statue doesn't pay the bills around here" ("And the Award Goes To"). The focus on labor in all its mundane details breaks with the highly sexualized working-girl stereotype that has long haunted popular culture, as Yvonne Tasker has shown, in "an insistent equation between working women, women's work and some form of sexual(ised) performance" (3). *My Life on the D List* departs from the frothy postfeminist version of work that Negra describes as a trend in contemporary television and film where women retreat from the cruelties of the public professional world and embrace traditional "women's work" in more private settings dealing with food, hospitality, or child care (86–116).

My Life on the D List dislodges all illusions that show business is romantic or glamourous in its everyday practices. The payoff for the hard work is often disappointing, and much of the comedy of *D List* resides in the absurdities that result when a promising A-list situation turns out to be a D-list debacle. In season 2 Griffin gets the good news that the city of Louisville is going to give her the keys to the city, but only ten people show up for a paltry ceremony on the steps of city hall, with the deputy mayor officiating because the mayor had a dentist appointment ("Going, Going, Gone"). In the same season she auctions herself off on eBay for a weekend at her Hollywood "A-list house" to raise money for charity and, she hopes, to garner major publicity. It's a bust. The high-bidding winners withdraw their bids and leave Kathy with a low-paying houseguest from Cleveland who is not especially impressed with her life ("Red State, Blue State"). By the end of season 5, when Griffin is far more established and popular, she's thrilled to be nominated to have her own star on the Hollywood Walk of Fame. Then she learns that she did not in fact make the final cut; instead, she's awarded a star on the lesser-known Palm Springs Walk of Fame, an honor she shares with Cheetah the Chimp, we learn in the episode's final shot ("Kathy Is a Star"). In short, the series continued to emphasize Griffin as the outsider and loser, the status she needed to maintain in order to assure her fans she had not become part of the power elite.

The *D-List* moments that are most uncomfortable are the failed performances early in the series. Heather Osborne-Thompson says Griffin exposes "what comedians refer to as 'dying' on stage," revealing "the part of being a comedian that many long-term performers allude to but never show." Osborne-Thompson's argument is that *My Life on the D List* works in the television convention of women comics who "perform their 'failures' as women" (281). Griffin's "failure" is her work as a female stand-up comic with a "shockingly personal stand-up style" that is offensive to middle-class audiences. Not surprisingly, says Osborne-Thompson, the most disastrous performances documented on *My Life on the D List* occur when Griffin "fails to connect with 'mainstream' audiences through material that seems to delight in attacking 'mainstream' sensibilities" (285). Because the mainstream sensibilities most often defied in Griffin's stand-up routines are heterosexual, it is worth noting the queer implications of Osborne-Thompson's insight about Griffin's "failures as a woman," given that these are the failures that her queer-friendly fans find hilarious.[12]

My Life on the D List documents one failed performance that is strikingly different because of its racial themes. A season 5 episode, "Kathy at the Apollo," covers Griffin's gig at the famous Apollo Theater in Harlem, emphasizing her nervousness about how she will appeal to a predominantly black audience. Preparing for her appearance, Griffin visits comedian-rapper-actor Katt Williams to ask for advice, noting Williams's impressive status as one of the top-selling touring comedians in the world. "He sells out *stadiums,*" she says in describing his importance. A favorite of the hip-hop community, Williams is known for his outrageous racial and political comedy, and his star status serves to expose the racial politics of the Holly-wood hierarchy. To wit, despite his astonishing success on the tour circuit, Williams is hardly a household name and is not what Griffin has in mind when she refers to the A list. Griffin's focus on mainstream stardom is a focus on whiteness in which Katt Williams simply doesn't register. The epi-sode strongly suggests that Griffin fails to comprehend this blind spot in her own shtick. Instead, she projects the limitation onto the audience, re-peatedly asking Williams if comedy is "color-blind" and if "funny is funny." Even when he says no, she continues to pose the question to others later in the episode, claiming she can't tell what race her audiences are because "they're just gay." However, it would take quite a bit of visual impairment not to notice the lack of racial diversity in Griffin's theater audiences.

Anxious about playing in Harlem, Griffin gets Al Sharpton to give the introduction at the Apollo. "You can't get blacker than that," she observes, but she gets a sense of her situation when, as a guest on his radio show that day, she got not a single call-in. "Where are my African American gays at?" she asks, apparently not thinking through the implications of a culture that developed the identity of the "down low."[13] Yet while black gay male fans did not respond on Reverend Sharpton's show, at least some of these fans showed up at the Apollo that night, because when Griffin opened her act and asked first for her "ladies" and then her gays, she did get an enthusiastic response. But it turns out that she misinterpreted or misread the Apollo's invitation and venue. She was actually the guest star on a family-oriented amateur night that included child performers who were still in the audi-ence when Griffin took the stage. As soon as she began to use profanities, the band played her offstage and she was escorted out of the building. The camera then focused on a young black woman being interviewed outside the theater, clearly irate, proclaiming she was "very offended" by Griffin's usage of foul language in a theater where children were present.

Several other *D List* episodes show Griffin using inappropriate language in front of children, and although the camera often scans the audience to show their discomfort, no other episode frames a protest so elaborately, with the young woman facing the camera, the lights and traffic of down-town Harlem in the background. The unmistakable effect is that Griffin offended not just this particular audience member but the entire black community. The episode ends with Griffin laughing about it in a phone call to Katt Williams, who seems especially amused that Griffin and her entou-rage were escorted out of the theater. But it's unclear what exactly amuses Williams; Kathy Griffin has been banished from the Apollo Theater, and the final shot of the group speeding away in the limousine suggests she's been exiled from Harlem, which in fact seems appropriate for a comic who insists or hopes that comedy is color-blind.

The Apollo Theater episode illuminates the specific racial dynamics of D-list humor, which refers to an A list that is implicitly white in its definitions of glamour. Women of color who become A-list stars such as Halle Berry and Jennifer Lopez usually conform to Caucasian ideals of skin color and facial features. As bell hooks comments about the camp world of *Paris Is Burning*, "The idea of womanness and femininity is totally personified by whiteness," and "The femininity most sought after, most adored, was that perceived to be the exclusive property of white womanhood" (147–148). hooks calls attention to the moment in that film when it's evident that no black drag queen wanted to be Lena Horne. Richard Dyer, discussing the racial value of white female stars, notes that Horne was "unplaceable" as a sexualized figure in Hollywood because she was a light-skinned black woman (*Heavenly Bodies*, 40). However, the whiteness of the glossy feminine ideal doesn't figure in Griffin's D-list comedy. She often quips that straight men are indifferent to celebrity gossip, but she does not concede that indifference to her comedy may have a racial register as well — that the misbehaviors of Lindsay Lohan or Paris Hilton may not be interesting to black audiences. So Griffin's comedy about white celebrity tends to duplicate the dynamic of *Suddenly Susan*, which often satirized white privilege without acknowledging whiteness as the underlying value.

Griffin is far more likely to target celebrities such as Britney Spears and Paris Hilton on the basis of class entitlement, characterizing them as "beautiful, skinny, young girls who have the world handed to them on a platter and now have a clothing line" (in Fonseca, "Most Annoying"). A good example is the Paris Hilton episode of *D List*, "Paris Is My New BFF," when Griffin tries to boost her own tabloid profile by going shopping with the sensational heiress. The episode is a parody of Hilton's own reality show on MTV, *Paris Hilton's My New BFF* (2008–2009), a competition to become Hilton's (temporary) new "best friend forever." This episode combines Griffin's celebrity send-ups with the D-list dynamic that positions her against a hopeless ideal. The comedy resides, in fact, in the nonsense of this ideal as well as in Griffin's awkward imitations of Hilton's sloppy extravagance. What Griffin misses is the racial specificity of Hilton's value as blond heiress and baby-voiced sex symbol, the ideal Dyer describes as "the most highly prized possession of the white man" (40). Instead, Griffin targets Hilton's over-the-top performance of celebrity, consumption, and femininity. The artifice of Hilton's poses when she pouts and cuddles her adorable purse-size dog becomes apparent when Griffin apes the same pout and shows up with her large, unruly dogs pulling her in different directions. When Griffin participates in one of Hilton's reckless shopping sprees, its foolishness is far more evident than its glamour—$14,200 worth of glittery gowns and boalike vests, all of which Griffin returns to the store as soon as she and Hilton part company. In all, the Paris Hilton episode provides rich fodder for the kind of satire Christian Lander has popularized with his *Stuff White People Like* book (2008) and website, which in turn suggests how whiteness is being gradually acknowledged in popular culture as an identity that is not universal.

Yet my overall claim about Griffin is that even though she fails to see how much of her beloved A list falls into the category of "stuff white people like," her comic mimicry of Paris Hilton, like her upstaging of Brooke Shields, mobilizes a subtle power shift. Ellen DeGeneres likewise enables a shift away from the feminine ideal, though in a very different register given her lesbian identity. DeGeneres hosted Paris Hilton on her talk show and mimicked her poses with hilarious results, partly because lesbian butch identity exposes the absurdity of red-carpet posing. Griffin's similar maneuver illustrates how her liminal relation to celebrity is closely linked to her relation to traditional gender and sexual roles. When Griffin dresses in Hilton-like fluff and follows her instructions on how to strike a seductive pose, the dragqueen effect underscores Griffin's alienation from femininity. The larger question, then, is the meaning of this playful slippage of cultural power, which is very much related to that in Griffin's dismissals of straight guys in her audience, a ploy in which they are, in a milder way, objects of laughter, held up as an entitled group that has lost its entitlement.

CAMPING IN THE D LIST

Griffin's joking self-identity as a gay man and as a failure at gender and heterosexuality align her with the marginality celebrated in camp humor. Camp is a particular outsider response to gender ideals, especially as seen in Hollywood and celebrity culture. Griffin's alliance with camp and with gay men is another clue to the murky ambiguity of her D-list world, in its simultaneous complicity with and defiance of gender norms. Griffin begins her memoir stating that her only male readers are gay men "and the occasional DL (down-low) husband" (3) and ends it expressing her anxiety about the extra five pounds in the bikini photo; she can mock the male gaze engaged in the peesh photos but not the gay male gaze that would criticize her for letting herself go. Likewise, certain strands of camp humor can cut with a misogynous edge.[14] However, Griffin's usage of camp, like the forms of camp humor now widely found in popular culture, mobilizes feelings and identifications that in the long run work in small but significant ways toward social change.

I am indebted in my argument to Pamela Robertson's work on camp as a feminist strategy for women and to Muñoz's concept of camp as a practice of disidentification. Both scholars understand camp as an inclusive and politicizing strategy that challenges dominant ways of thinking and opens up identifications across genders and sexualities. For Muñoz this strategy enables "dissing" as "a mode of enacting self against the pressure of the dominant culture's identity-denying protocols" (120). Like Robertson, Muñoz seeks to break camp out of its gay male frame of reference to include a variety of performances that subvert mainstream images and stereotypes. Muñoz is particularly concerned with the predominant whiteness of camp and in his examples seeks to establish connections across races as well as genders/sexualities in camp's politics of resistance.[15] I have indicated ways Kathy Griffin's comedy falls short of cross-racial references, and her uses of camp remain likewise fixed in wholly white frames of reference. Nevertheless, her elusive gender/sexuality identifications and her uses of celebrity gossip demonstrate how the insider/outsider comic can subtly shift ways of seeing and thinking.

Further exploring how the alliance of women and gay men can be theorized, Roberta Mock develops the concept of the "heteroqueer" sensibility to explain the attraction of certain straight women to the gay male milieu as a "non-oppressive femininity" (21). Like Robertson, Mock is interested in camp as the site where this relationship can play out, and her prime example is Bette Midler's campy performance of the femme that draws on "gay male performative codes rather than those usually associated with heterosexual femininity" (30). This is not Griffin's performance style, although the instability and flexibility of the gender roles and discursive positioning in her stand-up suggest her affinity with the heteroqueer. Mock is careful to delineate heteroqueer not as an identity but as a way of "doing" queer: "'Doing' queer means possessing the agency to defy and destabilize gendered behaviours, sexes, and sexualities through continuing and conscious decisions" (33).

Because Griffin is not herself a flamboyantly campy performer, I want to make clear that I am describing an alliance and a framework for her comedy rather than a performance style. Certainly there are campy flourishes in Griffin's work; on the cover of her 2009 memoir she poses with giddy fabulousness in a prom dress and crown, and she occasionally appears on worst-dressed lists, as she gleefully reports. But Griffin is more a fascinated spectator of camp performance than a leading player and more likely to act out her fan worship of Bette Midler, Liza Minnelli, or Cher than to partici-pate in Cher-style carnivalesque behavior or dress. Nor does Griffin openly embrace the campy fag-hag identity that Margaret Cho celebrates, which far more radically critiques and distances heterosexuality (Martínez, 137–159). Instead, camp is both a structure and an affect for Griffin, providing a way to situate her comedy in popular culture and describe how it feels, its particular blend of outsider edginess and bitchy triumph.

Camp's association with gay men is historical and debated. Most critics agree that camp was a specifically gay male practice for much of the twen-tieth century as a strategy of identification and continues to be important for the gay community. While some theorists claim it remains a gay male province, others are more willing to identify it as a queer practice, inclusive of nonheteronormative positions. For other critics, camp has lost its mar-ginality—and political power—because it is so widely available as an ironic response and postmodern style in popular culture. Slippery though they may be, definitions of camp usually include its focus on excess and arti-fice—the over-the-top gesture, costume, or narrative—and its appropria-tion of mainstream and popular cultural artifacts for alternative uses and readings.[16] The codings of gender are prime material for camp, although gender is not its only topic. Would-be celebrities—the undead of the D list, for instance—are campy as failed performances of stardom. Certainly the camp exclamation is perceptible in Griffin's remark about the irresistible allure of looking at a "snapshot of any celebrity's peesh." In a move often described as central to camp, Griffin has repositioned a pop-culture text, these online photos, for an alternative enjoyment, and her overdramatic exclamation of finding it "nearly impossible to turn away" is as excessive as the photos themselves in an over-the-top bid for attention.

Even more significant is the distillation of camp dynamics in Griffin's description of high school gender politics in making fun of cheerleaders while sometimes wishing to be one. Her response, turning to the doughnut shop as an alternative fun spot for the people not at the prom, acknowledges the mainstream location of power (the prom) and the pain of her isolation from it. While camp may be widely available as a humorous interpretation of popular culture, it retains this darker element of abjection in some of its representations. An early theorist of camp who specifically identified it with gay men, Jack Babuscio emphasized the dark side of camp humor, a "bitter-wit," he called it, that points to "self-hatred and low self-esteem" in the "awful-funny confrontation with the 'normal' world" (48). This is the darkness heard in Griffin's bitter complaint about the high school mean girl whose power is that she is pretty.

As a woman who is not gay but presents herself as not very successful at heterosexuality either, Griffin's position is similar but not identical to the gay male's awful-funny confrontation with the normal world identified by Babuscio. Through a comedy of insider/outsider edginess, she shares a dis-identification with standard gender roles that is foundational to some forms of camp. Muñoz opens up the conversations about identity and camp in useful ways by indicating the danger in proscribing camp as the exclusive property of gay men and in undermining its political effects by understanding it simply as style (128–135). Its power, he argues, is its status as "resemblance and menace" and its ability to negotiate between the embrace and total dismissal of normative identifications (136). Muñoz's larger argument is that alliances, hybridizations, and resistances are more valuable than circumscribed identifications and categories, providing an entry into Griffin's alliance with the camp style of gay men that nonetheless retains strong ties to a female heterosexual status.

Griffin's investment in that heteronormative status is evident in her endless plastic surgeries as well as in her emotional response to Jay Leno's crack about her appearance. That is, the queer, campy space of the D list or doughnut shop has particular emotional implications for the straight woman without a date for the prom. Pamela Robertson's treatment of camp acknowledges this female complicity in conventional gender roles as part of the complicated relationship of women to camp culture. Robertson traces a feminist camp tradition from Mae West to Madonna, emphasizing the subversive appeal of these performances for women. Her argument is that camp shares feminism's "critiques of gender and sex roles" and its interest in "gender construction, performance, and enactment" (6). The specific alliance of women and gay men is, for Robertson, part of camp's appeal and progressive agenda, although she specifies that feminist camp is not necessarily gay and that some forms of camp, misogynist or specifically gay male, are not in women's best interests at all (6–8). The pleasure of camp is a "guilty" one for women, says Robertson, because camp material so often sets up femininity as its object of laughter and derision, and some campy portrayals of the feminine are clearly misogynist. However, Robertson finds considerable evidence of female camp performance in which the woman "plays with her own image . . . without losing sight of the real power that image has over her" (17). Griffin's repeated citings of Julia Roberts and Nicole Kidman participate in this dynamic that acknowledges the real power of these images but also puts them into play in the D-list world where the hopelessness of living up to the ideals is comic rather than oppressive.

Robertson claims camp as a queer discourse in the broadest sense, inviting the inclusion of all those who experience "discomfort and alienation from the normative gender and sex roles assigned to them by straight culture" (10). She does not use queer theory as her principal tool of analysis, nor does she address the question of how feminist, lesbian, and queer positions differ in relationship to camp. Still, her argument provides insight into Griffin's alignment with gay male culture as well as Griffin's critical perspective on gender and celebrity. As the Julia Roberts and Nicole Kidman examples illustrate, Robertson offers an approach to the prickly ambiguity of Griffin's D-list identification against A-list feminine ideals by showing how camp, as performance and spectatorship, can provide for women a site of ironic play that is "simultaneously critical of and complicit with the patriarchal organization of vision and narration" regarding women's roles and bodies (14). This is the strategy that allows Griffin to turn Leno's remark, a sexist judgment about female beauty, into her own before-and-after joke, recognizing its sting but insisting she can roll her eyes about it, too.

Griffin's alliance and identification with gay men and camp humor shapes her focus on Hollywood and celebrity culture. Babuscio's 1977 claim about a gay sensibility attuned to campiness in cinema is widely disputed, but he was among the first to zero in on the elements of the red-carpet world dear to camp parody: the heightening of male/female contrast, an emphasis on style, and breathtaking theatricality (42–47). Cohan notes that in the decades before Stonewall, "movies and their stars supplied a rich source of readily available and immediately recognizable straight material for camp to rework toward more communal, queerer ends" (14). Though no longer the exclusive province of gay men, Cohan argues, camp continues to be "central to and definitive of gay culture" (19), with Hollywood cinema providing rich material for queer readings. Decades of film scholarship have shown how Hollywood cinema foregrounds and celebrates gender norms and heterosexuality, often in excessive forms. Stars who are camp icons "seem to wallow in the excesses of apparent heterosexual identity (Victor Mature, Marilyn Monroe)," as Caryl Flinn puts it (440). So while camp objects and performances are not limited to the world of celebrity and stardom, that world is particularly rife with camp material and has served as a nexus of knowledge and communication for the gay community.

Gossip about stars and celebrities has likewise been a key factor in gay identification and community. Patricia Spacks, in her extensive study on this topic, notes that gossip is a key element in all communities because it "facilitates self-knowledge by offering bases for comparison, . . . constitutes a form of wish fulfillment, helps to control competition, . . . and generates power" (34). During much of the twentieth century, when an openly gay identity would have meant the end of a public career, gossip served as a powerful circuitry of knowledge and gay history. For gay fans of Hollywood stars before the Stonewall era, gossip was a validating discourse and means of connection. Queer critics have often shown that gossip about celebrities' sexualities can have intensely personal meanings because the "secret" identity of a star makes a "secret" personal sexual identity less isolating and even empowering. Douglas Crimp describes the dynamic: "'Really, he's gay? She's a dyke?' 'Jodie's a dyke? Then maybe I'm fabulous, too'" (13). Gossip as secret knowledge about a star's gay identity could articulate the unspeakable and shape a marginalized community around this secret way of seeing and understanding (Weiss, 30–31; Mayne, 160–62). Gossip about celebrity gay identity continues to operate that way today, suggesting the prevalence of homophobia under the veneer of a supposedly liberal media and open-minded Hollywood.

The flip side of celebrity gossip's place in the gay community is its campiness, its pleasure in outrageous stories and melodramatic revelations viewed with irony. Writing about the similarities of camp and gossip as discourses, Joke Hermes argues that from the perspective of camp, the "truth" of gossip is beside the point because its pleasure is its take on life as "a farce, a comedy of manners." (308). Hermes emphasizes the importance of gossip in "communities that are held together by a shared camp sensibility, which can be read as a form of protest against prevailing norms and values" (309). So while celebrity gossip has political value as knowledge in the gay community, it has a parallel political value as the refusal to take knowledge seriously or to refuse the middlebrow reading of news items about celebrities as true or false.

Griffin herself claims gossip as a D-list activity of no interest to those in power. "I have nothing to say to [white, middle-age, straight men]," she told a *Newsweek* reporter. "They don't care that Gwyneth Paltrow named her kid Apple. They're not even sure Gwyneth Paltrow is a different person than Nicole Kidman" (in S. Smith, 70). Laughter about pretentious celebrity behavior stakes out a bond of identity and authority among those who, though marginalized in other ways, are in the know about how to read such news. While the white, middle-age, straight man has no need for this validation, his inability to get it further empowers the marginalized community for its privileged mode of interpretation. Gossip, Spacks explains, "embodies an alternative discourse to that of public life . . . [and] provides language for an alternative culture" (46).

It is not surprising, then, that gay audiences were Kathy Griffin's springboard to her niche topic of celebrity culture. In her memoir she describes how, when *Suddenly Susan* ended and she had to restructure her career, she relied on a strategy she'd used for her performances at the L.A. Gay and Lesbian Center. She would begin those performances by showing video clips of outrageous celebrity conduct: "Mariah Carey talking about her negligee room as if everybody had one" and "a makeup-less Julia Roberts braving Outer Mongolia to show how she likes to keep it real" (193–194). The clips were a gold mine of diva behavior and performances that were howlingly funny to an audience attuned to camp humor. Plucking the clips out of context and resituating them for a gay audience, Griffin could count on enthusiastic responses. Years later her comments to a journalist again explicitly linked her comedy about celebrity to her high school experience of bonding with the gays at the doughnut shop: "Hollywood is like high school. The celebrities I make fun of are pretty much the mean cheerleaders in school, or the mean jocks" (in Wiltz). In short, women who embody the ideal of "pretty" are the ones she is likely to find funny.

Griffin says the video clips at the Gay and Lesbian Center worked so well that she later used them in the more mainstream Laugh Factory club, also in Los Angeles, where she began to attract gay audiences for her performances, a crowd she preferred because they were "unshockable" and immediately got the nuances of her "rolled-eyes" voice-over (194). She describes the growing crowds at the Laugh Factory as primarily "the gays," with "the breeders folded in" (194). Griffin sees the video-clip strategy as the turning point in her career. Celebrity gossip became her leading theme, interspersed with stories about her own hapless attempts at glamour, including frank discussions of her many plastic surgeries.

Dyer has famously pinpointed glamour as the gold standard of "successful" gender performance for women: "Not being glamourous is to fail at femininity, to fail at one's sex role" (*Heavenly Bodies*, 163). He makes this claim as part of his description of Judy Garland as a camp icon because of her repeated performances of gender that fall flat. If, as Negra and Holmes argue, celebrity culture provides the stage where femininity is tested and expected to crash and burn, we can understand camp humor as expecting similar failures as evidence that success at being a woman is a staged performance, a package that can come undone. In the long run, this is the undoing of gender central to Butler's concept of gender as a surface sign or repeated performance that produces the illusion of a "real" interior essence (24–25, 134–141). Scholars often acknowledge Butler's critique as being central to post-1990 theories of camp as a queer practice that exposes gender as performative.[17]

Griffin's comedy, with its expansive gay identification, could be used as evidence for the ongoing argument that at least some forms of camp have lost their subversive edge and are now commonly available as a hip, apolitical style of humor and sophisticated perspective on popular culture. But it could also be argued that Griffin's gay-oriented camp style is popular because some members of mainstream audiences are willing to take on a more flexible gender/sex perspective. When Griffin doggedly recognizes her gays as part of the queering of her performance space, she summons an audience that gets her campy perspective on the celebrity scene and the travails of being a woman. This is a self-selected group, as is made painfully clear by Griffin's many performance failures chronicled on *My Life on the D List*.

What exactly, then, is the experience of this queered audience willing to be drawn into the D-list perspective of shared laughter about the failure of glamour, celebrity gossip, and the incongruous effects of sex and gender categories? Discussing the importance of camp humor in the early history of the gay community, Cohan speaks of camp's "formation of a queer *affect*: of taking queer pleasure in perceiving if not causing category dissonance," so that "camp intervened in the value-making process of culture productions . . . in order to reinvest them queerly" (18). His point is that camp practices made a difference in gay history, producing feelings and pleasures that shifted perspectives. Robyn Warhol, analyzing the consumption of sentimental texts in popular culture, makes a related argument about the production of "affective patterns," claiming that "repeated reading of specific pop-culture genres creates and perpetuates gendered feelings" (120). She wonders how, in the experience of these texts, the gender categories of "'masculinity,' 'femininity,' and "effeminacy' become more flexible, less prescriptive, less pejorative, and less rigidly tied to categories of sexual identity" (xviii). Her larger point here is that the repetition of a certain kind of textual experience has not simply a visceral but a political effect.

No doubt the majority of Griffin's audiences and fans show up to see how audacious and outrageous Griffin will be in her put-downs of celebrities, gossip scoops on stars, and secrets of stardom on the bottom rung of the ladder. Likewise, fans of her reality show looked forward to the behind-the-scenes antics and Griffin's comic, nonstop commentary on the entertainment business. But when they enter either space—the theater auditorium or the reality-TV world of the D list—they experience a world that is highly oppositional to mainstream ideas about gender, a world that dismisses straight men altogether. By staking out a liminal identity Griffin repositions the perspective not just on herself but on the A-list stars and bodies broadly considered ideal or "pretty" in all the powerful normative effects of that term. The D list instead offers an alternative pleasure, and it remains to be seen if this kind of entertainment nudges audiences into thinking of gender in more flexible, less prescriptive, less pejorative ways.

CHAPTER TWO

Feminism, Postfeminism, Liz Lemonism

PICTURING TINA FEY

SPECS APPEAL

TINA FEY IS THE MOST CEREBRAL OF THE WOMEN COM-
ics treated in this book, known for her wit as the acerbic
anchorwoman on *Saturday Night Live* and for the sophisticated humor of
her NBC sitcom *30 Rock*, hailed by critics as a brilliant satire of network
television. She is also the only one who had formal schooling in theater.
Born in 1970, she graduated from the University of Virginia with a degree
in drama in 1992 and then trained in improvisation with the Second City
comedy troupe in Chicago. She joined *SNL* as a writer in 1995 and made
her television debut five years later as the conservatively dressed co-anchor
of its "Weekend Update" segment, the first of a series of "geek girl" characters she would play. The most developed of these is her *30 Rock* character,
Liz Lemon, the brainy writer who eats Three Musketeers bars for breakfast
and repairs her bra with scotch tape. Fey has never been associated with the
foul language or lower-body humor of Kathy Griffin, Sarah Silverman, and
Margaret Cho, nor does she engage in the full-body mimicry that Wanda
Sykes performs or the slapstick goofiness of Ellen DeGeneres. Instead, Fey
is known for brilliant one-liners and her signature black-rimmed eyeglasses,
emblem of the sharp-sighted intellectual.

The eyeglasses became the central prop in the media buzz that has relentlessly focused on Fey's looks, an ironic turn for a comic famous for her
wit. When Fey became a regular on "Weekend Update," she soon was beloved for her "sassy sweetness—cloaked in stage-prop smarty-pants glasses,"
as one reviewer put it. "Men wanted to date this cute, hilarious nerd;
women wanted to be her" (Mitchell, 88). Fey's choice to wear glasses—
rarely seen on women in television—confounded the cliché from hun-

When Tina Fey debuted in 2000 as co-anchor of "Weekend Update" on Saturday Night Live, her black eyeglasses became her trademark as "geek goddess" with "specs appeal." Photo courtesy of Photofest.

dreds of movies in which the heroine removes her glasses and becomes instantly gorgeous, a beautiful sight rather than someone who can see. Instead, Fey kept her glasses on and delivered "poison-filled jokes written in long, precisely parsed sentences" (ibid.). By 2001 *Entertainment Weekly* was reporting the regard Fey had won for these "precisely crafted, pertly delivered zingers" but also for being "hot" and turning eyeglasses into sexy accessories (Baldwin). Journalists dubbed her "the geek goddess" and "the thinking man's sex symbol" and touted her "specs appeal."

The glasses became such a trademark that Fey and Amy Poehler used it as a joke in their acclaimed 2008 political sketch on *SNL* in which they impersonated Sarah Palin and Hillary Clinton, respectively. Poehler as Clinton angrily objects to Palin as a sexy figure who strutted into national politics with a "pageant sash and Tina Fey glasses" (Fey, *Bossypants*, 214). The joke alluded to the way former beauty queen Palin was described as a "Tina Fey look-alike" long before Fey agreed to impersonate her on *SNL*.

Because it soon became evident that despite the eyeglasses Palin was no intellectual, Fey's impersonations effectively played against the brainy "type" she'd established on "Weekend Update" and 30 *Rock*. The performances as Palin launched Fey into national politics and prominence. In polls conducted by the American Research Group in October 2008, voters repeatedly referred to Fey's impression of Palin even though no poll question mentioned Fey (Teinowitz).[1] Mocking Palin's lack of knowledge about international relations and geography, Fey's line "I can see Russia from my house!" was repeated so often that Palin later had to protest that she never actually made this claim.[2]

Fey was a household name by 2010, featured as a cover girl for magazines from *Mirabella* to *Vanity Fair*. The moniker ubiquitously used to describe her was "sexy librarian," the stereotype illustrating mild astonishment about desirability and studiousness in the same female body. Not surprisingly, the perceived contradictions around Fey's persona were pegged as part of the pretty or funny binary for women comics. "In an industry in which a woman can be either gorgeous or funny but rarely both, she's the rare exception," a *USA Today* writer noted in 2008 (Freydkin). The ambivalent attitude toward this supposed exception is evident in the remarks of a costume designer who told *Vogue* in 2010 that Fey made possible "the acceptance of the dark-haired girl, the acceptance of the sexy librarian, the girl with glasses who's smart but can be pretty" (Van Meter, 3). His comment inadvertently sums up the cultural expectation: the very idea of the pretty and smart girl who is not even blond is a stretch.

Fey's best-selling memoir, *Bossypants*, demonstrates her awareness of this perceived stretch as a cultural absurdity about gender; no matter how brilliant she is, no matter how funny, successful, and nationally acclaimed for her writing, pop-culture consumers and purveyors remain enthralled by what she looks like. The cover photo of *Bossypants* cleverly sends up the traditional pretty author photo in a grotesque mash-up of feminine and masculine physical features, the lovely female face with the heavy, hairy, masculine hands and arms. The *Bossypants* title is a moniker from childhood, a playground taunt, but the photo is an unnerving image about gender and power, how culture pictures and fears a woman who's "the boss," a reference to Fey's groundbreaking stint as head writer at *SNL* and her powerful roles as star, writer, and producer on 30 *Rock*, the sitcom she created. On the back cover, fake endorsements further satirize the focus on Fey's looks, intimating that even as an author, her appearance will be prioritized over her writing. Under the traditional back-cover heading "Praise for Tina Fey," the first two endorsements read:

"You'd be really pretty if you lost weight." — College Boyfriend, 1990

"Tina Fey is an ugly, pear-shaped, overrated troll." — The Internet

In the same vein, the first chapters of *Bossypants* satirize the cultural scrutiny of women's bodies and the resulting self-surveillance of women who feel compelled to fix their "deficiencies," which Fey spells out in a long list that includes "nasal labial folds" and "lunch lady arms" (20). All women are supposed to live up to impossible ideals, she writes, enumerating these ideals in another list that includes "long Swedish legs," "the hips of a nine-year-old boy," and "the arms of Michelle Obama" (23). In a book that comically skewers gender expectations about work, motherhood, and family relations, Fey makes clear how strongly they are grounded in the body itself. In an earlier interview she pinpointed these worries as the basis of her comedy, in a summary that has become formulaic for women comics: "I think I got interested in comedy because I wasn't the pretty girl in middle school" (in Jacobs, "Real Tina Fey," 87).

In all, Fey as a cerebral comic is deeply embedded in body politics and the anxieties about femininity that her image provokes and she, in turn, satirizes. The pretty versus funny dynamic has particular resonance given Fey's reputation as "Hollywood's token feminist," as critic Melissa McEwan has put it. In many ways this tension plays out as feminism versus femininity, especially on 30 *Rock*, where Fey's bumbling feminist character, Liz Lemon, is pitted against the glamourous performer Jenna Maroney (Jane Krakowski). Because Liz is the writer and Jenna is the star of the fictional television show, the setup broadly replicates the cliché of the funny one versus the pretty one, although 30 *Rock*'s gender politics is far too complicated to depend on such a reductive ploy. Both characters, for instance, are implicated in the series's satirizations of popular postfeminism, a highly influential model of contemporary femininity. 30 *Rock* is prominent in this discussion not only because Fey is so strongly identified with the feminist character she created for this show but also because it showcases Fey's most extensive comedy on gender politics, with entire episodes built around questions of feminism and postfeminism. 30 *Rock* has been the lightning rod for angry criticism about Fey's representations of feminism. Fey did not write every script for every episode, although she clearly had a hand in shaping and revising every script, as she explains in *Bossypants* (174–192). So while I focus overall on material written by and not simply performed by women comics, 30 *Rock* is a collaborative effort, with Fey a key player in this collaboration.

I draw on concepts of both feminism and postfeminism in my discussion of Fey's image and stardom, including her engagement in the postfeminist issues of femininity and glamour. The 30 Rock episode "TGS Hates Women" gets extensive analysis because it responds to feminist backlash against Fey and explicitly takes up the pretty/funny binary in its plot about a glamourous woman comedian who prompts feminist questions about looks and comedy. My argument about 30 Rock is that it is not, in fact, a feminist series but rather a series that tests and teases out representations of feminism. Central to those representations is Fey herself and the conflation of her character with 30 Rock's madcap heroine Liz Lemon.

"SUPERFUNNYSMART FEMINISM"

Fey's reputation as a feminist says a lot about the charged and contradictory meanings of the term itself. On the one hand, her status as a feminist icon has prompted both adulation and disappointment, with some critics complaining her comedy works against feminist ideals. On the other hand, some journalists who refer to her as a feminist often qualify the term to explain that it's a version of feminism that is consumable in popular culture. In April 2010 the Los Angeles Times called her a "feminist who isn't angry" (Sharkey, 4), and the previous month an article in Vogue described her as a star who brought to television "her particular brand of superfunnysmart feminism" (Van Meter, 458). Both characterizations paint "real" feminism as humorless and too unpleasantly contentious for mainstream entertainment; they also bolster the arguments of the feminist critics who see Fey's work as a superficial version of serious gender politics. However, the question at hand is not about the authenticity of Fey's gender politics but rather about how feminism as a theme and buzzword functions in Fey's stardom and in her work, particularly in relation to the glamourizations of her media image.

Fey herself is reluctant to use the "F" word in interviews and invokes it in Bossypants in a passage inferring that indeed feminism is an unpalatable element that must be quietly sneaked into comedy. This is an unusually long and detailed passage describing the SNL Sarah Palin–Hillary Clinton sketch with Poehler. The story of her decision to do the impersonation, the fine points of the writing process, and the replica of the script altogether take up seventeen pages. No other sketch or performance is described in so much detail, and no other script is included whole within the book. The sketch portrays Palin and Clinton "crossing party lines to address the now very ugly role that sexism is playing in the campaign," as Fey's Palin character piously puts it (210). The cleverness and feminist punch of the sketch lies in its illustration of how the double standard about attractiveness, no matter how sexist, still benefits the pretty one. Fey's Palin sweetly comments that she is "tired of words that diminish us, like 'pretty,' 'attractive,' 'beautiful,'" while Poehler's Clinton bitterly adds, "'harpy,' 'shrew,' 'boner shrinker'" (212). The extended treatment Fey gives to this sketch in *Bossypants* suggests she's especially proud of this work. Nor is she subtle about its meaning. "You all watched a sketch about feminism and you didn't even realize it because of all the jokes," she writes. "It's like when Jessica Seinfeld puts spinach in kids' brownies. Suckers!" (216–217). The punch line plays down the obviousness of the protest about sexism in the sketch while it also underscores how feminism is in fact mainstreamed in certain strands of women's comedy, folded in but not flagged as such because of all the jokes.

Fey's reputation as a feminist actually was cemented earlier in the 2008 presidential campaign, when Hillary Clinton ran against Barack Obama in the Democratic primaries. On an *SNL* "Weekend Update" special report on women and politics that spring, Fey satirized the sexist treatment of Clinton by the media and the ironies of women thinking they were now beyond feminism. "Women have come so far as feminists that they don't feel obligated to vote for a candidate just because she's a woman," Fey says in the monologue. "Women today feel perfectly free to make whatever choice Oprah tells them to." Fey points to media accusations that Clinton is a "bitch" and heartily agrees. "Bitches get things done," she says. She concludes with the much-quoted line "Bitch is the new black," which reinterprets the fashion cliché into a claim for the white, older woman over the younger, black man. The line is a clever appropriation of "bitch" as authoritative, forceful, and effective, an in-your-face rebuke to the tired cliché that assertive men are leaders, but assertive women are bitches.[3]

Fey's comedy has focused consistently on gender beginning with her work on *Saturday Night Live*, for which she was recruited from Second City. When she moved from behind the scenes to appear in the skits, she often zeroed in on women's issues. A *New Yorker* profile observed, "Gender has been Fey's ace since she arrived at 'S.N.L.,'" citing her material on topics that varied from bikini waxing and infertility to sexist stereotypes. Her delivery, the essay emphasizes, hits "like a lash" in jokes like this: "Hey, kids, it's the great women of U.S. history! Collect all ten!" (in Heffernan). Fey's joke is typical of the gender critique frequently found in her comedy; it takes a swipe at male versions of history but also at female complicity in the ways gender and history are represented and sold.

In a 2009 interview Fey characterized her agenda in comedy as "something to do with gender and telling the truth about women. At least, as truthfully as I can see it. To let them be flawed in the way they are flawed" (in S. Armstrong, 8). Some of Fey's most caustic comedy on *SNL* focused on these flaws, as in her famous "Mom Jeans" ad that lampooned sloppy fashion sanctioned by pieties about motherhood, "You're not a woman, you're a mom," or in the sly implication about responsibility in her announcement of a birth control patch newly available for women, "It's three inches wide and says GET OFF ME." Indeed, Tina Fey's brand of superfunnysmart feminism is known for its acidic bite. In her infamous *SNL* skit "Old French Whore," aging prostitutes as game show contestants tell comically gruesome stories until one of them drops dead. Some of her *SNL* colleagues in 2002 called her humor "hard-edged," "vicious," and "cruel" in her insights about female culture and sexist practices. In one of her "Weekend Update" stories on the sexual abuse of female prisoners by corrections employees, she reported it was a problem in every state except Minnesota: "So, ladies, if you wanna rob a bank but you don't want your cooter poked, head to beautiful Minnesota, land of ten thousand lakes" (in Heffernan).

Her first extensive treatment of "the truth about women" with all their flaws was her screenplay for the hit film *Mean Girls* (2004), which exposed Girl World, the shrill high school universe presided over by gorgeous bullies with the power to manipulate their peers and ruin lives. Praising the intelligence and wit of the film, reviewers often used the word "sociological" to describe the acuity of its observations; in fact, Fey wrote the screenplay based not on a fictional text but on a self-help book for parents, Rosemary Wiseman's *Queen Bees and Wannabes: Helping Your Daughter Survive Cliques, Gossip, Boyfriends, and Other Realities of Adolescence* (2002). Filling out the characters of Girl World, Fey shaped the sociology into a narrative about a high school trio of toxic, living Barbie dolls called The Plastics, who manage to seduce and entrap an intelligent young woman, twisting her values into superficial judgments about looks and popularity. In later interviews Fey claimed her sharp insights into Girl World came from Wiseman's study but also from her own experience of using her caustic wit defensively in high school—"lashing out at others to make myself feel better," she says in a 2009 interview, even if the meanness was "in my circle of loser friends" ("Oprah," 3). The fictionalized version of this appears in the *30 Rock* episode "Reunion," in which Liz remembers her high school days as a victimized nerd, while her high school peers remember her instead for her devastating wit and cruel quips. Fey, like Kathy Griffin, points to high school as an origin story about claiming an identity as an outsider—Griffin through the gay young men who eventually align her with camp humor and Fey through the development of a savvy and spiky wit.

Although the critical success of *Mean Girls* demonstrated Fey's skill as

a scriptwriter, she continued in cinema as an actor and as a voice in animated films, while her primary scriptwriting project as of 2006 was the
NBC sitcom *30 Rock*. Fey created the series about a weekly, late-night,
live-audience, comedy-variety show based on her experiences at *SNL*. *30
Rock* satirizes the corporate nature of network television, and gender politics is a key theme of the series as well, reflecting the widespread criticism
that *Saturday Night Live* operated as a clubby, masculine space where
women were not especially welcome, least of all in its first two decades.
In the 1990s a group of strong women comics in the cast (Molly Shannon, Ana Gasteyer, Cheri Oteri) helped establish a serious work ethic and
were given credit for turning the show around after some years of declining
quality (Shales and Miller, 485, 528–529). Fey is often commended for further changing the culture at *SNL* after she became head writer and made
certain that women comics were prominently featured in sketches and in
writing contributions. Janeane Garofalo, who briefly worked at *SNL* in the
mid-1990s and complained of the sexist atmosphere, lauded the "Tina Fey
regime" as an "exorcism" of the frat-boy mentality (Hefferman, 2).

On *30 Rock* the fictional late-night comedy series *The Girlie Show*,
called *TGS* by the characters, is transparently a version of *SNL* in which
a frat-boy mentality predominates through an old-boy circuit of network
executives. Fey produces, writes, and stars in the series as the main character, Liz Lemon, a thinly disguised version of Fey herself, a harried, super-
conscientious thirty-something head writer in charge of a group of unruly male comics. "She's mostly me," Fey has said about the character,
"with some neuroses and behaviors exaggerated" (in Freydkin, 9). Because
Fey's given first name is Elizabeth, the name Liz Lemon is a joke that's
self-referential and self-deprecatory, playing on the slang connotations of
"lemon" as "sourpuss" and "defective goods." Liz is characterized as a dour
drudge because she's the only sane and responsible authority figure in a
dysfunctional workplace, but the reference mocks her gender politics, too.
In the pilot episode, she's pegged as a "Third Wave feminist" by her boss
on the show, Jack Donaghy (Alec Baldwin). When Liz writes a best-selling
book, in the season 4 episode "Problem Solvers," she learns that in the Chinese version her name is translated "Lesbian Yellow Sour-Fruit," reflecting
the stereotype of the humorless, man-hating feminist.

The name is a cheap joke, but the Liz Lemon character also figures
in a more complicated satire of corporate and patriarchal politics. Her
feminist ideals are constantly undermined by an emotionally adolescent
team of male comedy writers and a sexist bureaucracy focused on profits
at the expense of quality and ethics. Liz Lemon caricatures the creative,
liberal-minded career woman with a "Big Ben–size biological clock," as

Donaghy puts it, who wants to have it all despite a pathetic romantic life of doomed dates and loser boyfriends. Liz's foil characters offer radically different ideas about professional women: her conservative and chauvinist boss Donaghy and her ultrafeminine colleague Jenna, who aspires to glamourous stardom. In short, Liz is located in a dense thicket of expectations, stereotypes, and contradictions about being a woman comedy writer in the masculinist, ratings-driven world of network television.

As a metafiction, television about television, 30 *Rock* is especially self-conscious about media representations of women. The intense and unusual referentiality of 30 *Rock*—its constant allusions to popular culture, other television series, feminist and postfeminist contentions, and national political debates—suggests the centrality of these discourses to the show's comedy. Likewise, 30 *Rock* is attentive to Liz Lemon as a fictionalized version of the real Tina Fey, famous as a female comic and comedy writer who succeeds not only in the male milieu of *Saturday Night Live* but in the larger male-dominated comedy business. Fey explained to a journalist in 2009 that in creating 30 *Rock*, "we wanted to make sure that everything we did with Liz Lemon rang true on some level—to me or to one of the other women in the room" (in S. Armstrong). So while the comedy and narratives of 30 *Rock* are frequently absurd, they are grounded in specific real-life histories and cultural contentions about women as producers of and images in media.

PICTURING TINA FEY

In the spring of 2009 30 *Rock* aired an episode with a subplot about Liz Lemon's photo on a magazine cover, openly engaging the question of Tina Fey's stardom and how she was represented. Riding a wave of publicity for multiple 30 *Rock* Emmy nominations, Fey appeared on the covers of four mainstream magazines between March and September 2008 and a fifth early in 2009, beginning a rich history of conflicting cultural pictures of the star comic. The conflict, in turn, illustrates the larger conundrum of women's bodies in comedy—the meanings of their bodies in conjunction with the meanings of their language and wit. The cover girl, the glossy image that sells newsstand magazines, usually involves the feminine ideal in one of its popular versions—upscale glamour, all-American cuteness, femme fatale sultriness, pouty insouciance, bad-girl sexiness—none of which fits Fey's brainy persona.

"Mamma Mia," the 30 *Rock* episode that takes on this conflict, reduces the issue to whether Liz Lemon wants to be seen as pretty or funny when

On 30 Rock *Tina Fey played Liz Lemon, the idealistic feminist identified as a direct descendant of the Mary Richards character on* The Mary Tyler Moore Show *of the 1970s.* 30 Rock *insinuated that women have done better since then but that network television has become much worse. Photo courtesy of Photofest.*

she poses for the cover of a magazine. But the theme draws on a larger question about Fey's looks and the looks associated with feminism. How do people picture the superfunnysmart feminist? The T-shirt slogan that has circulated in women's groups since the 1990s reads, "This is what a feminist looks like," implying there's uncertainty about this or that feminists look different from their stereotypes or that no two feminists look the same. Nevertheless, the slogan and T-shirt address the cliché that the feminist can be picked out from the crowd as the ugly one. This in turn proceeds from traditional feminist objections to conventional femininity that internalizes the male gaze and thus makes women complicit in objectification of their own bodies. In the episode "Secrets and Lies" 30 Rock plays along with the stereotype of the shabby feminist by portraying Liz in old-lady cardigan sweaters and a clothing style that her boss Donaghy dubs "small-town lesbian."

However, many versions of feminism and postfeminism have reclaimed female pleasure in femininity. Postfeminists in particular have recouped cosmetics and fashion as "a source of pleasure and power that is potentially resistant to male control," Jane Arthurs notes, offering "an alternative route to self-esteem and autonomy" (87). Generally, contemporary feminism shies away from the orthodoxy about makeup and feminine attire that informed the more militant dogmas of 1960s women's lib. Nevertheless, the nervousness about what a feminist looks like continues, as seen not only in the popularity of the T-shirt but in the circulation of alarming images such as the fanged woman on the cover of Mike Buchanan's book Feminism: The Ugly Truth. The cultural nervousness is about feminism's critique of gender roles and ultimately of femininity as a set of expectations that has worked against women's best interests. These contentions unsettle the most basic beliefs about identity and in the long run spur palliative moves such as picturing Fey, known for her feminism, as really a fashion-loving cover girl.[4]

In the "Mamma Mia" episode Liz and Jenna are chosen for a magazine photo shoot because of the wildfire popularity of their TGS skit "Dealbreakers," which Liz has written and Jenna performs. The skit is a wicked advice forum that tells women when to dump their husbands or boyfriends; it decides which female demands and desires are deal breakers in the relationships. While Jenna gets all the attention for delivering the lines, Liz is the brain and creator in the background, so she's happy to be invited to the photo shoot. Jenna warns Liz that she should avoid funny props and goofy poses because those inevitably are the ones chosen over the more flattering shots. "Open your mouth a little and try to look like Lindsay Lohan," Jenna instructs her, a subtle joke about postfeminist obsession with girlishness (Lohan is almost half the age of Jenna/Krakowski) as well as a reference to Fey's *Mean Girls*, in which Lohan starred. Wholly at a loss about how to pose, Liz hangs her mouth open in a facial expression that is vacant to the point of stupidity. But when the photographer hints that a funny photo rather than a chic one might be on the cover, Liz springs into action, dismissing Jenna's advice, dropping all vanity, and clowning for the camera without restraint. "You're the funny one!" the photographer cries, happily snapping away.

In Tina Fey's real-life career as a cover girl, humor about her images has propelled a number of witty cover photos. The 2007 cover for *Geek* magazine features the headline "Tina Fey Is Smarter Than You. Deal With It." In the photo Fey smiles cheerfully back at the camera, her arms crossed, signature black-rimmed glasses in hand, every inch the pretty boss to a roomful of adoring but terrified gearheads. For *Geek*, the way to deal with the threat of the intelligent woman, the woman capable of "poison-filled" zingers, is the "sexy librarian" image. In 2004 Fey appeared on the cover of the feminist, pop-culture magazine *Bust* wearing fishnets, heels, and a tiny black dress and crouching in front of a 1970s typewriter, with the headline "Tina Fey: Geek Chic." Fey's posture and over-the-top facial expression in the photo signal camp humor, a clue that this play at sexiness isn't serious, while at the same time the image melds sex and humor in a package reminiscent of the heroines of classic screwball comedies, romantic leads like Claudette Colbert, Carole Lombard, and Myrna Loy who were famous as "fast-talking dames." And this is exactly the point: Tina Fey's persona resists cover-girl imagery because, unlike the cover girl, she talks back. She can be reduced to a one-dimensional image, yet her more complex dimensions as quick-minded humorist are an inextricable part of her appeal.

Three of the 2008 magazine cover designs—in *Parade, Entertainment Weekly,* and *Rolling Stone*—acknowledged this resistance to traditional feminine poses by putting Fey in campy or funny scenarios that emphasize her role as a comic. *Marie Claire*, however, posed her more seriously as a fashion model for an issue that included tips on spring dresses, "extreme heels," and aging skin. Although the fashion-model pose works at odds with Fey's celebrity image, it also indicates the cultural work of appropriating Fey's star power into more conventional modes of femininity: she wears a tight-fitting trench coat, a windswept hairdo, and nighttime eye makeup; her mouth is slightly open in the traditional fashion-model hint of a half-smile at the camera, a move mocked on the *30 Rock* episode with her ridiculous attempt to imitate a Lindsay Lohan facial expression.

In the fall of 2008, following Fey's celebrated Sarah Palin imitations, *Vanity Fair* featured her on its January 2009 cover in an Annie Leibovitz photo as a tongue-in-cheek American girl wearing a kicky red, white, and blue majorette costume and carrying a gigantic American flag. The image combines classy and even classic iconicity with irreverence by mocking the nationalist iconography that drapes women with flags and names them Liberty or Columbia. Given that Fey is known for comedy that undercuts sentimental nationalism, the effect is ironic. Yet this cover photo celebrates a woman comic who commanded national attention during a presidential election and who looks appealing in a flirty little skirt. Leibovitz's visual wit thus puts multiple codes—patriotism, the all-American girl, the pinup—into comic spin in order to deal with the representation of an attractive woman known for what she says as opposed to what she looks like.

Surveying the blitz of Fey magazine covers during this time, one journalist argued that the "problem" with Fey as cover girl was the ambiguous status of her looks in the hierarchy of celebrity glamour. She "straddles the liminal space between Hollywood bombshell and geeky antihero," he writes. "She's no schlub, but she's also no Megan Fox" (Haramis), referring to the actor commonly regarded as one of the most beautiful celebrities of the decade. Fox is the same age as Lindsay Lohan, indicating that the cover-girl ideal runs a couple of decades younger than Fey, who turned forty in 2010. Even after Fey appeared on the cover of *Vogue* in a traditional fashion-model pose, a *Los Angeles Times* blogger cattily summed up the event as an aberration: "Decidedly unglamourous gal Tina Fey has received the highest blessing from the world's fashion bible—the writer and actress appears on the March cover of Vogue magazine" (Donnelly). In short, because Fey's celebrity is about her writing rather than her looks and because she can indeed "glam" up into a Hollywood bombshell, one strand of celebrity discourse keeps insisting that the real Tina Fey is more schlub than fox, just as another strand insists the real Fey is a fashionista rather than a feminist. The bigger issue here is the uneasiness about identifying a real Tina Fey for image-driven media when her celebrity is powered more by her words than by her image.

In an ironic blowback effect, Fey's media images became sexier and more conventionally feminine after the Palin performances launched her to heightened national attention in late 2008, as if Palin's beauty-queen status adjusted the lens on Fey as well. Even though the sexy librarian descriptions continued, the discourses began to tilt toward glamour, so she was praised for beauty "unusual" in a woman comic. *Glamour* magazine included her in "The 50 Most Glamourous Women of 2009," emphasizing that "her intelligence is glamourous." The comic or campy photographs gave way to high-fashion poses for the March 2010 *Vogue* cover, in which she is all decolletage and windblown hair. For the *Esquire* cover the following month, she is funny but decidedly sexy, tarted up in raccoon-eye makeup and a sleek, plunging dress, handcuffed to a cop—a high-class hooker striking a pose with the tell-tale fashion-model open mouth.

Part of the comic effect is the contrast of the trashy *Esquire* image with Fey's other comic personas, from prim "Weekend Update" anchor to goofy Liz Lemon to the harried suburban mom in *Date Night*, a film that premiered the same spring. The accompanying *Esquire* "interview"—a list of Fey's funny one-liners about herself—emphasizes Fey's comedy, and the slutty-girl photos accompanying the piece are all jokes: Fey standing on a table at a rowdy party, Fey presiding over a trashed room with a passed-out policeman in it. An inset quotes her description of how she turned down far more salacious poses proposed by *Esquire*: "I'm a mom. And my kid's going to find this someday. I don't want to be handcuffed to a bed in Esquire. What are you, nuts? I got to get my kid into kindergarten" (in Jacobs, "Real Tina Fey," 85).

Tina Fey as a slutty bad girl is funny, but it's a joke grounded in a cultural imagination of casting the very smart, very funny woman in a standard, feminine visual discourse. Interestingly enough, the slutty criminal motif was used three years earlier in *Maxim* magazine's photo shoots of Sarah Silverman, playing up her bad-girl image in a far more predictable way (Spitznagel, "Sarah Silverman"). *Esquire*'s costuming, making up, and staging of Tina Fey is nearly identical to that of Silverman as tarty criminal, in red high heels, hands up against a car, looking back at a cop. Certainly with Fey the comic effect is the contrast with her fussy persona; in both cases, though, men's magazine editors have chosen to imagine comic women with razor wits as the femme fatale, on the wrong side of the law, fetishized into a campy cliché about female danger. In short, magazine photos have tended to reclaim Tina Fey into more standard versions of femininity.

Fey's 2009–2010 media makeover occurred just as a great amount of attention went to her weight loss in the late 1990s before her debut on "Weekend Update." It was no secret that Fey lost thirty pounds before moving in front of the camera, as reported by *Entertainment Weekly* in 2001, when her celebrity was relatively new (Baldwin, 40). Though there are no before photos being circulated to document the makeover, Tina Fey was, by her own account, a moderately plump writer with a bad haircut when she moved to New York from Chicago in 1995. Maureen Dowd's January 2009 article in *Vanity Fair* was the first to go into detail about the before version of Tina Fey, saying she wore "knee-length frumpy dresses with thrift-store sweaters" and "maxed out" at 150 pounds, which is not extraordinary for someone who is five feet four; still, she was "quite round," her husband, Jeff Richmond, reported, remembering her as a "Rubenesque kind of beauty"

(11). Fey said she lost weight and got a better haircut because she "wanted to be 'PBS pretty'—pretty for a smart writer" (11), but when Dowd's article came out, a *Boston Herald* columnist immediately noted how the makeover story contradicts Fey's feminist image: "Here we thought you were the type of girl who would reassure us that being skinny wasn't important" (Falcone). Letters to the editor in *Vanity Fair* the next month under the heading "Funny Girl" likewise chastised Dowd for the focus on Fey's looks and weight. But once the before story was out it became a standard question or reference point, as seen in the 2009 interview in *O* magazine, for instance ("Oprah," 5) and the *Vogue* article in 2010 (Van Meter, 3).

Dowd writes that Fey's makeover "is the stuff of legend" (7), but the makeover as a larger cultural narrative is the more pertinent legend at hand, in that it offers a powerful way to deal with Fey's celebrity image. In her extensive study of what she calls "Makeover Nation," Brenda Weber has demonstrated how the makeover phenomenon promulgated throughout pop culture registers cultural anxieties about normativity, especially around gender. Women who have successfully transitioned to the ideal body feel they have finally entered authentic womanhood by "fully participating in scripts of bourgeois heteronormativity" (13). The makeover as a normative discipline is particularly relevant to Fey, whose wit and intelligence are often framed as anomalous for women.

In all its versions on reality television, talk shows, and advertisements, the makeover narrative of before and after results in the made-over subject achieving "greater competence and agency in the world, localized primarily at the site of gender" (Weber, 164). This is exactly the trajectory of Fey's story as presented by Dowd: Fey's emergence into competence and agency was her emergence on "Weekend Update" after her weight loss. So her writing career and work in Second City in the 1990s became the before part of the narrative. The absence of before imagery in one sense renders the heavier, bad-haircut Tina Fey outside of representation. The focus instead is what Weber calls the after body of the makeover, the "polished, refined, beautiful, and confident individual" made possible through physical transformation, so that "the body stands as the gateway to the self" (5).

Because Fey was visible to the public only as the after body at her "Weekend Update" debut, the ugly-duckling makeover story conflates Fey's wit and body as emergent at the same moment. Biographical articles and interviews describe Fey's longer career in comedy, but the visual discourse produces her as the comic who was always already the sexy librarian. In all, the discourses around Tina Fey as supersmartfunny feminist as well as the nonfeminine klutziness of her alter ego Liz Lemon suggest how the makeover story pulls her back into normative femininity. By 2009 Fey's pre-

SNL makeover discourse merges with the media makeover to produce, on the cover of *Vogue*, a model-gorgeous Tina Fey, the glasses gone, the hair loosened, even a facial scar airbrushed. Weber emphasizes that the bottom-line mandate of the makeover is "to do away with female bodies that do not act or appear feminine" (169). Fey's extensive media makeover is arguably the cultural reclamation of her femininity. While the Liz Lemon character acts out awkward and ungainly attempts at femininity, the star image of Fey compensates with more acceptable figurations of gender, making over the unacceptable elements of goofy but lovable Liz.

The glossy fashion-model photos of Fey are at odds with the self-deprecating persona in the accompanying interviews. The "Tina on Top" article in the 2008 *Marie Claire* with the fashionista cover, for example, is a fake interview by Amy Poehler that parodies the standard beauty-tips feature story, with Fey explaining she had plastic surgery in which "they loosen the skin on your whole body, and they pull it up over your head, and then basically tie it like a bread bag." For the *Vogue* story, Fey is asked about her status as an "unlikely glamour-puss" and says, "I don't fit the mold. Clearly, by asking that question they are kind of letting me know that I am an aberration" (in Van Meter). More bluntly, she told *Esquire* in regard to the sexy librarian image, "What I've come to realize is that when people say, 'The thinking man's whatever'—there's no such thing. The thinking man also wants to fuck Megan Fox" (in Jacobs, "Real Tina Fey," 87). In short, the written text gives ample evidence of Fey's wit and ironic distance from the photos, while the images themselves sometimes tell an entirely different story, as in the "serious" fashion magazines that offer a seriously glamourous Tina Fey.

Not surprisingly, Fey devotes an entire chapter of *Bossypants* to her cover-girl treatment, broadly satirizing the technologies, accessories, and cosmetics that go into the production of a finished image that will resemble "a young Catherine Deneuve" (156). Her advice for photo shoots is to lower the expectations of everyone involved: "Show up looking like an uncooked chicken leg and they can't help but be pleased with the transformation once they get all your makeup on you" (147–148). The technologies of glamour photography are satirized in an episode of *30 Rock* as well when Liz submits to a makeover so she can come out from behind her writer's desk and appear on the show, referring to Fey's camera debut on *SNL* in 2000. On *30 Rock* the makeover results in a horrific haircut, laser surgery for her eyes that nearly blinds her, and—in a gag moment in front of a supposedly high-definition camera—the exposure of enormous zits, scars, and wrinkles that send her into an *Exorcist*-style meltdown ("Dealbreakers' Talk Show"). The implication is that makeover technologies that produce chic Tina Fey cover girls are just that—technologies, graphics, choices of lens, and lighting that can produce monsters as easily as glamour girls.

The wrap-up of the "Mamma Mia" episode about magazine covers likewise can be interpreted as Fey's commentary on glamour and celebrity in relation to the woman comic. At the photo shoot, a chagrined Jenna steps back as the photographers crowd in on the funny one, their work resulting in a montage of Liz in a series of ridiculous poses with a rubber chicken. At the end of the episode Jenna disgustedly shows Liz the magazine cover touting Liz as "The Funniest Woman in New York." In the photo Liz wears a bizarre lederhosen outfit, a nod to Liz's interest in German culture and language referenced throughout the series, and is crouched over a toilet giving birth to a rubber chicken. The grotesquery is, in Bakhtin's terms, carnivalesque in its rude violation of boundaries: the female body as merger of human and animal, the toilet as the site merging waste and birth, and the entire scenario specifying the lower body as site of fertility, productivity, and culture—the woman comic birthing the classic comic prop of the rubber chicken. Instead of being embarrassed, Liz is thrilled. "I'm on the cover!" she says, beaming with self-satisfaction. Neither Tina Fey nor her character Liz Lemon is generally associated with bawdy, grotesque comedy, but the cover-girl episode of 30 Rock strongly suggests that for both of them, gender expectations about being pretty are rich comic material.

FEMINISM, POSTFEMINISM, 30 ROCK

30 Rock is not the first sitcom to pose the question of what a feminist looks like. It is the first to acknowledge the history of that question and to make the representation of feminism one of its running themes. 30 Rock situates Liz Lemon as the successor of the prime-time heroines Mary Richards, Murphy Brown, and Ally McBeal, television's high-profile interpretations of the liberated, single career woman in the 1970s, 1980s, and 1990s, respectively. The pilot episode of 30 Rock nods to this history by parodying the famous credit sequence of The Mary Tyler Moore Show, often considered one of the earliest extended representations of feminism on a prime-time series.[5] The 30 Rock pilot opens with a song that mimics the Mary Tyler Moore theme song as it follows Liz Lemon on the streets of Manhattan on the way to her office weighed down with a large box of hot dogs for which she's paid $150 in a misguided attempt to teach justice to some line jumpers at a street vendor's stand. While Moore's Mary Richards character was noted for her charm ("Who can turn the world on with her smile?" the theme song asks), Liz appears in a series of clumsy social en-

counters as she tries to give away her hot dogs to strangers and colleagues. As she admits to a co-worker, her grand gesture toward fair play has resulted in an overpriced box of wieners.

This opening sequence maps out the series's interest in—and cynicism about—television roles for women. As Liz arrives at her office, the corny song continues with the bouncy chorus "That's her, that's her, that's her," a wry reference to *That Girl* (1966–1971), another early series about a single career girl.[6] At this point the camera reveals that the tune is not background music for Liz Lemon or *30 Rock* but part of a skit being rehearsed for *The Girlie Show*. While Mary Richards on *The Mary Tyler Moore Show* struggled to become an associate television news producer with modest authority, Liz Lemon is the head writer for a major network show, later described in this episode as "a real fun ladies' comedy show for ladies." However, the skit in rehearsal is "Pam, the Morbidly Obese Over-Confident Woman," featuring Jenna Maroney in a fat suit—altogether, an ironic reversal of the *Mary Tyler Moore* standard of "quality television."[7]

The implication is that although women have come a long way from the days of Mary Richards, with television shows now written and produced by and for ladies, the result is tasteless skits about female bodies. *30 Rock* takes great pains to suggest that dumbed-down programming is the result of network pressure for ratings, but it also shows Liz constantly compromising her ideals as the cost of working for a national television network. Especially during the first two seasons Liz is "schooled and seduced" into sleazy network thinking, Emily Nussbaum observes ("Meta Follies"), and Liz would "protest, then cleverly make her case, before giving in." So the series often implies that women, even when in powerful positions, are complicit in sexist or morally bankrupt media.

Given the high expectations of Tina Fey's politics, feminist media critics in 2010–2011 expressed considerable disappointment with the series and with Fey herself because *30 Rock* so often undermines Liz Lemon's feminist ideals and replays the clichés of the feminist as frumpy, unfeminine, possibly a lesbian, or—as suggested by the *Bossypants* photo—secretly a man. The complaints often fell into the assumption that bad images of feminists and professional women are politically detrimental and out of place on a series that in most ways espouses a progressive ideology. The targets of these criticisms include Liz Lemon's hapless state as a desperate single woman, her lack of female friends and focus on male relationships, the ugly-feminist jokes, and the good-old-boys mise en scène that includes only one, habitually silent, woman writer on the staff.[8]

The complaints on blogs emerged in feminist scholarship as well. Joanne Morreale in an essay in *Feminist Media Studies* objects to the images of Liz

Lemon as a supposedly unattractive loser and to the 30 *Rock* narratives that make progressive claims and then recoup them, citing an episode ("The C Word") in which Liz's feminist stand backfires and she dissolves into tears and is carried out of the room. Morreale argues that this exemplifies how the series "addresses but does not challenge gender politics" (486), implying that "bad" images—the woman collapsing in tears—should not be represented on a show with a feminist agenda.

However, the episode cited by Morreale challenges gender politics in a more complicated way by showing its entanglement with racial politics. Generally, 30 *Rock* is fearless about making these connections between race and gender, especially regarding the relative power of women and black men in a white, patriarchal culture. In "The C Word" episode, Liz and her African American colleague Tracy are in very different positions because black men are rewarded for "acting white," but women are rarely rewarded for "acting masculine." Tracy is invited to a swank NBC golf outing, where he first loudly exclaims that he's the only black guest and quickly catches on that his own movie career will benefit if he performs as "white," or "plays the game," as Jack puts it. Meanwhile, Liz attempts to be a nurturing female boss because she's been taken to task for being stern and professional—that is, acting like a man. The staff quickly takes advantage of her new, feminine style, forcing her to stay up all night doing their work while they hand in flimsy excuses. Liz regains her authority by quoting a feminist speech from *Designing Women* before collapsing from her all-nighter. It's true that she has to be carried out of the office by Pete, but the point of this disaster is its parallel and contrast to the white speech Tracy gives at the country club, which is applauded and rewarded. The unsettling implication of the entire episode is that Liz playing the game like a man, being the tough boss, will not yield the same benefits as Tracy playing the game like a white man.

Far from claiming 30 *Rock* as a feminist text, my primary argument here is that it does a different kind of cultural work than expected by Morreale and others in representing a feminist TV writer complicit in profit-driven, sexist, mainstream media and in exploring the messy ways feminist ideals play out in institutions and popular culture. 30 *Rock* is noteworthy precisely for the centrality of feminism and gender politics in Liz Lemon's characterization as the awkward, unattractive loser, a standard trope about the comic protagonist as the insider/outsider, a liminal figure, sympathetic for being on the fringes of the power structure. Significantly, Liz Lemon is a liminal figure in relation to corporate and cultural power as well as to feminism, and 30 *Rock*'s comedy draws from both corporate and feminist politics.

Certainly Liz's feminist ideals are frequently lampooned. When Liz finds herself without a date on Valentine's Day, she protests the holiday by celebrating an alternative one, the February 14 birthday of American suffragette Anna Howard Shaw. "Valentine's Day is a sham created by card companies to reinforce and exploit gender stereotypes," she tells a puzzled little girl who's selling Valentine cookies. When the little girl demurs, Liz bitterly recites her history of romantic failures, making clear the Shaw holiday is a feminist booby prize for losers ("Anna Howard Shaw Day"). However, 30 *Rock* also targets the media sexism that makes feminist intervention necessary. In season 4 episode "Lee Marvin vs. Derek Jeter" Liz learns that she's an affirmative action hire and that *The Girlie Show* was picked up by NBC only because women's groups protested a show called *Bitch Hunter*. In cutaways in this episode and a later one, scenes from *Bitch Hunter* illustrate its over-the-top misogyny; Will Ferrell cameos as the macho guy with an automatic weapon breaking into a women's restroom and a bridal shower to hunt down "bitches." These scenes satirize popular Ferrell films like *Anchorman* (2004) that indulge in sexist jokes as retro— that is, sexism can be both enjoyed and dismissed because the age of serious sexism is over. It's a strategy that an *Entertainment Weekly* blogger called out the previous year, citing sexist Super Bowl ads and a misogynist scene in the Will Ferrell Broadway play *You're Welcome America* as examples of why "we still need feminism" (J. Armstrong, "ShePop").

The *ET* blog post subtitle was "Fun with Postfeminism!" 30 *Rock* has fun with postfeminism, too, particularly the version claiming that feminism is "over," accomplished, or no longer relevant, so women can focus on staying young well into middle age, as satirized through the character Jenna. The introduction to this book provides the history around popular postfeminism as a set of media representations touting a new liberated woman who no longer needs feminism. Various scholars agree that the tropes of popular postfeminism emphasize choice, consumerism, girl culture, individualism, traditional concepts of glamour, and the romanticization of motherhood, all of which are satirized on 30 *Rock*.[9] While traditional versions of feminism remain skeptical about femininity, popular postfeminism embraces it as a central ideal. Attention to fashion, makeup, diets, and fitness can be prioritized in this view because women now have the same opportunities as men and can use sexiness as part of their overall empowerment, as evident in the girl power trend of the 1990s. Far from deflecting the male gaze, the aim is to exploit it. Sarah Projansky finds that this "play with the heterosexual male gaze" is a strategy that "intensifies heterosexuality" in popular versions of postfeminism and secures femininity as one of its primary elements (*Watching Rape*, 80). The focus on

femininity carefully excludes certain bodies and classes, privileging whiteness, youth, heterosexuality, and budgets that can include $200 haircuts.

With its focus on conventional femininity, postfeminism is strongly tied
to fashion and girliness. The "'girling' of femininity," Tasker and Negra say,
is intrinsic to the postfeminist notion that "age is only acknowledged to
the extent that its effects can be erased by cosmetic surgery" ("In Focus,"
109). 30 Rock directly satirizes this ideal through the title of its fictional
series, The Girlie Show, as well as through its star, Jenna, targeted for her
staggering self-centeredness and delusional attempts to look like a twenty-
something. Jenna embodies the "girl discourse" that Projansky describes
as intrinsic to postfeminism: the glamourization of youthful femininity,
the crucial need for commodities to accomplish it, and the displacement
of adult concerns with the "fun" concerns of girls ("Mass Magazine Cover
Girls," 44–45).

The casting of Jane Krakowski is itself a clever allusion to postfeminism
because of Krakowski's previous role on Ally McBeal (1997–2002), a nearly
identical supporting role as a peppy blond who occasionally breaks into
song and trades heavily on her good looks. The eponymous heroine of Ally
McBeal, played by the wispy Calista Flockhart, sporting excessively short
skirts and indulging in a whimsical fantasy life, was literally a cover girl for
postfeminism in the 1990s. The June 29, 1998, cover of Time magazine pictured feminist history through the images of Susan B. Anthony, Second
Wave icons Betty Friedan and Gloria Steinem, and the fictional Ally Mc-
Beal labeled the "death" of feminism.[10] Because 30 Rock blatantly skewers
the girlie ideal through TGS and its scripts are weighted with complicated
allusions to popular culture, the nod to Ally McBeal seems as calculated as
the Mary Tyler Moore parody in the pilot as part of its agenda about media
representation of the liberated woman.

The Liz Lemon character participates in 30 Rock's crafty tweaking of
postfeminist clichés, especially the romanticization of marriage, motherhood, and family, all of which are perceived to be imperiled by the feminist
push to keep women in the workplace, assuming women are there only by
choice. Surveying postfeminist narratives and ideals of the late 1990s and
the 2000s, Diane Negra finds that these topics are the ones most likely to
garner sentimental or nostalgic treatments, often resulting in "retreatism"
from professional to family life, as seen in a number of television series such
as Judging Amy (1999–2005) and films like Sweet Home Alabama (2002)
about women giving up careers in the big city to move back to traditional
roles in smaller towns (15–46). In each of these narratives the woman finds
her true feminine self in making this move. Mocking the trend, 30 Rock at
one point has Liz follow her boyfriend to live in Cleveland, where she finds

that by Cleveland standards she's attractive enough to be a model for local department store ads ("Cleveland"). The move is short-lived. Liz's dreamy idealizations of marriage are satirized when, with no marriage in sight, she impulsively buys a $4,000 wedding gown that she wears to the office and ends up using for a "ham napkin," as she puts it, when she sits on the floor eating a sloppy sandwich while she works ("Seinfeld Vision"). In the series's last season, when she finally does marry, she wears her Princess Leia costume as her wedding gown, satirizing postfeminist fantasies about the magical wedding day and the bride as princess ("Mazel Tov, Dummies!").

If Liz Lemon is an unlikely bride, it is because she decides to get married only so she can finally adopt a baby. 30 Rock specifically targets postfeminist "baby panic" that pushes the biological clock and blames feminism for goading women into professional lives that cut short their opportunities to marry and have families.[11] Crazed by the ticking clock, Liz ends up accidentally kidnapping a baby on "The Baby Show" episode, and in "Señor Macho Solo" she dates a dwarf because she's too embarrassed to admit she mistook him for a child. Lampooning the romanticizing of motherhood, Liz fantasizes being a "kick-ass single mother like Erin Brockovich and Sarah Conner" when she mistakenly thinks she's pregnant ("Cooters"). In one of the most obvious parodies of a popular postfeminist film on this topic, Liz befriends Juno 32, a young woman in an online community of pregnant teens who have all named themselves Juno after the heroine of the 2007 film of the same name. Juno valorized teen pregnancy through an appealing, intelligent young woman represented as saner than the adults in her life. In the 30 Rock episode, Liz is the insane one, shamelessly manipulating the teen into thinking Liz herself would be a "cool" mother and trying to push the baby's father out of the picture ("Goodbye, My Friend"). Liz's irrational behavior satirizes the fetishizing of maternity that Negra finds in postfeminist narratives positing "motherhood as the all-purpose site of adult female subjectivity" (85).

30 Rock draws on the postfeminist tenet that professional accomplishment for women entails the loss of femininity. In that sense, the less obvious link between Mary Richards and Liz Lemon is the character Murphy Brown from the sitcom of the same name that ran from 1988 to 1992. 30 Rock cites this link in the "Baby Show" episode when Jack warns Liz about her maternal yearnings: "Don't go all Murphy Brown on me." Bonnie J. Dow asserts that Murphy Brown served as a "validation of women's progress" and an "exploration of the costs of that progress" and "the lessons of liberation" (Prime Time Feminism, 137). Brown encapsulated postfeminism at the moment before it developed its girlie side, when its primary emphasis was the sacrifices of family and romance incurred by successful

feminists. A divorced loner with few social skills, the Brown character was portrayed as a woman paying for a high-profile career, her ambition costing her romantic relationships and meaningful friendships, illustrating the "perceived conflict between femininity and personal success" (143). While Liz Lemon is not nearly as masculinized as the brassy Murphy Brown, a running comic theme is Liz's continual failures at traditional femininity or being a real woman. That is, the jokes rely on the popular perception of feminist-or-feminine. In the "Blind Date" episode her co-workers tell Liz she looks like Tootsie, the transvestite character played by Dustin Hoffman in the 1982 movie of that name. When Donaghy goes to her for romantic advice and introduces his question by saying, "Liz, you're a woman," she replies, "Yes. That doctor was a quack" ("Larry King"). This line of comedy references the postfeminist cliché about the successful woman not being a real woman while it also indulges in a joke about the more cartoonlike elements of the earnest, nerdy, feminist Liz Lemon.

Nevertheless, while 30 *Rock* often mocks feminism's earnestness and postfeminism's slickness, the Liz Lemon character is also involved in narratives that expose and trouble the contradictions of feminism and postfeminism. For instance, 30 *Rock* frequently foregrounds the white privilege and unconscious racism of the savvy, independent woman in ways overlooked in *Ally McBeal, Sex and the City,* and *Murphy Brown.* The middle-class whiteness of Second Wave feminism was scathingly targeted by that movement's critics, just as critics of postfeminism have attacked its focus on white, young, heterosexual women as its ideal subjects. Kimberly Springer argues that scholars "studiously" note the racism of many postfeminist narratives without analyzing exactly how whiteness functions in these texts as an enabling condition for the privileged heroines ("Divas," 249). 30 *Rock* is unusual in implicating Liz Lemon as a woman whose success is tied to her position as a "white lady from Whiteville," as Tracy calls her in one of his many indictments of Liz's unconscious racism ("Jack Meets Dennis").

Liz enacts that racism, for example, when she finds herself seated next to Oprah Winfrey on a plane and pours her heart out to the famous talk-show host, prostrating herself on Oprah's breast in a classic representation of the mammy and the "honey chile" ("Believe in the Stars"). Her unthinking bigotry is foregrounded in other ways as well in this episode: because Liz is hallucinating on tranquilizers she's taken for the flight, her seatmate is actually not Oprah Winfrey at all but a plump, young black girl, implying that for Liz, large black women all look alike. Granted, Liz is on drugs when this happens, but it's part of a larger pattern about how Liz Lemon sees or fails to see people of color. She mixes up the names of the black men on the set in "Do Over," and in "Somebody to Love" she reports her Arab neighbor to Homeland Security, certain he is involved in suspicious activities—putting maps on his wall, doing timed physical-fitness training—when he was merely preparing to be a contestant on *The Amazing Race*. So while *30 Rock* openly taunts the whiteness of postfeminism through the girlie, blond Jenna, it also raises the larger question of feminism in relation to race through the character of Liz.

30 Rock develops without necessarily resolving complicated questions about the varieties and complexities of progressive gender politics. The episode "Rosemary's Baby," for example, takes on the relationship of younger feminists and postfeminists to Second Wave feminism. Carrie Fisher guest-stars as Rosemary Howard, an older feminist who was Liz's girlhood idol, the female television comedy writer who broke the barriers in the 1970s so that decades later Liz could have a prestigious job at NBC. Liz arranges to have Rosemary work as a guest writer on *TGS*, where they are briefly bonded as feminists opposed to Jack's sexism and advocating for equal rights for older women workers. But it quickly becomes clear that their relationships to institutions and corporate life are very different. Liz is successful at NBC because she plays by the rules. Indeed, "Rosemary's Baby" begins with Liz being awarded the corporate "followship" prize for being a good follower, and she is about to reject it until she learns it comes with $10,000 in cash. As opposed to Liz Lemon's followship, Rosemary has retained the political contentiousness that energized her as a trailblazer in the 1970s, so in writing skits for *TGS* she insists on touchy topics like blackface or "an abortion clinic in New Orleans." Liz is shocked and defensive, telling her uneasily, "You can't do race stuff on TV. It's too sensitive." This is an inside joke, given *30 Rock*'s own edgy race stuff, but the point is that as the corporate-friendly postfeminist, Liz is uneasy with Rosemary's uncompromising politics.

As it turns out, Rosemary is an impoverished and dysfunctional alcoholic who rails that she sacrificed her personal life so women of Liz's generation could have prestigious jobs at NBC. "You wouldn't have a job if it wasn't for me. I broke barriers for you!" she shouts. "I sat around while my junk went bad, all for you! I didn't have any kids. You're my kid! You're my kid that never calls!" Liz Lemon is, in fact, Rosemary's baby in this sense, the product of a political movement that got at least a few women into the boys club of the television industry in the 1970s. But *30 Rock* doesn't represent that history; instead, it represents the 1960s–1970s feminist as the crazy lady who drinks wine from a thermos and whose offspring, the wretched Liz Lemon, "Rosemary's baby," is unnatural, born of a deluded mother who brings Satan—sell-out postfeminism—into the world.

What this episode accurately represents, through the framework of mothers and daughters, is the conflict between Second Wave feminists and twenty-first-century feminists or postfeminists as a struggle often pitched in emotional, generational terms.[12] In the end, the episode recuperates Rosemary's perspective even as it distances Liz from Rosemary's radicalism. First, it acknowledges Rosemary Howard's importance as a female role model by literalizing Liz's indebtedness to her. Liz arranges to pay Rosemary a monthly stipend "for forever." This is a gesture of social justice that distinguishes Liz from Jack—who would never contribute money to a social justice cause—and from Rosemary, whose conscience and radical politics have driven her into poverty. Second, the episode validates Rosemary's vision of edgy comedy through a racial parody performed by Jack (which won Alec Baldwin an Emmy award). In all, "Rosemary's Baby" is a savvy take on intergenerational quarrels within feminism but also on the ambivalent and multiple positioning of feminism itself—as a history and influence, as a dated set of strategies, and as a valid critique of sexism and racism in the entertainment business.[13]

LIZ LEMONISM

Feminist critics often point out that despite Liz Lemon's supposedly frumpy feminist looks, 30 Rock does little to disguise Tina Fey's attractiveness. Liz may wear old-lady cardigans, but she also wears low-cut necklines that remind viewers of Fey's cover-girl images (Morreale, 486). As this argument suggests, critiques of 30 Rock often conflate Fey with Lemon. In a frequently quoted criticism, blogger Sady Doyle in 2010 complained that Liz Lemon typifies the so-called feminist whose most active concern is "'body image' . . . without taking much note of the fact that as a white, abled, cis [conventionally gendered] person she conforms to the 'beauty standard'" herself. Doyle describes Liz Lemon's politics as a white, "privileged semi-feminism" utterly detached from issues of race, queerness, and disability. Doyle admits that her anger about the 30 Rock character is actually her anger at the larger phenomenon of popular, watered-down versions of feminism. The political interests of this would-be feminist, she says, are limited to "certain issues only as they pertain to her own personal life."

Newsweek blogger Kate Dailey quoted Doyle on this phenomenon and named it "Liz Lemonism," going on to compare its limitations to the more emphatic, straightforward feminism found in Amy Poehler's NBC series Parks and Recreation (2009–). Doyle's complaint overlaps with the concerns of Morreale, whose primary argument is that Liz Lemon ends up confirming rather than challenging the status quo. Yet a very different reading of Liz Lemonism has been posited in *Salon* by Rebecca Traister, responding to the online feminist critics of *30 Rock* and specifically to Doyle's disappointment in Fey's character. Traister argues that Liz Lemonism, far from being a flawed, tepid version of feminism, is *30 Rock*'s satire of that very phenomenon—the privileged, would-be feminist. The limitations of Lemon as "a gutless, self-interested semi-feminist," says Traister, are jokes that appear in the series almost every week ("Tina Fey Backlash").

Doyle's protest of Liz Lemonism as politically reprehensible and Traister's recognition of Liz Lemonism as satire speak to the tension about how feminism can or should be represented in comedy. The portrayal of the *30 Rock* heroine as a gutless, self-interested semi-feminist makes feminist fans uncomfortable, Traister says, because it evokes the problem of feminism and comedy about women—where to draw the line about female targets of ridicule or satire. Traister further contends that Fey herself has drawn controversy because she is "a professional comic . . . not a professional feminist," and the anger about Fey's work on *30 Rock* demonstrates "the intensity of longing for a perfect feminist idol." Certainly the mixed signals around Fey—the longing for and nervousness about feminism in popular culture—are demonstrated in the high stakes of the looks of this perfect feminist idol, given multiple cultural pressures to picture her as nonthreatening, mainstream, and even glamourous.

As Fey's most developed and sustained comedy about gender, *30 Rock* functions not as a feminist text but as a slippery text about contemporary feminism, lampooning girl-culture popular postfeminism and politically correct feminism that is blind to its own privileged status. Liz Lemonism, I would argue, satirizes both feminist hypocrisy and postfeminist bourgeois angst. Yet Doyle is right to suspect a privileged, middle-class politics looming under the surface of *30 Rock*'s comedy as its perimeter in imagining social change. This dynamic can be glimpsed in the season 5 episode "Brooklyn without Limits," when Liz buys jeans from an independently owned boutique and is smugly proud that she's not patronizing a big corporation and is supporting an American company: the label on the jeans says "Hand Made in USA." She finds out the label is misleading; it actually means the jeans are made by the "Hand" people, Vietnamese slaves owned by Halliburton on the island of "Usa." Liz agonizes because these are the only jeans that have ever made her look good, and she's bought multiple pairs. She is at first adamant that the nasty socioeconomic story behind the jeans is irrelevant, but her political conscience gets the best of her, and in the end, she takes them all back. In the final scene, she is wearing her beat-up overall-style jeans that balloon her backside into two basketball-size globes—a visual joke that could well have been labeled "This Is What a Feminist Looks Like."

The episode mocks and valorizes political correctness, and the payoff is a joke about how hideous political correctness looks on Liz's body. However, the darker joke is the absurdity of how global capitalism is masked in everyday transactions, and the episode positions the audience to sympathize with Liz's political conviction rather than the indifference of Jack Donaghy, who sees nothing wrong with Halliburton making a buck where it can. Yet what the episode—and generally the trajectory of 30 Rock—does not acknowledge are the limitations of Liz's liberalism. She doesn't stage a protest, write letters to Halliburton, or do an exposé of hideous labor practices, any of which a traditional social-change feminism might entail. Instead she makes a personal choice about her looks, money, and commodities—on the one hand, a traditional feminist axiom that the personal is the political, and on the other hand, a far less ambitious political move that accepts personal power as the only viable kind of agency, so that social issues become personal ones, spun on the axes of appearance and consumerism. This is the Liz Lemonism that slips under the radar of fans like Traister who appreciate the satire, and its implications are more unsettling than the bad images of Liz repairing her bra with Scotch tape or eating entire blocks of cheese as a late-night snack.

"TGS HATES WOMEN"

I conclude with a detailed analysis of the season 5 episode "TGS Hates Women" because it alludes to the controversies around Fey's feminist reputation and focuses on the feminism versus femininity issue—specifically, sexy women comics who are accused by feminists of exploiting their attractiveness to get media attention. While "Rosemary's Baby" portrayed Liz as the ever-compromising postfeminist in relation to the older, traditional feminist, "TGS Hates Women" cleverly flips the generation gap in the other direction. In the latter episode, Liz is the older feminist up against the sexy young writer and performer Abby Flynn (Cristin Milioti), who is being hailed by young postfeminists as "the freshest female voice in comedy." The episode successfully lampoons both sides of the issue but backs away from a closure, demonstrating 30 Rock's willingness to explore controversies of feminism and representation without attempting to resolve them. However, the awkwardness of the closure, protested by reviewers as bad writing or a cop-out, suggests a larger unease about how or whether feminism works as a viable critique of popular culture.

Bloggers quickly noted that the episode seems to have been a response to online feminist criticisms of Fey and her series. The plot begins with Liz stunned that a well-known feminist website, *JoanofSnark.com*, has accused *TGS* of hating women. "It's this cool feminist website," Liz says, "where women talk about how far we've come and which celebrities have the worst beach bodies—Ruth Bader Ginsberg!" The website, shown in a cutaway, is a parody of the real-life *Jezebel.com*, which advertises itself as "Celebrity, Sex, Fashion for Women. Without Airbrushing" and immediately acknowledged the reference: "thrilled and honored to be parodied by *30 Rock*" (Hartmann, "Joan of Snark"). *Jezebel* perhaps typifies the semifeminism or Liz Lemonism decried by Sady Doyle, given its coverage of traditional women's magazine topics as well as protests against airbrushing and sexism in media. As part of *30 Rock*'s parody, a later cutaway shows *JoanofSnark .com* links that include "She-mail: Free email for feminists" and "Fashion & Beauty: Because you're a goddess," clearly a jab at glamourous versions of postfeminism. Because the cutaway is brief, the details are impossible to see without pausing the image, showing a distinct expectation for viewers who are invested in these issues of feminism and representation and showing *30 Rock* itself invested in this elaborate joke about how, exactly, contemporary feminism is being defined and practiced.

That question is picked up and fine-tuned into the question of what feminist comedy entails, although the first scenes give obvious answers by satirizing sexist comedy clichés. Liz is disturbed by the accusation that *TGS* hates women because, she says, the previous few shows were entirely focused on its female star, Jenna. The scene then cuts to two of Jenna's skits showing her as Amelia Earhart crashing her plane and Hillary Clinton deciding to nuke England, both disasters happening because these women suddenly got their periods. Realizing these are sexist jokes, Liz quickly explains that they are "ironic reappropriation," but she stumbles and admits she's "not sure anymore." She goes on to say that *TGS* "started as a show for women starring women. At the least, we should be elevating the way women are perceived in society." At that moment, Liz gets her period, goes crazy, and fires everyone in the room. Typical of the metacomedy on *30 Rock*, these jokes target misogynist humor and the problem with ironic reappropriation as a rationale for circulating sexist images. At the same time, they deploy irony by positioning Liz—and certainly Tina Fey—as responsible for keeping the misogyny in circulation. This opening also refers to the set of expectations that followed Tina Fey to *30 Rock*—that it would be a show "for women" and even a show "elevating the way women are perceived in society"—the piousness of the latter statement marking it as a satirical take on the gender representation on both *TGS* and *30 Rock*.

The satire of sexism continues in the following scene with Jack. When Liz asks him if he thinks she hates women, his reply is a lecture on how women are "genetically predisposed" to compete with each other for "strong, powerful men like myself," a parody of certain supposedly scientific explanations of female behavior. Jack pompously explains that if you breed this competitiveness out of women, you end up with "a lesbian with hip dysplasia." In the same scene Jack ruminates on the proper life goals for an ambitious young woman: "a doctor's nurse, or a lawyer's mistress, or the president of the United States' shopping assistant." Not surprisingly, he refuses Liz's request to hire Abby Flynn as a guest writer until he sees a photo of the blond, buxom comedian that prompts him to agree immediately. As this scene demonstrates, egotistical masculinity is an easy target for feminist comedy.

Liz exclaims that hiring Abby will be a "fem-o-lution," but the earnest feminist sisterhood collapses when Abby arrives at the studio flaunting her miniskirt and pigtails. To Liz's horror, Abby uses a cutesy baby voice to flirt with the writing staff and bounces her ample cleavage by jumping up and down on a trampoline, where she's joined by an enthralled Jack. The baby voice and pigtails allude to Sarah Silverman, known for her cover-girl good looks, and Milioti is made up to resemble Silverman as well. However, the trampoline confirms the Abby Flynn story as a reference to the 2010 feminist quarrels around comic Olivia Munn, a former *Playboy* model who appeared in a bikini on the January 2010 cover of *Maxim* and in a photo shoot that included suggestive poses on a trampoline. Munn was hired by *The Daily Show* in 2010 after *Jezebel* criticized it for being an old-boys club despite its liberal politics (Carmon). But feminist forums (Itzkoff, Williams) protested that Munn is not as funny as other available women comics, and Munn received even more salacious attention when she appeared on the January 2011 *Maxim* cover wearing a small T-shirt and transparent underpants (Hartmann, "Olivia Munn's Groin"). The debate about Munn's looks versus her talent generally overlooked the image and persona that launched her to fame: between 2006 and 2010 she co-hosted *Attack of the Show!* on the G4 network in which she represented the girl geek as articulate and techno-savvy, updating viewers on video game news, reviewing new games, and confidently situating herself in a notoriously all-boy milieu. So her hire on *The Daily Show* taps this previous persona of the brainy computer whiz even if it was overshadowed by her career on men's magazine covers.

Tina Fey has acknowledged Munn as the subtext of the "TGS Hates

Women" episode and admitted the controversy was about her looks. In a radio interview Fey remarked that if Munn "were kind of an aggressive, heavier girl with a LeTigre mustache posing in her underpants, people would be like, 'That's amazing. Good for you.' But because she is very beautiful, people are like, 'You're using that.' It's just a mess! We can't figure it out" (Fey, "Tina Fey Reveals All"). The mess Fey decries is the way the pretty/funny binary has evolved into market demand for women comics who are drop-dead gorgeous and the feminist suspicion about how good looks trump comic talent in casting decisions. The mess is also the feminist critique of Fey herself, who is suspiciously good-looking to play a Liz Lemon character who is supposedly drab and unattractive. In fact, defending her ubiquitous bikini images, Munn has invoked Fey as a comparison: "Hey, Tina Fey has been on the cover of Vanity Fair and Entertainment Weekly, and she always looks like a bombshell. . . . It is possible in this world to be pretty and funny and successful all at the same time" (in Spitznagel, "Daily Show's Olivia Munn"). Still, "TGS Hates Women" loads the question by making it clear Abby's good looks are her only power. Her jokes are terrible: "You know what sucked about my last lesbian orgy? Right in the middle of it, one of us had to get up to go use the bathroom, and then we all had to go," she says to the fascinated TGS male writers, who chuckle at her supposed wittiness while Liz fumes.

The looks controversy is played out in a brilliant scene that pits Liz's feminist moralizing against what she calls Abby's "baby hooker" act. Deciding to educate Abby, Liz meets her in Central Park in front of the statue of Eleanor Roosevelt, "champion of the rights of women and the lid on my high school lunchbox," she proclaims. In what follows, Liz's self-righteous pitch is grounded in standard feminist discourse about sexiness as a construction rather than a natural behavior: Liz implores Abby to talk in her "real voice" and to drop the "sexy baby" act, the gross jokes, and the pigtails. In response, Abby insists she really is a sexy baby and that she can't help it if men are attracted to her, as illustrated by a homeless man who is watching her and playing with himself. More cunningly, Abby poses a question that makes an indirect reference to Tina Fey's own star image and its sexualization: "What's the difference between me using my sexuality and you using those glasses to look smart?" The line cleverly cites Fey's star history in which the glasses have not simply made her look smart but have been central in her "specs appeal" glamour. Even if her images are not as sexualized as those of Olivia Munn/Abby Flynn, they conform to mainstream standards of attractive femininity embraced by popular postfeminism.

Unlike earlier scenes that satirized sexist comedy in a recognizably feminist dynamic, the park scene complicates the question of feminism and comedy by characterizing Liz's feminism as judgmental moralism but also a valid perspective. When Abby protests that her image is her own career and none of Liz's business, Liz replies, "Except it is, because you represent my show, and you represent my gender in this business, and you embarrass me." This is a fairly straightforward assertion that representation matters and affects more than the individual artist or performer. Far from undermining this perspective, the script follows up with a demonstration of how embarrassing Abby's performances can be. The homeless man yells "Kiss!" and Abby, after reiterating her position on sexiness, says, "Shall we give the gentleman what he wants?"—leaning toward Liz with her tongue outstretched.

Unfortunately, after setting up the topic of feminism and representation so richly, a preposterous plot turn dismisses it altogether. As it turns out, Liz Lemon is proven correct in her feminist conviction that Abby Flynn's sexiness is a performance. On the Internet she finds footage of the "real" Abby Flynn, who is actually Abby Grossman, a far funnier and less glamourous comic. Liz triumphantly posts the footage on *JoanofSnark.com*, but her strategy backfires with terrible consequences. Abby furiously confesses that she had taken up the blond baby hooker persona to disguise herself from her abusive ex-husband, who is trying to kill her. Liz's posting has already alerted him about Abby's location at the *TGS* studios, so Abby must flee for her life. Liz Lemon's feminist intervention is a disaster, and even though abusive male power, the horrible ex-husband, is actually at fault, the end result is that it looks like Liz and *TGS* both hate women.

In the NPR interview in which she discusses "TGS Hates Women" and the Olivia Munn controversy ("Tina Fey Reveals All"), Fey admits the episode "confused and sort of delighted the Internet in a way." The reference here is to the episode's mixed online reviews and outrage about the ending, which was perceived by many as a cop-out. "That story is so loaded and complex that I was really glad that we did it . . . because it sort of opens up more questions than it answers," Fey continues. For her part, she thought Liz was "in the wrong" to criticize the young comic's use of her sexuality, but she also thought it was a "tangled-up issue . . . and we didn't go much further saying anything about it other than to say, 'Yeah, it's a complicated issue and we're all kind of figuring it out as we go.'" The raw process of figuring it out demonstrates the tendency of 30 *Rock* to make tentative explorations of gender issues rather than to take a feminist stand about them. My argument here has been that the dynamic of 30 *Rock* is not in fact feminism but the contesting and disputing of popular ideas and versions of feminism—quite literally "figuring it out as we go."

A good example of this dynamic is the way "TGS Hates Women" represents the contradictory ways that power circulates in gender relations and in popular culture. Traister, who praises the episode for "slicing and dicing nearly every angle of the arguments that crop up any time anyone tries to talk about gender, popularity and perception," pinpoints a line that she characterizes as a "truth" about gender. When Jenna wants to destroy Abby Flynn out of pure jealousy, Liz says, "No, Jenna, that's exactly the problem: men infantilize women and women tear each other down." Traister notes approvingly that there's "no contradictory punch line here. Liz spoke the truth!" ("'30 Rock'"). Traister is accurate in characterizing the seriousness of Liz's comment on how women lose power. Yet conflicting concepts of women and power are central to this episode's thematic. Liz does not have the power to hire Abby until Jack sees a photo of Abby's cleavage, and when Abby comes on board, her sexuality is powerful. Liz believes she is helping Abby Grossman restore her power as a "strong, smart, beautiful woman," she tells Jenna, but even though Abby Grossman's comedy was funnier, she clearly had no media power until she became the baby hooker Abby Flynn.

These intriguing contradictions are shut down when they are trumped by the power of the abusive ex-husband, and tellingly, the comic energy of the episode shuts down at this point, too. Traister's exclamation about Liz speaking the truth about women and power is a reminder that the best and wittiest comedy in this episode is in the sharp barbs at all sides of the issue—Liz's moralism, Abby's sexy-baby pose, and Jack's sexism. In contrast, the weakest scene is the final one, when Liz is flummoxed by the dramatic revelation of the death threats from the maniacal ex-husband. "I thought it was, like, pressure from society," she says feebly. The episode ends with Liz meekly getting the writers back to work: "We were on page six where Wonder Woman gets her period." That is, the episode circles back to its opening joke as if the entire question of the sexy woman comic had not been raised, indicating an inability to articulate what is true about feminist critique of sexualized representation.

In the episode's exploration of feminism and comedy, a subtle detail tips a hat to the political comedy of the Rosemary Howard character from the earlier "Rosemary's Baby" episode, who—though last seen as impoverished and possibly psychotic—turns out to be successful after all. The first cutaway to *JoanofSnark.com* shows that the website is advertising Rosemary Howard's play: "I'm Only Laughing Because It's Funny—Now on Broadway." When Rosemary (Carrie Fisher) was introduced in "Rosemary's Baby" she had just published a book with that title. This follow-up reference also alludes to Fisher, whose 2008 memoir *Wishful Drinking* was adapted as a one-woman Broadway play in 2009 and was still on tour when "TGS Hates Women" appeared the following year. By acknowledging the success of Rosemary (and Carrie Fisher), the allusion confirms the value of the Second Wave feminist as a successful comic—even as the ad appears on the website praising Abby Flynn as "the freshest female voice in comedy." After all, "TGS Hates Women" undermines the funniness of Abby Flynn's comedy but not its marketability. Likewise, the episode successfully takes some witty swipes at sexism, although satire of sexism is much easier than the questions of what feminist comedy entails, the impacts of progressive as well as sexist representations on television, the gender politics of sex-as-power postfeminism, and the moral authority—or audacity—of feminism in criticizing that stance. This ambitious set of questions exemplifies the complicated gender politics that I see operating in *30 Rock*, which never settles on a definitive answer for what feminism or the feminist looks like.

In her memoir, *Bossypants*, Fey represents herself as neither a feminist nor a postfeminist; however, there is a good deal of critical thinking about gender in her story of being a geeky girl making her way through the ridiculously macho worlds of Second City and *Saturday Night Live* and then surviving *30 Rock* stardom while breastfeeding and throwing birthday parties for toddlers. And certainly her sardonic takes on glamour, having it all, and even baby panic satirize postfeminist clichés. In her closing chapter she reveals her gender politics most blatantly in her passion about the need to change the climate for women in show business. In the sexism of that world, Fey says, even if a woman isn't using her feminine wiles to get ahead, she's being "sexually adjudicated" by network executives who "really do say things like 'I don't know. I don't want to fuck anybody on this show'" (271). The only answer, she says, "is for more women to become producers and hire diverse women of various ages. That is why I feel obligated to stay in the business and try hard to get to a place where I can create opportunities for others" (272). Meanwhile, at the age of forty, Fey sees herself slipping into the category of the "crazy" lady in comedy. "I have a suspicion," she says, "that the definition of 'crazy' in show business is a woman who keeps talking even after no one wants to fuck her anymore." This is a version of a line from the Rosemary Howard episode of *30 Rock*, and Rosemary Howard is, of course, the crazy lady with a social conscience.

CHAPTER THREE

Sarah Silverman

BEDWETTING, BODY COMEDY, AND
"A MOUTH FULL OF BLOOD LAUGHS"

TOTALLY CUTE WHITE GIRL

MORE THAN ANY OTHER COMIC COVERED IN THIS book, Sarah Silverman challenges the pretty versus funny dynamic at its very root—the cultural identification of women with their bodies. Silverman performs gross-out comedy that defies cherished ideals of femininity but also confronts contempt for the female body as filthy or degraded. So her comedy takes on the extremes of how women's bodies are stereotyped, as messier than male bodies because of menstruation, childbirth, and lactation yet more idealized in versions of femininity that deny bodily functions altogether. The latter facet of the pretty/funny tradition in comedy has allowed male comics to engage in bathroom humor with the understanding that men don't need to be pretty about these things. So when in her 2010 memoir, *The Bedwetter: Stories of Courage, Redemption, and Pee*, Silverman describes her enthusiasm for bathroom humor, she acknowledges the gender transgression: "I have—not just for a female, but any human being—an inordinate love of farts. . . . Fart jokes make me happier than just about anything in the universe" (95). The qualification "not just for a female" cites the traditional expectations about femininity that Silverman gleefully smashes in her performances. As culture critic Paul Lewis puts it, "Show Silverman a taboo about sex, excrement, or the body and she'll show you how it can be transgressed in a punchline."

Indeed, Silverman's comic performances often provoke discomfort, using the body as comedy's ground zero and inviting laughter at its unruliness. When Silverman's cable sitcom premiered in 2007, a *Salon* review of its first few episodes complained that "*The Sarah Silverman Program* has all of the charms of a joke with an audible fart as the punch line" (Havrilesky). Equally disconcerting are Silverman's reminders of the body as the source of prejudice and bigotry. She frequently lampoons the attribution of dirt and smelliness to bodies marked as "other" because of social, ethnic, or racial difference. In her concert film *Jesus Is Magic* (2005) Silverman tells her audience about a Mexican woman who confronted her for saying Mexicans smell bad. "I had to explain to her," Silverman says patiently, "that you can't smell yourself." This is the comedy of political incorrectness that *New York Times* reviewer A. O. Scott describes as "a form of political correctness in its own right," aiming to mock both bigotry and "hypersensitivity" about bigotry ("Comic"). At its best this comedy carries an unambiguous political punch. One of Silverman's most-cited routines in *Jesus Is Magic* is an unsettling joke about white privilege and the invisible, racialized labor that produces luxury items such as diamonds. In this bit she praises the beauty of a jewel found only "on the tip of the tailbone of Ethiopian babies" and expresses regret about the "moral issue" of the badly treated unions "that debone the babies." Silverman's blasé delivery speaks what is usually silenced: indifference to the exploitation of nonwhite bodies for Western commodities.

Describing the dynamics of Silverman's offensive comedy, Scott observes that "everything she says is delivered through enough layers of self-consciousness—air quotes wrapped in air quotes—to make anyone who finds it offensive look like a sucker" ("Comic"). However, the layers of air quotes do not entirely disarm Silverman's outrageous commentaries, which can easily be read as the racism, homophobia, and intolerance they parody. In short, her politically incorrect comedy is a high-wire act with the risk of falling flat into cruel, not-so-ironic racism, a problem Silverman addresses at length in her memoir. She has also used criticisms of her political comedy to illustrate her own self-consciousness of her privileged status as white and "pretty." In 2001 she found herself in a high-profile media controversy about her use of the term "Chink" in a joke on *Late Night with Conan O'Brien* (1993–2009). In *Jesus Is Magic* she describes the controversy and deadpans, "What kind of world do we live in where a totally cute white girl can't say 'Chink' on network television?"

As this suggests, Silverman's girl-next-door prettiness is a major component in the shock effect of her comedy. *Slate* critic Sam Anderson remarks, "She's pretty in a way that baits journalists into bodice-ripping Harlequin descriptions" such as "babelicious." Describing Silverman's persona and comedy, the headline of a *New York Times* article declared, "From Sarah Silverman, an Adorable Look, Followed by a Sucker Punch" (Newman). The sucker punch involves the gender expectations of pleasantness and politeness from someone who looks "adorable"—shorthand for palatable,

Sarah Silverman, seen here in her 2005 concert film Jesus Is Magic, provokes comments on the contrast between her feminine good looks and her usage of gross-out and politically incorrect humor that is usually considered masculine comedy. Photo courtesy of Photofest.

nonthreatening femininity: "Her beauty . . . lets her get away with being gross," Judith Newman writes. Along the same lines, reviewer Ruthe Stein for the *San Francisco Chronicle* calls Silverman's feminine appearance a "gimmick," explaining that "she doesn't look like someone who'd be spouting obscenities and insulting minorities." Chris Nashawaty, in *Entertainment Weekly*, similarly comments on "the disconnect between her feminine beauty and the decidedly unfeminine spew that comes out of her pretty mouth." In *Rolling Stone* Vanessa Grigoriadis describes her as "being almost too cute—a Jewish Cameron Diaz," and Stephanie Zacharek of *Salon* notes the "alluring" quality of Silverman's looks, the Breck-girl hair and "creamy glow" of her skin, "in direct contrast to the stream of unthinkable thoughts that issue, uncensored, from her lips, the sort of things that nice girls shouldn't think, let alone say" ("Sarah Silverman").

The comments on the disruption of gender stereotypes, the unfeminine spew from a pretty mouth, indicate just how entrenched traditional stereotypes remain. Gross-out humor and the comedy of political incorrectness have been male turf, associated with stand-ups such as Daniel Tosh and Dave Chappelle and films and television series aimed at and starring adolescent boys and adolescent grown-up men: *Porky's* (1982), *American Pie* (1999), *Superbad* (2007), *Beavis and Butthead* (1992–1997; 2011–2013), *South Park* (1997–), and *Blue Collar TV* (2004–2006). As affronts to good taste and middlebrow manners, gross-out and politically incorrect comedy overlap in these texts, which likewise defy respect for race, ethnicity, sexual orientation, disability, and religion. These politically sensitive subjects, as well as AIDS, abortion, 9/11, and the Holocaust, are featured topics in Silverman's stand-up comedy and on her cable sitcom, *The Sarah Silverman Program*, treated with uniform lack of reverence.

Silverman's unthinkable thoughts revolve around the abject body and the abjecting dynamic of racism. From the perspective of cultural-studies criticism, her comedy occupies the realm of what Bakhtin calls the "material bodily lower stratum," jokes "with an audible fart," as compared to the greater reliance on wit, or cerebral, "upper-body" humor, on *30 Rock*. Bathroom or gross-out humor occasionally surfaces in the latter show but was a constant element on *The Sarah Silverman Program* and even likely to be the basis of the narrative, as seen in episodes with names like "Doody" and "Pee." This is an embrace of abjection in a very different register from Kathy Griffin's *D List*, where Hollywood hierarchy is at stake and abjection means being ignored by publicists and booked at corporate conferences. Silverman's comedy instead engages cultural hierarchies about far more basic experiences, the body itself, in which abjection means the leaky, smelly, lower body and her show's surreal stories about wetting the bed, marrying a dog, and swallowing a dried-up hermaphrodite baby penis.

I examine *The Sarah Silverman Program* in detail because of Silverman's extensive input and writing on the show and also because, as a sitcom on a cable network, it subverted traditional ways of "emplotting" the transgressive comic heroine, to use Kathleen Rowe's term, in narrative. The Silverman character on the show is an extension of her comic persona. "I play a version of myself," she said in an interview, "a character with that great combination — ignorance and arrogance" (in Clements). As her primary shtick, Silverman remains in character as an obnoxious personality blind to her own ignorance and arrogance. *The Sarah Silverman Program* was structured around this self-absorbed persona and the thinnest of premises — the immature slacker Sarah, her slovenly gay male neighbors ("gaybors"), and her devoted sister Laura (real-life sister Laura Silverman), who pays Sarah's rent and all her bills. Like *Seinfeld*, it was a sitcom about "nothing" but it was propelled by the audacity of an attractive woman in the lead as a crude, tactless reprobate.

In her memoir Silverman describes her career as singularly focused on comedy and an outsider identity. She was born in 1970 into what she describes as one of the few Jewish families in Manchester, New Hampshire (220). Her stand-up work began in 1991 when she dropped out of college to pursue comedy full time. In addition to small parts in films and television, her early career included a one-season gig (1993–1994) as a writer and bit performer on *Saturday Night Live*, where her on-air time was limited and none of the sketches she wrote got on the show. Her *SNL* colleague Michael McLean remarked that this was not surprising given that Silverman doesn't do characters or anything outside her own comic persona (in Goodyear). This strategy worked to her advantage when she appeared in the 2005 anthology film *The Aristocrats*, a performance that attracted a national audience.

The Aristocrats featured more than ninety comedians doing variations of a filthy anecdote about the live-sex performance of a show-business family. One of the few female comics in the film, Silverman delivered a risky and original take on the joke — claiming she was herself a member of that show-business family and that during that time she was raped by Joe Franklin, the elderly radio and talk-show personality. Her serious demeanor during the delivery of this revelation gives no hint that it's part of the very dark gag. *Slate* reviewer Sam Anderson writes that "Silverman was the only comic in the film who met the challenge of the joke: She pushed it too far." The same year, Silverman's outrageous comic persona came to large-scale public attention with her film *Jesus Is Magic*, which interspersed music videos, comedy skits, and animated sequences into her stand-up performance. Garnering reviews and articles in national venues, including a profile in the *New Yorker*, the film was the turning point in Silverman's career. It enabled her to broker *The Sarah Silverman Program*, which debuted two years later.

As the pretty comedian who fouls conventional notions of prettiness and uses shock tactics as "funny" exposures of bigotry, Silverman fits into the pattern of women comics who challenge or satirize femininity as part of a broader rebuke of conservative politics. Silverman's comedy has been cited and appreciated by feminists and queers. *Bitch Magazine* writer Kathleen Collins names Silverman as a feminist, arguing that her "raw, direct manner forces you to confront every politically incorrect utterance and really think about what she's getting at." In Alessandra Stanley's early review of Silverman's television series in the *New York Times* ("Cruel, Clueless"), she proclaims the show "a feminist milestone" for its boldness in having a female character whose "material is as raw and profane as any man's, but served up slyly." A 2008 article in the lesbian magazine *Curve* claims that while most reviewers focus on "the racial aspects" of her comedy, its "subtext" marks her as "honorary lesbian" and queer. The subtext, writer Lori Selke finds, is Silverman's involvement with bodily taboos. "She's not afraid of the word 'cunt'" and is "obsessed with pussy . . . and 'doody' and farts and everything below the belt," Selke notes with tongue-in-cheek earnestness. "Who else but a lesbian would manage to incorporate a joke about her sister's pubic hair into the first episode of her TV show?" This argument draws on the concept of lesbian as outlaw, an outsider to the laws of heterosexuality and gender, but more generally as a disruption of cultural systems and assumptions, a fitting description of the Silverman persona.[1] On *The Sarah Silverman Program* the Sarah character's disrespect for the law—any law—is foregrounded by having her policeman brother-in-law, Jay, as her primary adversary, always suspicious of Sarah's propensity for mindless speeding, shoplifting, or abduction.

In the *Curve* article Selke additionally claims that Silverman can be understood as queer, comparing her raunchiness to that of queer performers Margaret Cho, Lea Delaria, and Sandra Bernhard. Unlike these comedians, though, Silverman explicitly denies lesbian or bisexual proclivities, explaining in her memoir that she has no "interest in vaginas, other than for their comedic value" (52). Nor does she inhabit Kathy Griffin's queer detachment from heterosexuality. However, she shares with Griffin a substantial gay following, given her politics and the gay-friendly nature of *The Sarah Silverman Program*, which regularly lampooned homophobia and came down especially hard on opposition to gay marriage ("Night Mayor," "Vow Wow"). When the series faced cancellation in 2009 after its third season, the gay-lesbian network Logo saved it by subsidizing the budget. In her memoir Silverman credits the inclusion of gay characters for this gesture by Logo (188), but even beyond those characters the series flaunts a subversive sexual politics cited by a later article by Kristin Smith in *Curve* on "our favorite straight comic," praising the "gender-bending" dynamics of the series and songs like "The Baby Penis in Your Mind."

Silverman's alignments with queers and feminism demonstrate the edginess of her work and suggest the political implications of her gross-out and politically incorrect comedy. My argument is that the connection between these topics—the abjected female body and the abjections involved in racial/ethnic identities and hierarchies—is dirt or pollution, as elaborated in scholarship by Mary Douglas and others who have described the ways the body and social populations are mapped and coded to form rankings of status and privilege. Douglas describes "dirt" as a cultural perception of "matter out of place," the pollution of a system, whether that be a system that organizes the body or cultural groups (35). Silverman herself links the domains of body and race through her frequent self-identifications as "dirty Jew" or "hairy Jew" or, as she sings in one of her sitcom episodes, "half monkey, half Jew." Picking up this startling image, I focus on each of these components: comedy grounded in the female body, perceived as inherently dirty or bestial (monkey), and comedy grounded in racial/ethnic identification (Jew). Finally, I address the problems presented by Silverman's racial comedy and her own response to those problems. My framework is Bakhtin's work on the carnivalesque, which addresses the abject and grotesque body and provides a rich entry to questions of the female body, comedy, and culture.

HALF MONKEY

Silverman's song with the line about being "half monkey, half Jew" occurs in the 2008 episode "Pee," which centers on the character Sarah's bedwetting problem. This is Silverman's signature topic, given its centrality in her memoir, *The Bedwetter*. In her book Silverman describes the problem of being a bedwetter well into her teens, and in the audio commentary for "Pee" she confesses that the problem returned for a while after she was fired from *Saturday Night Live*. The book's fake introduction, written by Silverman in the third person in the tradition of celebrity promotions, represents her as a leaky body and potty mouth: "She has peed on mattresses up and down the Northeast Corridor and has used the topic of human excrement to vault her from obscurity into the global fame she enjoys today" (xiii). This is a parody of the rise-from-obscurity narrative, rewritten as a rise through and with the materials of human waste, celebrating rather than repressing the excremental. Conventionally a topic of embarrassment rather than comedy, bedwetting is a disquieting self-identification for any celebrity, though its connotations are particularly relevant to the Silverman persona. Naming herself "the bedwetter" is a joke that characterizes her as a body that is fallible, porous, soiled, and adamantly unashamed. Bedwetting is the body's punch line, the leaky condition of childhood and old age. It marks the body as unpredictable and unreliable—in short, as comic.

Bedwetting is a key signifier of Silverman's comedy also because it is a social transgression, a pollution taboo, the spoiling of sheets and mattresses, an affront to adult domestic space. Douglas describes in anthropological work often cited by scholars of literature and culture that dirt and disorder are the "materials" of cultural systems, the elements that create boundaries and systems. Dirt is "matter out of place," Douglas writes. Cultures designate as "dirt" the elements that violate and pollute social categories—food bits and stains on clothing, bathroom items in living areas (35–36). Bedwetting is specifically characterized as matter out of place in "Pee" when Sarah's sister Laura lectures Sarah about her inability to be a responsible adult. "In our society," Laura says primly, "adults are expected to put their waste in a toilet." The imperiled mattress and bedclothes in the episode are those of persnickety Officer Jay (played with super-straight macho bluster by Jay Johnston), Laura's boyfriend and later husband, who is pressured into allowing Sarah to sleep at his place to take care of his pet turtle while he and Laura are away.

The narrative of "Pee" resists the conventional structure of a sitcom, which would restore order (continence) and promise a cure. Instead, the episode depicts fantasies about the joys of lawlessness and the pleasures of transgression. Terrified of wetting Officer Jay's bed, Sarah stays awake all night. Eventually she hallucinates that the pet turtle speaks, and this encourages her to steal Jay's gun so she and the turtle can run away together "like Thelma and Louise," as the turtle puts it. The Thelma and Louise reference amplifies the gendered lawlessness of Sarah as bedwetter: it's not nice, not feminine, to wet the bed, especially the bed of a policeman. In a panic, Sarah accidentally shoots the turtle, sparing Jay's bed but killing his prized pet. The episode ends not with a cure for Sarah's problem but rather with Sarah happily wetting her own bed again and having a warm, soggy dream, a fantasy of being underwater with her little dog Dougie, who is "half Chihuahua, half pug," while she herself is "half monkey, half Jew." She and Doug happily float through the water as fellow hybrids and mongrels, cartoon characters well outside the world of law and taboos about pee.

Silverman's embrace of bedwetting has gendered meanings in that the female body, which bleeds, gives birth, and produces milk, is perceived as leakier than the male body. Douglas argues that pollution taboos about liquidity—treacle, viscosity, stickiness—spring from the threat to "solid" concepts of oneself: "I remain a solid, but to touch stickiness is to risk diluting myself" (38). Feminist scholars have often noted how perceived female porousness has been linked to moral weakness and corruption. Tracing this line of thought from Aristotle, Jana Evans Braziel shows how Western philosophy has condemned the "excessive liquidity and compositional porosity of the female," linking these traits with moral "softness," self-indulgence, and vice (239). Strikingly, moral weakness is characterized by Aristotle as "incontinence," perceived as a trait inherent in the leakiness of the female body (240). Similarly, Elizabeth Grosz contends that the female body has been constituted as "uncontrollable, seeping liquid; as formless flow; as viscosity," although male bodies are leaky and unstable in other ways. Indeed, she says, this cultural representation of the porous female body is a disavowal of "the liquidities that men seem to want to cast out of their own self-representations" (203). For Braziel and Grosz, who both deploy Deleuzian concepts of how bodies are coded and territorialized, the perceived liquid nature of the female body is not simply a factor in cultural misogyny but an indicator of how profoundly this concept challenges Western ideas of autonomy and absolute boundaries of the individual. My point here is that Silverman's repeated violations of pollution taboos and her embrace of her identity as bedwetter disturb fundamental ideas about the human entity as "bounded" while also challenging and disarming a sexist tradition of seeing women as less than human for their "liquidity."

The celebration of the open, porous body has been famously described by Mikhail Bakhtin in his work on the carnivalesque, which has provided substantial insights on antisocial and subversive comedy. As described earlier, Bakhtin's focus is the profane strand of Medieval carnivals that foregrounded the grotesque body rather than the beautiful, "classic" body in the dissonant aesthetic of "grotesque realism." The grotesque body is characterized by its open apertures and protuberances, its voracious consumptions and excretions. As opposed to the classic body—the ideal that is represented as contained, smooth, and complete—the comic grotesque body is "ever unfinished, ever creating" because it consumes, digests, reproduces (Bakhtin, 26). Likewise, Bakhtin contrasts the cerebral upper body, associated with the "higher" functions of thought and emotion (the heart), to "the lower stratum of the body, the life of the belly and the reproductive organs" (21), associated with shame and filth. The raucous comedy of carnival reverses this ranking with the effect that "the body turns a cartwheel," the buttocks taking the place of the face and the anus taking the place of the mouth (373).

Silverman literalizes this cartwheeled grotesque body in the grand finale of *Jesus Is Magic* in which she sings a chorus of "Amazing Grace" from three orifices—mouth, anus, and vagina, holding the microphone alternately to each. Her long hair glistening in the spotlight, her curvy figure accentuated by hip-hugging jeans and a tight black top, she looks robustly sexy, well within normative concepts of classic female attractiveness. She earnestly tells the audience her song is "inspirational" and then enacts an outrageous fantasy of a lower body that can "speak"—in fact, sing. When the lyrics of the song proclaim "how sweet the sound," her voice (actually the gruff voice of her comedian colleague Brian Posehn) seems to emit from her rear end, which she backs up to the microphone. She puts the microphone to her crotch, too. Singing with her vagina and anus, Silverman performs the cartwheel that remaps the body, scrambling the larger cultural mapping that values the mind (the head) over carnality (belly, anus, vagina).

For Bakhtin the cartwheel effect is jubilant and profoundly antiauthoritarian. Body parts are no longer ranked as higher and lower but are rather seen in relation to each other, symbolizing the potential undoing of the larger social body.[2] Silverman's tour de force cartwheel that relativizes the mouth, anus, and vagina is especially significant given the cultural history of the lower female body as dirtier and more disgusting than the lower male body. Scholars of scatology and obscenity often point to female anatomy as the source of "the obscene," quoting Saint Augustine on the architecture of female genitalia: "Inter urinas et faesces nascimur," that is, "We are born between urine and feces." In the twentieth century George Bataille, writing about the nature of disgust and the connection between waste and reproduction, used the Augustinian dictum as support for what he sees as the biological basis of shame in the female body: "The sexual channels are also the body's sewers." Their "shameful" nature has been long acknowledged in Western theology: "St. Augustine was at pains to insist on the obscenity of the organs and function of reproduction" (57). Freud points to the same words from Augustine to explain human "repugnance" to "the sexual function" (*Civilization*, 53).

If these examples seem arcane, consider Comedy Central's censorship of *The Sarah Silverman Program* as reported by Silverman in her memoir. The censorship policies expressed far more squeamishness about female anatomy than male anatomy, she complains. Words like "penis," "balls," "scrotum," and "shaft" can be spoken with "essentially no limit," she says, "but female anatomical language is a big, flapping red flag (so to speak)." The network regularly cut the words "vagina" and "labia" even though anatomical language about male genitalia went unchallenged (189–191). Given the cultural function of censorship as the index of what is unspeakable, Comedy Central's censorship in 2007–2010 essentially replicated the misogyny about the female body traceable from Augustine through Freud.

These social meanings of the female body as repugnant and obscene, shameful and morally degraded are repeatedly confronted in Silverman's comedy. In a routine she often performed in Los Angeles in the 1990s, for example, she would appear on stage wearing khakis on which she'd spread red paint in the crotch area. She would do a somersault, hear the audience gasp, and hasten to assure them that she didn't get her period, as they must have feared. "I had anal sex for the first time tonight," she would tell them cheerfully (in Goodyear). The shock of the joke comes from citing two taboo topics and casually ranking one as less objectionable than the other but also connecting them through their shared semiotics of the blood on the seat of the pants. The boldness of the skit is Silverman's refusal to be ashamed of either one as an object of degradation or contempt.

Although Bakhtin's work often cites the cultural importance of the female lower body in the carnivalesque aesthetic, feminist scholars like Mary Russo have foregrounded his indifference to gender issues, especially the social meanings of the female body as repugnant and obscene.[3] Kathleen Rowe's work on the unruly woman in comedy demonstrates how Bakhtin's grotesque realism seamlessly reinforces the contempt for women implicit in Western traditions that identify the female body as de-filed, filthy, and lower than the male's.[4] In this masculinized understanding of comedy, Rowe asserts, "men transgress in their actions; women transgress in their being, through the very nature of their bodies, not as subjects" (34). As discussed earlier, Rowe is interested in transgressive comedy that enables female agency and is not simply ascribed to the very nature of women's bodies. She finds this comic subjectivity in two kinds of female bodies: the excessive grotesquery of the Mae West, Miss Piggy, Roseanne Barr tradition and the conventional femininity of the heroines of roman-tic comedy. The latter look as "adorable" as Silverman and match her in feistiness, too, threatening the status quo with their outrageous behavior and mouthy dissonance. The twist, however, is that Silverman defies both of Rowe's unruly woman models, inhabiting neither the outrageous or out-size body nor the traditional marriage plot, as *The Sarah Silverman Program* repeatedly illustrates.

In her memoir Silverman disparages the narrative roles usually offered women comics in movies and sitcoms as invariably versions of the same madcap but ultimately disposable character she calls "the Suze" — "the bitchy ex-wife; the lead character's cunty girlfriends . . . or the quirky best friend . . . two-dimensional Suzes whose sole purpose is to facilitate more complex three-dimensional roles" (178). The point about those Suze roles is that they are the ones usually available for outrageous women comics in traditional — that is, socially acceptable — narratives, as seen in the Suze role Kathy Griffin played on *Suddenly Susan*, a role for which Silverman in fact auditioned (Silverman, 177). So although she has the conventional good looks of the romantic heroine, Silverman refuses to be "emplotted," as Rowe puts it, in the narratives that make the subversive heroine accept-able for prime time.

The plots of *The Sarah Silverman Program* are worth noting because they so fiercely resist both sitcom and gender clichés about suitable stories for the perfectly adorable white girl. In the "Vow Wow" episode Sarah attempts to marry her dog Dougie, singing a romantic song about their future: "Will we eat each other's doodies, will we use a fork and knife . . . when I become your wife?" The marriage is called off only because Dou-gie ditches her at the altar, chasing after a skateboarder at the moment he needs to go through with his vows. Even when the plots on the show are supposedly resolved, the outcomes are dubious. In "Joan of Arf" Sarah is arrested for an "unlawful interspecies relationship" because she licked her dog's ass to find out why he considers it so "delicious." In court the judge makes a decision by licking the dog's ass, too, and then declares bestiality legal "but only with animals of the opposite sex." In "Doody" Sarah and her sister are shocked to learn their mother's grave has been desecrated by the nerdy bullies JoJo and Stencil, but the mother's ghost comes back to tell them she and Stencil "have a complicated relationship." And in "Wowschwitz" an attempt at a Holocaust memorial turns violent when Sarah is shot by a Nazi. But her little dog Dougie has time-traveled back in history and killed Hitler, with the happy result that—as anti-Semites have long maintained—the Holocaust never happened. These resolutions are mockeries of sitcom clichés, and the plots are travesties of social norms. In contrast to the romantic-comedy heroine who eventually conforms to the law of Oedipus, as Rowe points out, Sarah is never fully situated within the law; she has 2,000 parking tickets ("Face Wars") and is repeatedly arrested or being threatened with arrest throughout the series.

Routinely undertaking socially unacceptable narratives, the Sarah character on the show often violates the boundary taboos that Rowe associates with the comic unruly woman. Drawing on Douglas's insights about dirt, Rowe uses the Muppet character Miss Piggy as a caricatured example of the unruly woman who "destabilizes the line between animal and human," a boundary policed by numerous taboos about relationships with and uses of animals (41). On *The Sarah Silverman Program* Sarah violates the human-animal boundary in the episodes involving unlawful interspecies relationships with her dog and transgresses other boundaries as well. Her sloppiness with social boundaries leads her to join inappropriate groups: AIDS victims ("Positive Negative"), the homeless ("There's No Place Like Homeless"), black people ("Face Wars"), child contestants for a junior beauty pageant ("Not Without My Daughter"), and what she calls "the retarded" ("A Fairly Attractive Mind"). And in one of the most bizarre plots of the series Sarah enacts multiple pollutions; told that she was a hermaphrodite at birth, she accidentally swallows her supposedly amputated baby penis, poops it out, and then wears it on a necklace ("The Proof Is in the Penis").

On the one hand, this is gross-out comedy at its most farcical, pacing Sarah through the antics of a cartoon character. On the other hand, the outlandish violations of social norms and taboos demonstrate comedy at its most antisocial, and this is where we can see the gendered stakes of what Silverman is doing. Critics have long underscored comedy's anarchic strain and its impulse toward chaos. The overthrow of rules and regulations is usually associated with "comedian comedy," the mayhem machines of the Marx Brothers, Jerry Lewis, John Belushi, Adam Sandler. Gross-out comedy is likewise a form of social mayhem because the rules it violates are taboos involving basic distinctions in designating oneself as human and setting up boundaries of what-I-am-not (the body's excrement or discarded skin, nails, amputated parts), as Douglas and others have discussed. But antisocial comedy has traditionally been male. Comedy scholar Geoff King notes that women are far less likely to be cast in the role of comic anarchist because gender — women and men in their proper roles — is the anchor of the broader social contracts. King finds that the comic woman anarchist "represents a more serious challenge to the gender hierarchies on which so many social relationships are based" (133). My point is that these profoundly antisocial narratives involving pollution taboos enact a radical subversion of gender, challenging the kind of sitcom narratives appropriate for the "totally cute white girl."

This subversion is an interesting twist on the pretty versus funny dynamic of traditional sitcoms. *The Sarah Silverman Program* episodes often exploit Sarah's prettiness by placing her in narratives that grossly pollute bourgeois rituals and customs concerning femininity. The best example is the episode about a junior beauty pageant in which Sarah ends up coaching a little girl to be "pretty" by teaching her a song about poop. It's also an episode that slyly develops the comedy of grotesquery by revealing the beauty pageant itself as grotesque. Sarah first dresses up as a hideous little girl à la Bette Davis's monstrous grown-up child star in *Whatever Happened to Baby Jane?* (1962) — giant bow in her hair, tight curls, short baby-doll dress. It turns out that the adult Sarah enters the contest every year despite her obvious ineligibility because of her own failure in the competition when she was a child. The monstrosity of her appearance is matched by the grotesque child contestants who appear later — eight-year-olds in makeup, dresses, and hairstyles appropriate for glamourized adult women.[5]

Sarah "adopts" an orphan and coaches her for the pageant as a stand-in for herself. As the title of this episode hints, "Not Without My Daughter" lampoons mother-daughter melodrama not only through the cynical use of little Heather as Sarah's wish projection but also through the joke revelation that the little girl is actually Sarah's daughter, the eight-and-a-half-month "abortion" Sarah describes without understanding the connection.[6] While the horrific revelation is that Sarah doesn't know the difference between childbirth and abortion, the pageant itself touts outrageous boundary violations as well, between childhood and adulthood and between ambitious mothers and little girls who masquerade as sexy adults. The episode pointedly satirizes acceptable versions of femininity as white and middle class; while the title of the Little Miss Rainbow pageant suggests diversity, most of the contestants are creamy blonds who wear their hair piled up into fluffy beehives, and even the two girls who may be Asian are dressed as white fantasies of the China doll.

Tutoring little Heather, Sarah teaches the would-be beauty queen an entirely inappropriate song about "pooping at the mall," a particularly unnerving pollution of prettiness, given that the mall is a place for accessorizing and enhancing femininity. Obviously, this ditty is about matter out of place even though the song is a reminder that the mall is a place to poop as well as to shop. Putting the connection into a song is itself a violation of genre. But *The Sarah Silverman Program* featured several of these disturbing songs, such as "The Baby Penis in Your Mind" in the hermaphrodite episode. Unlike scripted dialogue in a show, songs are meant to be exportable, to stand on their own, to be remembered and repeated as popular texts. The successful ones are catchy and endlessly replicated.[7] And the songs from *Sarah Silverman* were available as separate videos on the Comedy Central website as of July 2010. Moreover, these are melodious ballads sung in Silverman's lovely voice—an attractive woman singing mellifluent songs about taboo topics—her body's seepages and, in the case of the baby penis, its grotesque, unnatural appendage. Silverman sang songs in *Jesus Is Magic* with the same disconcerting effect. The hybridity of this comedy—the loveliness of her voice and appearance, the shocking content of the songs—is precisely the point: a reminder of the threatening messiness of the female body that is repressed in the representation of the attractive woman singer with lily-white skin.

Discussing hybridity in this way, I draw on Peter Stallybrass and Allon White's development and rethinking of Bakhtin's carnivalesque. The authors find that while Bakhtin sometimes describes the grotesque as simple inversion—the cartwheel effect that reverses high and low—he also delineates a more complicated form of grotesquery that fuses together two or more contrasting elements into "new combinations and strange instabilities" (58). One of their primary examples is a circus-clown act that substitutes a piglet for a human baby, "forcing the audience to acknowledge the interchangeability of pig and baby" and the tenuous boundaries of the human and the animal. The audience is thus prompted "to enjoy what it had always 'known' but found it difficult to acknowledge" (59). This is the effect of the Silverman episode "Vow Wow," in which Sarah's decision to marry her dog recognizes an interchangeability of human and animal companions.

More than that, though, Silverman's startling fusions of the beautiful and the repulsive perform a function that Stallybrass and White recognize as a necessary part of bourgeois culture. These hybrid performances redraw and recall boundaries, exposing the elements that are repressed—the messiness and incompleteness of the body—in order to reclaim the body in culture as seamless and materially autonomous. Like the circus act with the piglet baby, Silverman's song about swimming happily in warm water celebrates the pleasures of the leaky body, "forcing the audience to acknowledge what it has repressed in order to become what it is" (59). Along the same lines, the song Sarah teaches the would-be little beauty queen about pooping at the mall concedes that what one does publicly at the shopping mall—prettifying, perfuming, and coiffing the body—obscures what one does privately as bodies that consume, digest, and excrete.

Singing about this, turning a secret into a public, repeatable text, is what Stallybrass and White call a "reverse or counter-sublimation, undoing the discursive hierarchies and stratifications of bodies and cultures" maintained by the dominant classes (200–201). This is not necessarily a politically progressive move, they caution, because the transgression may well be a site where dominant culture "squanders its symbolic capital" to "get in touch with the field of desire" it represses in order to have power. The enjoyment of Silverman's comedy is no doubt part of this dynamic of squandered symbolic capital, but Silverman's play with these power dynamics has gendered inflections. The mall-poop song pollutes and disrupts traditional discourses and narratives about feminine behavior encapsulated by the mall, where the female body is prettied up for the type of display seen in little-girl beauty pageants. In this context, Sarah teaching Heather a poop song has political resonance beyond bourgeois countersublimation. The antisocial nature of the song pushes the audience to consider the social norm at stake here—eight-year-old girls tarted up to compete against each other. As a wholly unnatural practice, is this less disgusting than a poop song?

A parallel example of this disruption of feminine representation is a sequence in the episode "Batteries," which originally was intended as the series pilot. In a restaurant brunch scene Sarah enthusiastically participates in a farting match with her friends but is horrified when she poops instead. Wishing it had never happened, she launches into a whimsical song and is transported into a romantic music video in the style of Celine Dion or Alanis Morissette, in which Sarah appears in a flowing white gown at sunset on a beach singing a smarmy song about her wishes for love among all peoples and for world peace. But when God appears and asks her to pick one wish that he will grant, her wish is that she had farted instead of pooped. So the romance and sentimentality of the musical sequence, that is, standard tropes of femininity, are instantly deflated in a return to gross-out comedy.

Sarah's wish also points back to the oozing, secreting body repressed in popular discourses of femininity. So there is a cultural logic to Sarah's moment of horror, represented in a montage of her embarrassed expression and the shocked faces around the table, being instantly redirected into the music video of the idealized female body. But the comic reversal, Sarah's wish that God does grant, dismisses the romanticized discourse and returns to the farting contest being won by Sarah. The relationship between the two scenes and the two bodies—one soiled and out of control, the other pristine and pretty—is hybridity, an acknowledgment of the cost of the idealized representation, in this case the cultural need to idealize and romanticize the female body. The abjected body sits in poop at the restaurant, and the more socially acceptable version of that body floats through a clichéd seaside landscape in a billowing white dress.

The hybridity of appeal and repulsion, the attractive and the objectionable, is central to Silverman's comic persona and routines. The song in "Pee" about being half monkey may have been a sly reference to her cover photo on the men's magazine *Maxim* the previous year, in June 2007, which startlingly illustrated her hybridity as sex object and object of revulsion. In the photo she wears a strappy, body-hugging T-shirt and bikini bottom, her chest thrust forward and her arm cocked in a traditional swimsuit pose—except that she is stepping into or out of a gorilla costume, its hairy leg coverings pulled up to her knees and the gorilla head near her feet on the ground. She also seems to be scratching her rear end. The headline is "SEXY BEAST: Sarah Silverman—The New Kong of Comedy!"

Silverman's cover-girl career provides an interesting contrast to Tina Fey's. In the previous chapter I argue that representations of Fey are frequently glamourized, more and more without irony, as part of a cultural appropriation that claims her as acceptably feminine. Fey's persona is conducive to that appropriation. The sexy librarian, the witty heroine hiding behind her eyeglasses—these are cultural figures that can be stylized into conventional cover girls. Not so Sarah Silverman, whose comic persona is too vulgar and offensive for middle-class, fashion-model iconicity. "Fashion" is itself a comic hot button for Silverman, who appeared at the 2009 Emmy awards show in a designer gown that she herself disastrously "tweaked" with alterations, resulting in a dress that in her own words made her look "like a fucking crazy blue house" or even more resonantly, in light of her lower-body comedy, "built to look like I possibly had some kind of elephantitis of my lower half" (Silverman, 121). In a 2007 interview for *Esquire*, she explains that even when she thinks she's wearing "a nice outfit," it ends up as a tabloid photo example of bad taste. "I just look like a transvestite when I try to dress up," she says (in Sager). There is little chance of rehabilitating Silverman onto the cover of *Marie Claire*.

In her cover-girl photo for Maxim in June 2007, Sarah Silverman is a hybrid creature, both beauty and beast. The following year she described herself as "half monkey, half Jew" in a song she sang on The Sarah Silverman Program.

Given her public persona of "dirty" girl or "dirty rotten princess," as a *Rolling Stone* article title put it, it's not surprising that Silverman's publicity images are often raucously sexy; she poses in underwear and swim tops that emphasize her substantial bust and long waist, and in some of these photos, she peeks shamelessly into her briefs. However, the look with which Silverman is most often associated is the baseball cap and T-shirt with a team number on it, the casual look she employs to avoid the transvestite effect. The *New York Times* article about her "adorable look" calls it the dress style of "a 14-year-old boy" and pinpoints its evocation of a specific "dude" fantasy: "the hot tomboy-next-door who will laugh at your potty jokes, punch you in the arm and then make out with you." The cute-tomboy look, Newman argues, serves as a "buffer" for the "brilliant, jaw-dropping, deliberately shocking jokes about racism, abortion, and rape" ("From Sarah Silverman"). The *Rolling Stone* "dirty rotten princess" article likewise credits Silverman's boyish style as part of her appeal, with language suggesting the tomboy look is a buffer not only for the raw comedy but for the raw sex appeal: "She has the best qualities of both sexes—the silly, sexually charged affect of a confident girl, and the silly, kid-around conversational banter of a guy" (Grigoriadis). The bantering guy is far less intimidating than the sexually charged, confident girl, just as the busty woman in the bikini bottom is less threatening than the gorilla. While all these discourses acknowledge Silverman's disquieting sexual power—the gorilla-suit photo, the tomboy fantasy, the mix of both sexes—they also picture her as a hybrid, boy/girl or beauty/beast. Silverman's own song about hybridity, describing herself as half monkey, half Jew, spins these characterizations into the realm of the grotesque.

The *Maxim* cover-girl photo of Silverman as the sexy body emerging from the gorilla suit plays with this grotesquery as well as the beauty/beast hybridity. The hybridity also speaks to the cultural work that Stallybrass and White claim as central to bourgeois representation, which in this case is specifically gendered: the exposure of what is repressed—fear of female sexuality, the female beast—in the pleasure of the curvaceous swimsuit-clad body. In the photos accompanying the feature article inside, Silverman is posed in campy and comic versions of the criminal or femme fatale. Dressed as a tramp in a clingy T-shirt, she shoplifts a can of soup into her shorts; tarted up 1940s style in bright-red high heels and pencil skirt, she stares back at a policeman who's ordered her to place her hands on a car. The glamourous fetishizations of the femme fatale are more common strategies to handle the threat of the sexualized female body, while the gorilla shots are far more direct about this threat. On the cover photo, the gorilla head on the floor is given a dialogue balloon that delivers an inane macho joke in an attempt to put the little woman in her place: "Knock knock. Who's there? Gorilla. Gorilla who? Gorilla me a cheese sandwich, babe!" But the menace is unabated in the inside photo in which Silverman's face is distorted into a snarl as she lifts the gorilla suit around her hips. The snarl does not diminish her sexiness; it acknowledges its dangerous edge.

HALF JEW

Just as the line about "half monkey, half Jew" carries the sting of an ethnic slur, the gorilla costume has resonances about race as well, in centuries-old traditions linking apes, gorillas, and monkeys to Jews and in Silverman's own self-disparaging jokes about her Jewish identity. "We grew up in a place with very few Jews," she told a *New York Times* reporter in 2007. "I didn't look like the other kids. I had hairy legs, hairy arms, hair everywhere. I looked like a little monkey" (in Solomon). In the interview accompanying the *Maxim* photo the same year she makes a similar comment, although the Jewish reference is curiously omitted, perhaps because the gorilla-suit photos would take on offensive connotations. Instead, her remark is about a more general privileging of whiteness: "I grew up in blonde New Hampshire. I was dark and hairy, and kids called me Ape Arms." However, when asked in the same interview if Jews are "capable of being anti-Semitic," Silverman replies, "Please. No one hates Jews more than Jews" (in Spitznagel, "Sarah Silverman," 97). Her monkey, ape, gorilla self-descriptions follow the tradition of self-deprecating Jewish humor, which has been described as masochistic and abject but also as a coping and bonding device that affirms community and identity.[8] Given Silverman's defiance toward cultural attitudes about female sexuality and the lower body, her self-description "half monkey, half Jew" can be seen as an extension of that defiance of abjection, her own version of Jews hating Jews.

In *The Bedwetter* Silverman is far more graphic and insistent in using images of monkeys and hairiness to describe Jewishness. One of the titles she considered for the book, she says, was "Tales of a Horse-Faced Jew-Monkey" (128). "I was the only one with hairy arms and 'gorilla legs,'" she writes about her childhood, claiming that a grade school kid would throw coins at her feet as you would for a trained monkey (220). Comparing herself to blond celebrities like Paris Hilton and Britney Spears, she calls herself a "dark, hairy backwoods Jew" (163). The images of a Jew-monkey and a little girl with gorilla legs are grotesqueries with specific racial dynamics, illustrating how bodies, like any sign, have meaning only within larger systems. The little girl's hairiness is not so much a physical quality as a cultural one; it registers as unattractive because she is in "blonde New Hampshire." Later, the adult comic is dark and hairy because she inhabits a world that privileges blonds like Hilton and Spears. As Mary Douglas puts it, the human body works as "model" or "symbol of society" on which are mapped social boundaries, anxieties, and concerns (114–115). The mark of difference on the body of a member of an ethnic minority, such as hair where other arms or legs are hairless, becomes a sign of matter out of place and a way to police the pollution and dirt of the outsider.

Dirt, in fact, is the link between Silverman's performances of abject Jewish identity and the abjection of the lower body. In Western thought, the qualities ascribed to the female body—bestiality, filth, and lower status—are also the qualities traditionally ascribed to ethnic or racial others, including Jews. In *Jesus Is Magic* Silverman plays on this when she says, "I'm a bad Jew, a dirty Jew," complaining that Jewish women have been excluded from porn to satirize the usual protests about how minorities are underrepresented in pop culture. In a cutaway, a half-naked Silverman lies face down on a bed, crying "Fuck my tuchas! Fuck my tuchas!"—comically transposing the "dirtiness" of the Jew to that of the sexualized woman. The sexual woman as outlaw and "dirty thief" is enacted in other ways in the *Maxim* photographs of Silverman as the arrested femme fatale and the slutty shoplifter, but her dirtiness is also suggested by the gorilla-suit outfit, which openly marks her as bestial. In the "Pee" episode and song on *The Sarah Silverman Program*, Silverman's line about being half monkey, half Jew entirely submerges her female identity into the hybrid of animal and racial identities. But "female" is the missing link because women's bodies have been slurred as "bestial," and Jewish bodies have been slurred as "womanly." While the female body has been perceived as lower and more bestial than the male body, the Jewish male body has, in turn, been perceived in anti-Semitic ideologies as more "feminine"—weaker and more dissolute—than the "European" male body. In the iconography of that line of racism, Jewishness is itself female and hence contemptible.[9]

Silverman sometimes uses her Jewish American identity as her authorizing voice in both her anti-PC and her racial comedy. A. O. Scott of the *New York Times* criticizes this as an easy move. "Like many young, otherwise deraciated Jewish comedians, Ms. Silverman falls back on her ethnic identity as a way of claiming ready-made outsider status," he observes ("Comic"). But the history of stand-up comedy is actually deeply indebted to the ready-made outsider status of Jewishness, John Limon writes, arguing that the abjection of Jewish identity in the middle of the twentieth century was key to the development of this entertainment genre (1–2, 6–8). In *The Bedwetter* Silverman devotes an entire chapter, titled "Jew," to this outsider status, explaining that despite her numerous references to her Jewishness throughout the book, she didn't want the reader to "get close to the end and discover that the thing was written by a member of an ethnicity that disgusts you" (217). Reinforcing this, Silverman quotes some of the anti-Semitic smears and insults she has received in letters and e-mails (193, 230). Certainly her Jewish identity was foregrounded in her video "The Great Schlep," one of her best-known productions. The YouTube video went viral in autumn 2008, a tongue-in-cheek rallying of young Jews to "schlep" down to Florida and convince their grandparents, suspicious of a black man with the middle name Hussein, to vote for Barack Obama. Playing up stereotypes of liberal young Jews and fawning Jewish grandparents, Silverman claims she is singly responsible for getting all of Florida's electoral votes to go to Obama that year.

At other times, as mentioned earlier, Silverman can play the totally cute white girl, tapping the assumption that skin color and image trump all other modes of identity. "People are always introducing me as 'Sarah Silverman, Jewish comedienne,'" she told *Rolling Stone* in 2005, turning it into a similar race joke. "I hate that! I wish people would see me for who I really am: I'm white!" (in Grigoriadis). Exploring the "enigmatic space" of Silverman's Jewish American identity, critic Aaron Tillman traces her links to Jewish comedy and particularly to the stereotype of the Jewish American princess evident in the Silverman persona of the obnoxious narcissist. But Tillman's main point is Silverman's inconsistent deployment of Jewish identity, which he characterizes as a "Rube Goldberg crazy straw" that is pragmatically mobile, so that "when convenient, she's 'one of the chosen people,' while at other times, her superiority complex comes from being white or straight or smart or thin" (73). Tillman makes an important point about the lack of a coherent ethnic or racial identity in Silverman's work, but Silverman often returns to her Jewishness as the baseline of her comedy and especially her comedy on race. Her chapter "Jew" concludes with her statement that she has "accepted being identified as Jewish" and realizes she cannot "get away from that" unless she undergoes "some major hair removal" (232), ending her chapter and the book with the self-deprecating Jewish humor that loops back to her status as hairy gorilla.

The monkey, gorilla, or ape as derogatory racial image is associated with African Americans as well as Jews. And while the oppression of both groups is parallel in many ways, their experiences of bigotry in the United States are markedly different, given the history of slavery and the relative economic power of Jews, especially in Hollywood, where racial stereotypes have been powerfully reproduced. In fact, Silverman's gorilla-suit cover photo subtly references Marlene Dietrich's infamous gorilla-suit scene in

Blonde Venus (1932), broadly read as the fetishization of whiteness through African and animal imagery.[10] The substitution of Silverman in this mise en scène profoundly inflects its meanings given that, unlike Dietrich's platinum and racial whiteness, Silverman's Jewishness places her on the side of the African and the beast. The usage of derogatory monkey or gorilla imagery for both Jews and blacks is a tradition and iconography found in European texts at least since the eighteenth century. Sander Gilman's study *The Jew's Body* discloses that Jews and blacks have a long history of conflation as "apelike" not only for their darker skin but for their supposedly unique origin in Africa.[11] Jews and blacks are the most salient targets of white-power groups, as Michael Billig illustrates in his research on humor websites linked to the Ku Klux Klan. On those sites, anti-Semitic jokes are found alongside "nigger jokes" and cartoons of African Americans as apes or with ape or gorilla heads (273). Silverman herself is featured regularly on white-power websites as an example of the offensive Jew.[12]

Conversely, Jews and African Americans have developed comic traditions that deflect bigotry, sometimes through self-deprecation, sometimes through gallows humor or clever riffs on stereotypes. Jewish humor has been characterized as a pervasive and highly influential mode of American humor, well established by the 1960s when African American humor began to be mainstreamed as well.[13] Joseph Boskin argues that present-day American comedy has been most shaped by these two groups "whose relationship to the dominant culture has been and continues to be that of the outsider" (57) and for whom comedy has been a powerful tool of self-identification and political savvy: "Jews and Blacks share most deeply the humor of the oppressed" (56).

In short, the genealogy of Silverman's performance as a dirty Jew and her self-description as Jew-monkey connects her to African American imagery, slurs, and comedy in several ways. This is more than esoteric history because Silverman pushes those connections in certain strands of her anti-PC comedy, which in turn are the places where her race comedy becomes risky, crossing over from Jewish self-deprecation—the tradition within which she can speak as an insider—to the more dangerous territory of jokes about blacks told by someone who is not. For Silverman and other anti-PC comics, including black comics like Dave Chappelle, the deadpan use of derogatory language and racist commentary aims to challenge bigotry but also the multicultural, liberal policing of bigotry by speaking—and thus exposing—the unspeakable. Silverman says in *The Bedwetter* regarding the use of the word "nigger" that "the more offensive the hate word, the more sharply it highlights the idiocy of the speaker" (144).

The problem, however, is that racial and ethnic slurs have emotional valences and are charged with pain and malice. The intention of the comedy may be disclosing the idiocy of the speaker, but there's no guarantee the slur will be interpreted that way. *Slate* reviewer Anderson points out regarding Silverman's racial comedy that "meta-bigotry" is a "dangerous game" because it "can look suspiciously like actual bigotry." British reviewer Alice O'Keefe saw Silverman's stand-up in 2008 in London and wrote that Silverman "leaves the stereotypes unchallenged. A racist could sit through a whole Sarah Silverman gig without feeling offended."

Silverman's comedy about the relationships of Jews to African Americans exemplifies the problems of intention, location, and identification. At its most obvious as anti-PC comedy, her humor often links Jews and blacks not as fellow oppressed minorities but as competing victims. In *Jesus Is Magic*, for instance, she plays Jews against blacks in a one-upmanship of persecution: "If black people were in Germany during World War Two, the Holocaust would have never happened. Or, not to Jews." But far more interesting is a joke in her stand-up repertoire that ups the ante by bringing in the unspeakable slur: "Why do so many Jews drive German cars? Is that like black people calling each other 'nigger'?" (in O'Keefe, 46). The joke is about working against one's own interests, which is often the dynamic of self-deprecating black and Jewish humor. But the punch line is the use of the word "nigger." So the joke is also metacommentary about who is entitled to use bigoted language and ultimately about whether black people calling each other "nigger" is on the same footing as the nonblack comic who talks about it. Unspoken here is the status of that comic as a fellow "insider" minority member, one of the Jews buying German cars. The joke hinges on Silverman's authority to say the word "nigger," even as a quotation, because of her Jewishness.

Yet the use of the offensive word here has a different effect than the word used to highlight the idiocy of the speaker, although it contains the same emotional charge. For one thing, the parallel bad behavior in the joke, Jews buying German cars, is simply not as contentious or prickly as the question of who is entitled to use racist language. The "interpretive margin" in this joke, to use Richard Raskin's concept of dealing with slippery interpretations of ethnic and racial humor (88), runs from risky to racist. This is the margin of all anti-PC jokes, but this particular joke is especially self-conscious in its positioning of the Jewish speaker in relationship to bigotry about blacks, illustrating—if not broaching the limits of—the shared outsider status of these groups.

The Sarah Silverman Program episode "Face Wars" is a revision and expansion of the Jew versus black joke that does a better job of playing with the interpretation and uses of an offensive racist signifier, in this case, blackface. Blackface is a tradition and symbol that in its own way is as emotionally unsettling as the word "nigger," as seen in the uneasy reception to Spike Lee's *Bamboozled* (2000), a satire about this racist practice. Silverman's "Face Wars" uses the clichéd sitcom plot of trading places. The narrative is launched from Sarah's belief that she is a victim of a hate crime because she can't book a tennis court at the local country club. It turns out Sarah is not a member of the club, so the episode begins by lampooning hypersensitivity about anti-Semitism. Complaining about her treatment while at brunch with her friends, Sarah begins an argument with a black waiter about which minority has it worse, Jews or blacks. This is when the two decide to trade places and races for a day.

Both their disguises are ridiculous. The waiter sports a huge, white, fake nose and pastes side curls (*peyos*) around his face. But Sarah, instead of "blacking up" as an imitation, sports a stylized symbol of blackface: a black oval mask with huge, white lips painted onto her face. The mask effect sharply foregrounds how the disguise or mimicry has always been about racial power dynamics. Rather than trading places, Sarah adopts the stereotype that has most offensively symbolized American racial history. The ongoing joke is that Sarah doesn't understand that this symbol is equally offensive to blacks and whites. When white pedestrians show revulsion at the black mask, Sarah is horrified. "I had no idea how cruel white people could be to us!" she cries. When she tries to join the choir at a black Baptist church, they too are revolted and toss her out. "Forsaken by my own people!" Sarah exclaims.

In a satire of superficial liberal gestures, Sarah's blackface is interpreted by a well-meaning pedestrian as the start of "a dialogue about race," citing a political phrase that began in the Clinton administration in 1997. When Sarah is arrested for her 2,000th parking violation, the sympathetic bystander videos the incident but catches only part of it so that it looks like Sarah is the victim of a hate crime. Facing the cop in her absurd blackface mask, she asks, "Do you have a problem with me being black?" "Yes, it's revolting," says the cop. This video clip is played on a local newscast without a shot of Sarah's blackface, so the clip seems to be showing a racist cop instead of a cop disgusted by racism. This gag about the disastrous results of taking a comment out of context is a reference to Silverman's arguments about her joke being likewise misinterpreted during the 2001 "Chink" controversy. In "Face Wars" the misinterpretation lampoons the knee-jerk reactions of liberals who quickly organize an antiracist protest movement in Sarah's defense.

Drawing this farce to an extreme closure, Sarah becomes a martyr when she's accidentally shot by policeman Jay, who can't figure out whether his gun's safety is on. In the hospital, making a rapid recovery, Sarah is still wearing the blackface makeup, but when her sister is interrupted in the process of wiping it off, the resulting effect is Sarah wearing an Adolf Hitler mustache. The offensive sign of blackface is seamlessly transformed into the offensive sign of Nazism, a parallelism of black and Jewish histories that the German-car-purchase joke makes less successfully. In a more general way, "Face Wars" is able to draw out and satirize the messiness of race humor's intentions and interpretations by making blackface the sign and not the location of antiblack bigotry, as seen in its usage by the protesters who adopt it as the ironic symbol of a dialogue on race. It's clear that only white people are interested in this use of the symbol and could possibly think the protest is effective, while black people have no investment in this kind of irony. The closing scene of "Face Wars" adds one more critical note by revealing how focus on the big, obvious stereotype can draw attention away from racism in its more subtle forms; the attendant from the country club appears at Sarah's hospital bed to admit that her intentions in turning Sarah away really were anti-Semitic. Repentant now, she warmly promises that Sarah can play tennis at the club any time she wants—except during peak hours.

BLOOD LAUGHS

Permeating "Face Wars" is suspicion about humorless liberal piety, a suspicion that is foundational for anti-PC humor. But racist humor, like the jokes that show up on white-power websites, taunts the humorlessness of liberal piety as well. Billig points out that the headline of the *Whitesonly* site, "Nigger Jokes and more Politically InCorrect Fun," is introduced by the disclaimer "Not everything must be deadly serious" (273). At times Silverman's blasé comments about her anti-PC comedy are as thin as this dismissal. In 2007, when a *New York Times* reporter asked if Silverman saw her work as "social commentary," she replied, "I don't see it as anything. I try not to look at it. Deconstruction is a comedy killer" (in Solomon). In the *Maxim* interview Silverman likewise scorns analysis: "I'm going for the laugh, wherever it comes from. Beyond that I'm not calculating. I'm not trying to offend people—I'm trying to surprise them" (in Spitznagel, 97).

However, in *The Bedwetter*, Silverman provides far more thoughtful self-analysis of her "politically incorrect fun," to the point that she risks—and talks about risking—the fun itself. Deconstruction may be a comedy killer, but she titles one chapter section "I Will Now Deconstruct Myself" (155), a darkly ironic subhead that introduces a decidedly unfunny commentary about her own experience of being hurt by racist humor and how her comedy emerged from that experience. Although much of *The Bedwetter* delivers Silverman's history in the bratty, deadpan voice of her comic persona, her analyses of race are the places where she steps out of that persona and positions herself as a Jewish American female comic performing radically anti-PC comedy.

Silverman's most extensive commentary about race and comedy in *The Bedwetter*, a full fifteen pages, examines the 2001 dispute triggered by her appearance on *Late Night with Conan O'Brien* when she used the word "Chink" as part of a story about how she got out of jury duty. She quotes in full the joke as she'd originally written it:

> I got a jury duty form in the mail, and I don't wanna do jury duty. So my friend said, 'Write something really racist on the form so they won't pick you, like 'I hate niggers.' I was like, Jeez—I don't want people to think I'm racist, I just wanna get out of jury duty. So I filled out the form and I wrote, 'I love niggers.' (143)

Reviewing her material before the show, the producer informed her that NBC couldn't allow the word "nigger," so she decided she'd use "Chink" instead. Curiously, he told her that although that word was also verboten, "spic" was an acceptable alternative (144). But Silverman decided "Chink" is a funnier word and used it anyway, precipitating a flood of protests from the Media Action Network for Asian Americans and eventually a televised debate with one of its representatives, Guy Aoki, on *Politically Incorrect with Bill Maher* (1993–2002). Silverman includes in her memoir a photocopy of her preparation for *Politically Incorrect* showing her extensive notes and questions around her key point: "Is the use of offensive words such as 'chinks' always wrong in any context?" (151).

The dynamic of the "Chink" joke, which lampoons the skewed logic of racism, is typical of the Silverman persona that purports to be insensitive to bigoted language and thinking. The joke is intended to be about bigots, not about the Chinese. Nevertheless, it deploys a derogatory word with offensive and emotional impact, leading journalists to describe possible interpretations of this strategy in polarized terms. Writing for *New York Magazine*, Will Leitch observes that "the confusion over whether she's exploiting stereotypes or puncturing them is what gets her into trouble." That is, if Silverman uses the joke for a laugh, but the cost of the laugh is continued circulation of the slur, then she is exploiting the stereotype even if her intention is to puncture it. Another journalist poses the question in even starker economic terms, asking if Silverman's humor is "subverting racism through race parody, or . . . exploiting racist stereotypes to make a buck?" (Wright, 43). The structure of these speculations presents antithetical options: the comedy is doing subversive cultural work, or it takes advantage of racial tensions to make a buck and, in effect, continue the bigotry.

However, neither comedy nor racial ideologies work so clearly through trajectories of either subversion or complicity, as Silverman shows in her own complicated response in *The Bedwetter* to similar questions about her anti-PC comedy. In the chapter that takes up the "Chink" incident, Silverman at first defends her position as doing worthwhile cultural work, comparing it with that of the 1970s Archie Bunker character from *All in the Family* (1971–1979), part of Norman Lear's "progressive" television productions, "delivering comedy with a social message." Then she makes a significant turn from this argument with another comparison, claiming that her jokes about race need to be read in contrast to "real" racism in media, in representations she describes as "oblique." Progressive comedy, she says, is more nuanced today than it was in the 1970s with Archie Bunker, but racism is mainstreamed into media in more subtle ways, too. She argues that racism is most often found not in public statements praising the Ku Klux Klan but rather in statements implying that President Barack Obama is a Muslim or native African, that is, not a native-born American. This happens in mainstream media such as Fox News, which she characterizes as "a twenty-four-hour-a-day racism engine" where the racism is "all coded, all implied" (154).

In effect, Silverman is distinguishing between what Stuart Hall has called overt versus inferential racism. Overt racism, says Hall, entails "openly racist" rhetoric or images, while in popular culture one is more likely to find inferential racism, "apparently naturalized representations . . . which have racist premises and propositions inscribed in them as a set of *unquestioned assumptions*" (36). Silverman's comedy about race often zeroes in on unquestioned assumptions, as in the "Batteries" episode of *The Sarah Silverman Program* when God appears as a middle-aged, black man. "Are you God's black friend?" she asks—lampooning the convention of casting blacks as buddies or comic seconds to white leads. In the same episode, when Sarah steals batteries from a convenience store the shopkeeper gives the police a lengthy description of the shoplifter as a white female, but the cop phones it in to the dispatcher as "black male."

When *The Bedwetter* was published in June 2010, Silverman's comments on the oblique nature of racism were quickly reduced to a sound bite about Fox News as "a twenty-four-hour-a-day racism engine." In response, a Fox spokesperson said Silverman's anger was "understandable" because her television show wasn't being renewed and her memoir wasn't doing well: "We sympathize with her need for attention considering her book is languishing near 300 on Amazon.com" (in *Huffington Post*). Silverman wrote the comments about Fox well before her show was cancelled (and later reinstated) and certainly before the book could have languished on Amazon. Nevertheless, this lack of logic was no deterrent to media more sympathetic to Fox than to Silverman. Missing Silverman's comparative point about racism in media, the Comcast media-entertainment site declared that Silverman was being "called out for stereotyping," for which "she essentially blamed Fox News and tea partiers" (Krakauer)—an interesting added detail in that the tea party movement is not cited in the Silverman book at all. The story prompted more than 600 comments on the Comcast site, mostly furious arguments about what constitutes racism, with a good deal of name-calling. A story in the *Huffington Post* reported the quotation from the book and Fox's response without editorial comment on it (Shea); it drew nearly 7,000 responses, generally more civil than the responses on Comcast but equally passionate in the debate about racism in television news, the role of Fox News in conservative politics, and liberal responses to race problems.

The impassioned debates about Silverman's comment and Fox News's response dramatically illustrate the controversial status of Silverman's race comedy and the touchiness about race and representations of race during this time. The sensitivity would be demonstrated on a much larger scale with the Shirley Sherrod incident in the summer of 2010 when conservative groups circulated a video of a black U.S. Department of Agriculture employee making what sounded like a racist statement at an NAACP meeting. In a turn of events uncannily similar to the "police racism" video clip in "Face Wars," it was revealed that the Sherrod clip had been taken out of context and, far from being racist, was an exhortation about the dangers of racism by black administrators. However, before the entire speech was reviewed, Sherrod was fired, so the hasty actions of the putatively liberal Obama administration were criticized as roundly as the hasty judgments of the groups attempting to expose Sherrod's supposed bigotry against white people.[14] My point here is that during the time Silverman was writing and then published *The Bedwetter*, with its lengthy self-analysis about race and comedy, American race relations and discourses on race were especially tense, given reactions to the presidency of Barack Obama, heated debates on immigration, the rise of the populist tea party movement—nicknamed "the white people's party"—and the Obama administration's own cautiousness about race issues. By honing in on race comedy in her book at exactly this historical moment, Silverman set herself up for polarized reactions that matched the politics of the times.

In discussing the "Chink" incident in the "Fox News" segment of *The Bedwetter*, Silverman's shift in language becomes less personal yet more thoughtful. Using language sober to the point of being academic, she describes her work as "comedy with a social message" and demonstrates a subtle understanding of how racism circulates as a set of "codes." Even more academic is her description of her own position in comedy about race. Reflecting on the "Chink" incident, she realizes the story is not only about comedy in culture but "about me, and my choices as a comedian." In a surprising move toward metacriticism, she draws on the Heisenberg Uncertainty Principle to explain the effect of self-consciousness about race on her comedy. There's "this thing in physics called the observer effect," she says, which explains why "the presence of the observer changes the thing" (154), so that once she's "too self-aware," her comedy is "tainted" (155). Yet the most remarkable element of this analysis is the abrupt reversal she makes at this point. She had introduced her foray into quantum physics by saying it explains why "I never want to deconstruct what I do" (154). But on the next page, in the section titled "I Will Now Deconstruct Myself," she tells a story of how she was once "upset" and "hurt" by an anti-Semitic joke told by a friend (155). Her feelings, she claims, "haven't changed," but she now knows how "to embrace the things that scare and upset me" as the topics of her comedy—"the Holocaust, racism, rape, et cetera" (156). She says her comic persona "at once ignorant and arrogant allowed me to say what I didn't mean" (157).

This is a shift from intellectual to emotional analysis, or a shift into affect: what it feels like to be the butt of a racist joke and to confront things that scare and upset her and, on the other hand, what it feels like to have a strategy about those issues: "For me, it was a funny way to be sincere" (157). Silverman's acknowledgment that the issue is emotional, or at least involves emotion as much as politics and cultural codes, is also an acknowledgment of the feelings of her main opponent in the "Chink" incident, Guy Aoki, the spokesman from the Media Action Network for Asian Americans who debated her on *Politically Incorrect*. In her autobiography Silverman includes a copy of the letter of apology she sent to Aoki but says, "Reading this now, I wince at how my self-righteousness seems to match his" (145). Summing up her feelings about him, she characterizes him as well intentioned but out of date, someone who should have been around to attack "Stepin Fetchit, Amos and Andy, and Al Jolson" rather than the more subtle discourses of racism in the twenty-first century. Her section subhead for this summary is a smart-alecky dig: "Guy Aoki: Heart in Right Place, Head Up Wrong Place" (153). Two pages later, though, she writes about her own experience of being upset when her friend made an anti-Semitic joke. She delivers the confession about her hurt feelings and offers a two-word, one-sentence, one-paragraph response: "I know" (155). And what she knows, by implication, is how Guy Aoki feels, no matter where his head might be.

The emotional aspects of racial humor are described even more vividly earlier in *The Bedwetter* when Silverman details her repugnance upon being confronted with a racist interpretation of her work. In a "horrifying" moment, she says, a well-known musician approached her gushing about how much he loved her comedy and confiding, "You have the best nigger jokes!" (93). Describing this phenomenon of "laughing at the wrong thing—the ugly part of the joke—the part intended for irony or insidiousness," Silverman quotes a former boyfriend in calling it "a mouth full of blood laughs" (93–94).

The visceral quality of this metaphor, the bitter taste and physical repulsion of the mouth full of blood, returns this discussion to abjection and specifically to pollution taboos: blood in the place of food, matter out of place. The boundary violation in this case is especially disturbing for its ambiguity; when someone in the audience takes pleasure in the racism that was intended to be mocked, are the blood laughs in the mouths of the laughing audience member? Or is it the performer, someone accustomed to getting laughs, who gets instead a vile taste when a racist joke goes awry? The messiness of the metaphor is exactly the point; if the performer felt no guilt at all, there would be no alarming aftertaste no matter how guilty the racist in the audience.

Silverman delivers this anecdote about the horrifying reception of her racial comedy at the beginning of a chapter called "Make It a Treat: My Guide to Drugs, Alcohol, Sex, and Other Things That Have the Potential to Be Gross" (93). The chapter is essentially a disclaimer about her relationship to gross comedy topics, from racism to rape to poop, blatantly asking fans not to confuse her comedy routines with her personal ethics or tastes. So she introduces her anecdote about the racist musician by describing her alarm at fans who misinterpret her "doody jokes" and want to send her "pictures of their poop and other extremely disgusting things. It gets worse" (93). The "worse" is the famous musician who loves her "nigger jokes," and her conclusion to the story is a return to her introduction—"I'm going to try to get the message out: I'm not interested in seeing pictures of anyone's bowel movements" (94). It's a rhetorical move that, like the ambiguous mouth full of blood, has a disturbing resonance—the musician's revelation being equated with the revelation of a poop photo. It also makes the connection I find most striking about Silverman's comedy, the linking of bodily and social abjection. In this case she finds both the musician's comment and the fans' poop photos disgusting, polluting, out of place in her "comedy with a social message." But she is also acknowledging the Rube Goldberg crazy straw of interpretation. All the good intentions of postmodern irony may return as a mouth full of blood.

The blood laughs share with other metaphors the grounding of Silverman's comedy in the body and in abjection: the show that smells, the comic as bedwetter, the identity as half monkey, half Jew. But Silverman's comedy is also bodily in its embrace and defiance of this abjection, its assertion of sexuality and sexiness that radically challenges the binary of pretty versus funny. These are characteristics she shares with Margaret Cho, whose comedy similarly celebrates the aspects of the female body culturally designated as not pretty.

CHAPTER FOUR

Margaret Cho Is Beautiful

A COMEDY OF MANIFESTO

COMEDY AND AUTOBIOGRAPHY

IN HER 2009 PERFORMANCE FILM *MARGARET CHO: BEAU-*
tiful, Cho tells the story of a radio-show host who asked her what
she would do if she "woke up beautiful—blue-eyed, blonde, five foot eleven
and one hundred pounds." Her comic response is about the physical im-
possibility of being that tall and thin: "I wouldn't get up because I'd be too
weak to stand," she says, but she adds on a more serious note that she feels
sorry for him because he must not "see much beauty in the world." *Beau-*
tiful, like much of Cho's comedy, pushes an agenda about race, tolerance,
and body politics, with the goal of expanding ideas about physical beauty
in order to see more, not less, beauty in the world. So the radio host's remark exemplifies the mainstream ideals Cho opposes, but his comment is
also striking for the racist basis of its assumption that a body like Cho's—
the Asian body, unlikely to be tall and blond—is automatically excluded
from standards of beauty.

Margaret Cho, like Kathy Griffin, anchors her comedy against the ideals
of white femininity and conventional ideas about being pretty, and both
comedians align themselves with a queer perspective in taking that stand.
Cho jokes about being "raised by drag queens" in an encore in the filmed
live performance *I'm the One That I Want,* and Griffin refers to herself as
an "inspiration" to drag queens as part of her performance of supposedly
failed femininity in her *Official Book Club Selection* (342). Both are indifferent to heterosexual men as audience members and are skeptical about
them as sexual partners. Griffin's comment that straight men are like Martians matches Cho's denial of the existence of straight men altogether. "If
it were not for gay men, I wouldn't talk to men at all," she says in *I'm the*

One. "I'm scared of straight men. I am heterophobic. Do you know any-body who's straight anyway? It's so weird, it's so subversive to be straight. If I'm talking to a boy who's cute and straight and single, I'm like, are you a unicorn?" Brian Lewis finds that this statement flips all the conventions of sexual norms so that for Cho "the queer becomes normalized, and the straight becomes 'subversive.'" This strategy parallels Griffin's taunts at her concerts when she dismisses straight men in the audience as either non-existent or as the group not intended for her performance.

Yet despite the similar status of Griffin and Cho as gay favorites, their perspectives on being beautiful are very different, and Cho is far more radi-cal in her attacks on the pretty versus funny dynamic. Griffin embraces her D-list identity and camps it up, but as I explain in my chapter on Griffin, she never disputes the authority of the list itself. Cho, in contrast, dismisses the Hollywood ranking system altogether as part of the political charge of her comedy, in which she makes vehement appeals for social change and for celebrating queer, diverse, and raced bodies as "beautiful," as she puts it in the performance film of the same name. Her story about the radio host also highlights what Griffin does not acknowledge about the whiteness of the A list as implicit in its notion of glamour.

Their physical transformations indicate how differently Griffin and Cho work in relationship to that ideal. As the comic outsider clawing her way in, Griffin remodeled herself through surgeries so she gradually conformed to A-list specs—if not blond, then at least tucked, proportioned, and scaled through surgeries, diet, and exercise into the taut face and "bangin' bikini bod" she reveres. In her 2010 stand-up routines Griffin admitted that she was slender because she was "always hungry," although the hunger was certainly also the alienated yearning of the campy outsider. Cho, in con-trast, discarded the rankings from the start, bluntly insisting that race itself determined where she could land on that list, as China doll or exotic fix-ture. She eventually lost weight because, she said, she didn't obsess about food and didn't fall into cycles of diets and weight gains (in Quinn). In the episode "Dr. 90210-Cho" of *The Cho Show,* her 2008 reality TV series, Cho contemplates plastic surgery but instead opts for tattoos, which exten-sively cover her body in dazzling colors and ornate designs. Turning away from the story of rankings and rejection, Cho declares herself the author of her own story, which she names *Beautiful.* Far from pushing her body into A-list ideals, Cho further queers it, marking it up as artwork and a site of play.

Cho's backstory is that her attempt to be beautiful by the standards of network television nearly ended her life. Her crisis and turning point was her stardom in the short-lived ABC sitcom *All-American Girl* (1994–1995).

Born in 1968 to Korean immigrants in San Francisco, Cho dropped out of high school and had been doing stand-up comedy for five years when at the age of twenty-three she caught the attention of television producers willing to support a new gimmick—the first sitcom about an Asian family, focused on a character based on Cho herself, the rebellious American daughter of Korean parents. However, the ABC executives demanded she lose thirty pounds in two weeks to film the first episode. The sudden weight loss hospitalized her with kidney failure, but she continued to diet so she could carry the series. In spite of this, tabloids sniped about her looks and her weight, and the show attracted incessant criticism of its supposedly Korean content, first for not being "Asian enough" and then for not appealing to enough white viewers. When *All-American Girl* was cancelled due to poor ratings, Cho claims it confirmed her lifelong anxieties about her physical appearance and about being Asian American. As a result she entered a self-destructive spiral of uncontrollable drinking from which she says she was lucky to come out alive. Ironically, then, Cho was nearly killed twice in attempts to be the all-American girl. Of all the sad stories about the funny woman's relation to being pretty, Cho's is exceptionally grim.

Cho made a triumphant re-entry into show business a few years later not in spite of this humiliating experience but because of it. Her come-back in 2000 was the stage performance and concert film *I'm the One That I Want*, followed by the 2001 memoir of the same title. In all three texts she describes her original interpretation of her sitcom disaster as proof she was too unattractive and too Asian to fit in with the beautiful white faces she loved on network television. But the main thrust of the book and the concert film is her fierce refutation of that interpretation and her rereading of her experiences through the lenses of feminism and queer identification. In her story an agenda emerges that critic Dan Bacalzo characterizes as "taking control of the production of truth," specifically by "position[ing] herself to intervene in existing discourses around representation" (44). More than any other comedian in this book, Cho savages the sexism and racism of primetime prettiness and makes it raucously funny.

I'm the One That I Want, as live performance, film, and book, constitutes a unique multimedia autobiography that is central to the meanings of Cho's comedy and stardom. Certainly most stand-up comedy is broadly autobiographical, and comedy writers often produce autobiographical books as well, such as the ones by Kathy Griffin, Sarah Silverman, and Tina Fey. However, unlike most celebrity memoirs, Cho's autobiography—in the print and performance versions—is not the story of her life so much as her radical reinterpretation of that story. It is precisely this reinterpretation that made her career possible. In all the versions of *I'm the One That*

I Want Cho tells her story of the failed sitcom in the context of American racism and the tyranny of unrealistic body ideals for women, ferociously renouncing what she herself had previously wanted—whiteness, the size 4 body—in order to make a claim for her self-esteem and for her own identity as the one she wants. In her later comedy she enlarges the scope of this topic, targeting mainstream prettiness not only for its implicit racism but for its relation to other hegemonic ideals about the body in culture—its sexuality, nationality, physical ability, age.

My argument is that Cho's comedy targets the racism and heterosexism of prettiness by engaging in the passionate autobiographical mode of manifesto, charged with life-or-death urgency and focused on the celebration of the bodies not often visible in mainstream culture—queer, raced, diverse, disabled. Bacalzo in his study of Cho says autobiography is always a "truth game" that gives the "illusion of authenticity" but is actually a strategy with specific purposes and effects (44). Theorists of autobiography, including feminist critics, concur that self-representation is a version or interpretation of facts that works toward specific meanings. In her come-back texts Cho self-consciously critiques the standard Hollywood story of the rising star by exposing the racism and misogyny embedded in the Hollywood ethos and defying that mainstream story with a manifesto about body image, self-esteem, the need for political voice, and the celebration of diverse bodies as beautiful. Cho's comedy continued in this didactic mode. Her subsequent concert films led up to impassioned and highly rhetorical short speeches that take a stand and refuse to represent the status quo. This is the defiantly marginal positioning of manifesto rhetoric.

Cho's topic is nearly always the body—its pleasures, frustrations, and looks. Her comedy is known for its sexual explicitness, drawing on intimate physical details linking the otherness of the Asian body and the queer body. Her stand-up routines include descriptions of sex acts with men and women as well as her experiences with S&M clubs, colonics, and quirky practices like anal bleaching, all of it treated comically but also positioned in terms of Cho's outlaw persona. In this way Cho stakes out a more radicalized audience than does Kathy Griffin, whose risqué speech is limited to her reckless use of the word "fuck" in concerts and on network television. Cho puts her body where her mouth is, so to speak. Her routines are shocking not so much for liberal use of expletives as for her graphic narrations of her sex life, from her advice on how to hurry a man's orgasm during oral sex to her admission that her favorite sexual act is "eating ass."

Cho offers these intimate details in order to insist on the visibility of the queer Asian body in popular culture, a body that isn't "supposed" to be there, that doesn't shore up the blond, heterosexual ideal. In effect she pushes the public/private boundary for political gain, profoundly taking up the Foucauldian concept of body politics, that is, power relations centered on the body. She is quick to satirize the stereotypes that signify these power relations through clichés about Asian bodies. In her 2008 reality show, *The Cho Show*, she says her favorite joke is her Asian chicken salad routine. In this joke, also seen in her 2004 concert film *CHO Revolution*, Cho lampoons the nervousness of a flight attendant who offers "Asian chicken salad" to everyone on the plane but freezes when he gets to Cho. Suddenly faced with a "real" Asian, he decides that the politically sensitive solution is a quick cover-up. "Chicken salad," he says meekly.

Cho then acts out his fantasy fear: a dragon lady who examines the salad with imperial disdain and then looms over him to cry, "This is not the salad of my people!" She pauses, glowering, hunching up as if ready to spring, and then intones dramatically that the people of her "homeland" use "mandarin orange slices and crispy won-ton crunchies." Embodying the Asian female monster, Cho turns her hands into claws and screws her face into a squinty contortion, brandishing an invisible sword that would slash the attendant in half. A petite, attractive woman, Cho can give the impression of hugeness and hideousness, reinforcing the comic contradiction of the skit—the imaginary dragon lady demanding ingredients mostly associated with Americanized versions of Chinese fast food.

The joke is a witty and satirical take on "authenticity" and Asian American identity. The overreaction of the dragon lady and the nervousness of the flight attendant point to a contentious political history of how Asian culture and bodies are represented in the West. This routine foregrounds the importance of her body in Cho's comedy—an implicit sign of racial difference that embarrasses the flight attendant and at the same time a body overdetermined by stereotypes of tiger woman and dragon lady. She says in *CHO Revolution*, "I don't want to be in any musical where there's a helicopter."[1] In her stand-up performances Cho often lists the clichéd movie and television roles to which Asian women have been limited; in her 2005 book, *I Have Chosen to Stay and Fight*, she extends the list into three pages of trite character types, including "worldly wise acupuncturist," refugee, peasant, Killing Fields victim, manicurist, ghost, dry cleaner, geisha, a woman with a chicken under her arm, or the woman who says "Welcome to Japan, Mr. Bond." She refuses these roles and scripts because, she says, "my story is never going to be told by anyone but me" (*I'm the One*, 44–47). The manifesto nature of this statement—the defiant stand, the announcement and challenge—makes clear that Asian American identity is always already a D list of background characters, names that no one can pronounce and faces no one remembers.

Margaret Cho, seen here in her 2004 concert film CHO Revolution, repeatedly challenges her assigned identities by queering not only her sexuality but also her race and defying how her body should be seen and read. Photo courtesy of Photofest.

Throughout her work Cho repeatedly challenges her assigned identities by queering not only her sexuality but also her race, defying how to "see" and read her body, as the Asian chicken salad joke suggests with its scenario of her body evoking an "authentic" Asian identity and her mockery of what that identity means for non-Asian audiences. Ernesto Javier Martínez analyzes the complicated links between Cho's queer and racial performances, describing what he calls her "faggot pageantry" that often depends on her play and subversion of racial stereotypes (151–158). That is, Cho confirms and confounds ideas about racial difference. She frequently talks about the racism she encounters in everyday life. "Living as a minority in America feels like dying of a thousand paper cuts," she says in *CHO Revolution*. Most notably, she claims that early in her career her Asian identity was thrown up to her as the obstacle to her possible success. When she first arrived in Hollywood, an agent refused to represent her, telling her, "Asians will never go anywhere in this business and you really are wasting your time" (in Southgate). Even when she did have her own show and her own agent, a man in her publicist's firm told her that "the Asian thing puts people off" (*I'm the One*, 203), a comment she turns into a comic routine in the film version by throwing herself into a fake martial arts performance as a parody of what non-Asian people imagine "the Asian thing" looks like.

Cho nevertheless also challenges the idea of racial identity, as in a routine in the film *Notorious C.H.O.* (2002) when she takes up the cliché that Asians all look alike so white people can't tell them apart. "*I* can't tell us apart," she admits. "Why do you have to tell us apart?" Jeffrey Carroll discusses this within Cho's strategy "to undercut the simple binary" of racial identifications with "a hint of identification with an audience of multiple kinds, multiple identities" (270). This is the same strategy as in the Asian chicken salad routine, he says, "that draws meaning out of its mixed parts . . . its comic undercutting of a fixed sense of center" (271). In the same concert film, though, Cho insists on her citizenship, the "American" component of the dual identity—and the one prone to slippage in the history of Asian Americans in the United States, as Lisa Lowe has documented.[2] In her *Notorious C.H.O.* film Cho talks about how her Asian American identity became more suspicious after 9/11 because she is perceived by Americans as implicitly foreign. Cho cites the disturbing history of mistreatment of Asian women by Americans in wartime, at the same time proclaiming she is a "fucking American." In this she quite literally is using her sexuality as a way to refuse to be terrorized, Michaela Meyer points out; claiming both citizenship and strident sexuality, Cho "violates the expectations and norms associated with Asian identity." Meyer emphasizes that from an Asian perspective Cho as a mainstream entertainer is a savvy insider of American culture as much as she is the suspicious other for Americans (285). Given that Kathy Griffin similarly exploits her insider/outsider position, Meyer's remarks suggest the profound inflection of race on that positioning.

This complicated approach to race is central to Cho's demand that her audience see her body in a different way and rethink the meanings of her body as "Asian" and "Asian American." Rachel Lee argues that Cho often reverses the white gaze, making audiences suddenly aware of—and uncomfortable with—the pleasures of white spectatorship (118), or in the case of the Asian chicken salad, aware of how they see Asian bodies.[3] Cho's success since 2000 is predicated on her ability to make audiences rethink how to see her as an actor, a comic, an American, an Asian American. At the beginning of her concert film *CHO Revolution* she literalizes this transformation by discarding first a fancy headdress and then a sleek, bobbed wig, saying, "You know I would never get this chinky of a haircut." A gifted mimic, Cho uses her entire body for impersonations of her Korean mother, gay men, and gay black men; Martínez notes that Cho often toys with stereotypes as a way to make connections between racial and gay oppression (151–158). But the recurring theme of her comedy is her own body, its racial meanings—as reflected in the flight attendant's nervousness—and its queerness, its overall positioning outside the gender ideals of American culture.

For Cho the celebration of her body as nonwhite and queer is a claim to power, a performance of pleasure outside the grid. And Cho herself remains outside the grid in terms of her demographics. By 2010 Cho enjoyed a decidedly "niche stardom" composed of mainstream recognition and popularity centered in the LGBTQ community. She told a reporter, "I would love to go mainstream, but my comedy is too edgy. It's always too dirty. It's always too filthy" (in Calhoun). By then a favorite of queers and feminists, Cho appeared as the author of essays in women's studies books and anthologies,[4] as a participant in gay pride parades, and as a performer in women-oriented burlesque and belly-dancing venues. In 2008 journalist Steven Mazey summed up Cho's "not-for-the-easily-offended" comedic range in saying it covers "politics, race, celebrities and sex, including graphic descriptions of her own experiences with men, women and a few battery-operated devices."

My approach to Cho emphasizes the centrality of the body in her work: the body in addiction and recovery, the body as sign of racial and sexual difference, and the queer body celebrated as desirable, desiring, and as Cho has stressed, beautiful in ways that have nothing to do with mainstream standards of beauty. Cho's comeback texts, the film and memoir *I'm the One That I Want*, laid out the ideological attacks on mainstream prettiness that Cho has used since. My premise is that her performances are characterized by their mode of manifesto, an autobiographical tactic that disrupts conventional understandings of who is entitled to a voice and a stand. By its nature as political rhetoric, the manifesto speaks for others and is keenly aware of the collective nature of its concerns. The other narrative and collective identification Cho makes in the book version of *I'm the One That I Want* in particular concerns her recovery from alcoholism. She was able to interpret her experience with network television and mainstream Hollywood through a feminist lens only because she was able to sober up, and her memoir suggests that feminism was the spiritual framework that enabled her recovery.

RECOVERY AND MEMOIR

In the final episode of *The Cho Show*, Cho makes a triumphant return to the high school that expelled her when she was seventeen because of her failing grade-point average and excessive absenteeism. Cho is warmly received in her meeting with students there, and she comments later in her voice-over that she was particularly pleased with her ability to inspire them. The clips from that inspirational meeting include one that shows a female student asking why Cho was willing to undertake a drastic and nearly fatal weight loss for her 1990s television series. Explaining why she'd been desperate for mainstream success, Cho tells the group, "The dream in me was so strong I couldn't wake up" ("Cho Place Like Home"). In an interesting twist to the usual clichés about the dream of success and the American dream, Cho instead emphasizes the illusive nature of the dream and the urgency of waking from it in order to go on with her real life.

Cho's emphasis on inspiring the students in her former high school re-iterates the didactic nature of her come-back nine years earlier in the per-formance film and book versions of *I'm the One That I Want*. Describing her experience with *All-American Girl* as something from which she had to wake up, Cho suggests how deeply and sweepingly she reinterpreted her own life. Cho's book takes the shape of a recovery narrative of the kind best known in twelve-step programs because her failures in 1995–1996 trig-gered abusive and self-destructive drinking. Far more detailed and serious than the film version of *I'm the One*, the book recounts the extent of Cho's drinking, its consequences, and the profound changes that resulted from her being in sobriety. Recovery stories are usually told as those of spiritual awakening, so Cho's language about not being able to wake up during her sitcom years is aligned with this type of narrative. I will return to this narra-tive structure later because it explains some of the collective identifications in Cho's book as well as its highly didactic conclusion. More generally, Cho's alcoholism was a significant factor in her comeback story because, she emphasizes, her excessive drinking was directly tied to her self-hatred, her failure to have the ideal body and be the all-American girl.

Cho's awakening is also blatantly political. Her awakened perspective, drawing from feminist, queer, and Asian identity politics, empowers her to celebrate her body and defy the norms that would marginalize it. This means that even though her story is about a rise to stardom, she is writing and performing against the grain of the traditional rise-to-stardom narrative that legitimizes Hollywood or network television as the fitting reward for the emerging star. Instead, her story follows the pattern of consciousness-raising narratives that rally readers and audiences toward social change.[5] Feminist scholars of autobiography have been particularly interested in memoirs in which the individual life story is offered as inspiration for a larger political agenda. Cho's work closely resembles the strategy described by Sidonie Smith as autobiographical manifesto, "in which the revolu-tionary subject can insist on identity in service to an emancipatory poli-tics" (157). The manifesto autobiography aims to disrupt the status quo, undertaking "new interpretations as a means of wresting power" and fore-grounding the power relations of subjectivity (163). Smith focuses on written rather than performed texts, but she is interested in "out-law" autobiographical genres, the forms that resist traditional narrative form, and Cho's comedy shows striking parallels to the "flamboyant performance" in certain manifesto styles described by Smith.

Cho becomes a revolutionary subject as she takes her stand against an entertainment industry that judged her as too fat and too Asian to succeed. Her network television series *All-American Girl* epitomized those hegemonic discourses by offering sitcom-friendly Asianness and the svelte star body as the hegemonic ideal—what audiences should want. Refusing those ideals, Cho repudiates the racist, sexist, and homophobic assumptions nestled behind the image of the all-American girl; in doing so she repudiates the kind of success she had wanted so desperately. Her proclamation "I'm the one that I want" expresses an embrace of success on her own terms and a pointed rejection of mainstream desires and images. This is the manifesto aspect of her story, the call for resistance as a "revolutionary gesture," in Sidonie Smith's terms (182).

The film and book versions of *I'm the One That I Want* describe personal transformation and link it to a call for social change. Smith explains that the autobiographical manifesto is inherently oppositional. Its author wants to make things happen, to contend against the norm, to demand public space and recognition for an identity that has been dismissed or reduced to a stereotype or a cliché. The purpose is to "incite . . . self-conscious encounters with the politics of identification" that would otherwise assign the writer to a fixed position as object or as representative of a minority (158). While the book version works as manifesto in its political stand against the status quo, the film version of *I'm the One That I Want* does so in its rhetoric, building up to a rowdy crescendo of affirmations and Cho's strident declaration of her right to a voice and visibility. Cho's comedy continued in this manifesto style of disruptive assertions and radicalized accounts of her experience, as evident in the titles of her concert films *CHO Revolution* (2004) and *Assassin* (2005) and her later book *I Have Chosen to Stay and Fight* (2005), a quotation from 1970s political radical Patricia Hearst. Even the more hegemonic title of Cho's later film *Beautiful* (2008) refers to her political appropriation of the word to assert the value of the queer body, positing its beauty as an oppositional force to oppressive politics.

Critics have generally prioritized the *I'm the One That I Want* film over the memoir, probably because the film demonstrates Cho's talent as a comic performer and, as her come-back performance, inaugurated a series of her successful concert films. The film illustrates Cho's ability to perform comically a number of incidents that, as recounted in the book, are serious or even grim. Praising Cho's performance techniques and theatrical presence as intrinsic to "staking claim to her own image," Bacalzo asserts that in comparison, "the book is an engaging read, but it is an entirely different writing strategy from the one Cho employs in her stage work," where audiences can see how Cho's "manic energy and comic exaggeration transform her pain into humor" (47–48). However, Rachel Lee gives the book version more credit, noting that by creating a stage performance, a film, and a book, Cho takes in multiple kinds of audiences—readers and spectators—and eludes a "decidable" version of her story, which instead "leaks" across genres (126). My argument here amplifies the specific ways Cho's story leaks across genres by analyzing them as two modes of autobiography—recovery and manifesto—that form a loop: Cho's book invites readers to reconsider the film through the lens of the recovery story that made the film performance possible.

Cho's book engages the conventional rise-to-stardom elements of the outsider, the alienated child, and the awkward adolescent who stumbles into adulthood and whose talent eventually enables her to succeed against the odds. However, Cho specifies that the odds are loaded with racist and sexist ideals. The feelings of alienation and self-loathing, the conditions that led to her alcoholism, are directly tied to her self-perception of failure against those ideals. And popular culture is the scene of her self-perceived failure—literally the world of images, in a Lacanian sense, that provides an ego ideal and illustrates how sharply she falls short of it. Cho opens her memoir by remarking on how tiny she was at birth: "At 5 pounds, 6 ounces, I was the Calista Flockhart of the newborn set" (1). Flockhart, who played postfeminist heroine Ally McBeal, was famous for her girlish slenderness, the size o body that set the standard for women television stars on shows such as *Friends* (1994–2004). The Flockhart reference is grimly ironic, as Cho reveals that her weight became a serious problem with her own televised representation.

The television she watched soon taught Cho that she would always be excluded from the ideal bodies she saw there: "One of my earliest memories is the day I realized I was not white, and therefore not like the people I saw on TV," she writes. She remembers being "really shocked" as a child that she did not resemble her "friends on the screen" (102–103). Her recurring adolescent fantasy was preparing for a school dance in a magically Caucasian body, "lining my big, big eyes with Aziza by Prince Matchabelli" and letting her "naturally curly chestnut hair" fall over her shoulders. The anecdote is remarkable as an exemplum of misrecognition, an investment in a fantasy cruelly opposed to her mirror image: "Then in the mirror I would be confronted with the awful reality that I was not that. It was almost too much to bear." Her insight about this fantasy is that it never extended to getting to the dance or enjoying the event itself. Instead, the scenario was "all about getting ready, looking a certain way, about not being me" (15–16). This anecdote resounds hauntingly in Cho's experience on *All-American Girl*, which unfortunately entailed looking a certain way and not being herself.

The story of *All-American Girl* takes up the central chapters of *I'm the One*, detailing the nightmare from which Cho needed to wake up. Cho's breakthrough into network television came after dreary years of doing stand-up routines on the road and humiliating experiences in Hollywood. On *Star Search International* she was asked to be more "authentic" by being "more Chinese" despite her protest that she was Korean American, and she remembers a makeup artist who rolled his eyes at the hopelessness of working with her (87–88). With the help of savvy agents, Cho found herself at the center of a bidding war for TV rights to a sitcom in which she would star as the wayward American daughter in an immigrant household.

For any stand-up comic, the offer of a network sitcom is a sign of arrival, of mainstream success. For Cho the stakes encompassed personal and racial identity: "If I got love from millions of people, then how could I still hate myself? . . . Maybe it was okay that I wasn't white, tall, thin, blonde, gorgeous, or a guy. Maybe my ship was coming in. Maybe I would make it okay for Asians to be on TV" (104). What Cho did not foresee was that network television had not reworked its ideals of what female bodies and Asian bodies should look like. In the performance film and the memoir, the crisis and turning point is the phone call Cho gets telling her, after the screen test, that the network had a "problem" with "the fullness" of her face and that she had to lose a substantial amount of weight, in whatever way possible, before the pilot was shot. The memoir repeats, word for word, the show-stopping question Cho poses for her audience and readers: "How do you keep going when someone tells you there is something wrong with your face?" (107). The shame of this rebuke confirmed her lifelong insecurities about her looks; she remembers her first and last ballet recital when she was eight years old, when her father told her she was "the fattest ballerina" (112).

In her later stage performances Cho uses a quip that sums up her experience with network television: "They asked me to lose weight to play myself." Encapsulating the cruelty of this system, being the star of her own sitcom was the experience of not being herself on several levels. A few months into the series she received a phone call from her then boyfriend, Quentin Tarantino, who was stunned to see an episode of *All-American Girl* in which her character decides that she shouldn't make fun of her own family and embarrass them in her routines. In her stand-up comedy Cho had used her family as material for topics of ethnicity and being second-generation Asian American. "They took away your voice!" Tarantino tells her. "Don't let them do that! You fucking live to publicly embarrass your family!" (131).

The false note about Cho as a comedian was symptomatic of larger problems with the script and the premise of the series. Even while the series was being shot, Cho realized that *All-American Girl* was not a very good show, either as a sitcom or as a representation of an Asian family: "The jokes weren't so much stereotypical as stale," she recalls (112). In an interview included on the DVD of *All-American Girl*, released in 2006, Cho attributes the blandness of the comedy to the anxiety about race that permeated network decisions. Because of the pressure about creating the first Asian American television family, she says, the overwhelming concern was "all about race" rather than about character development, comedy, or what she calls "television-ness."[6]

At the same time, Cho says in the interview ("All-American Girl: A Look Back with Margaret Cho and Amy Hill"), Asian American viewers who weren't accustomed to seeing themselves represented on television demanded that the show be "perfect." Eventually an "Asian consultant" was hired to help with the authenticity problems in the scripts and on the set, although in retrospect, Cho says, the problem wasn't authenticity but a racist perception that "there is one defining, 'authentic' Asian-American experience" (*I'm the One*, 140). In her *I'm the One That I Want* film performance she says the network's idea of authenticity involved an abacus on the set and chopsticks in her hair.

Cho's story is not the only evidence that ABC was less than respectful toward the diversity issues it claimed to embrace. In an interview with the *New York Times* during the show's early weeks, a network executive talked awkwardly about the characters coming from "the Far East," using such vague language that the interviewer wondered if the executive knew "exactly which part of the Far East they're supposed to be from" (Southgate). And as the show faltered, the network turned away entirely from concerns about Asian identity. Instead, because the series was criticized for its inability to connect to white audiences, ABC ordered a casting change that eliminated almost all of the Asian characters. By that time ratings were so low that it was evident the show wouldn't be renewed for a second year. In Cho's memoir she recounts that she was especially hurt by the Asian American community's accusation that she had failed as an Asian American and by the tabloid cruelty about her looks, suggesting that she had failed as a woman and a would-be star.

Determined to succeed as a network star, Cho began her cycles of dangerous behavior: crash diets, excessive workouts, and diet pills, followed by migraines and panic attacks. She took to excessive drinking to quell the anxieties: "My poor face . . . would flush bright red from all the vodka and pills I downed so that I could pass out and not look at it anymore" (108). At this point the memoir takes on the structure of a recovery narrative, with Cho's self-destructive drinking increasingly foregrounded in relation to her despair about having "something wrong" with her most personal identity, her Asian face. When she describes drinking as a way to escape this shame, it's clear that her recovery story is enmeshed in issues of representation, racism, and gender ideals.

Ironically, Cho continued to invest in the dream of Hollywood stardom as the answer to her self-hatred. "Looking for self-esteem outside myself and thinking I would find it in Hollywood was insane," she writes (90). The language of "insanity" signals what Robyn Warhol and Helena Michie call the "master narrative" of the conventional recovery story of addiction recovery programs. Warhol and Michie are writing of the specific narrative form found in the meetings and writings of Alcoholics Anonymous, the original twelve-step recovery methodology. My intention here is not to characterize Cho as an alcoholic (as defined by Alcoholics Anonymous or by any clinical, psychological, or other standard) nor to claim her memoir is really a recovery narrative with the truth about Cho as an addict in recovery. Cho refers to herself as being "in sobriety" several times in her performance films, and in her book *I'm the One That I Want* she freely uses the language of recovery programs to talk about her drinking, its consequences, and the process of sobering up. She does not identify herself as a participant in a recovery group, and indeed, a basic tenet of AA is its eponymous anonymity.[7] Rather than essentialize Cho's memoir as a recovery story, I propose that the recovery narrative conveyed in its final chapters invites the reader to consider the entire work as a recovery from the shame and marginalization that drove Cho to excessive drinking. And while traditional recovery narratives usually come from a twelve-step program perspective, emphasizing spirituality as the path to sanity, Cho's recovery is instead rooted in the perspective of feminism and queer identity, enabling her to embrace her identity and body outside conventional categories of gender and race.

Warhol and Michie explain that the recovery story is a specific kind of autobiography that identifies and internalizes the master narrative that enables sobriety. The recovery story is also a practice that requires retelling and hearing other versions of the same story so the accumulated stories work as "an autobiography-in-common that comes to constitute a collective identity for sober persons" (328). As a teleology, recovery is a powerful autobiographical tool because the narrative includes and even embraces the most abject elements of the narrator's history: blackouts, losses, failures, legal problems, disgrace. All these details point forward to a moment when the narrator understands those dark times in the larger perspective of health and sanity. Warhol and Michie describe recovery stories as "retrospective narratives designed to interpret the past in the light of a more enlightened present identity" (330).

Cho's account closely adheres to this pattern, beginning with the traditional "drunkalogue," the gritty details of blackouts, humiliations, and loss of control that are evidence of powerlessness over alcohol. Cho writes that she would "average two or three hangovers a day, drinking to get over the first one, getting drunk, falling asleep, waking up in the middle of the day with another one, drinking it away and getting a headache again" (*I'm the One*, 169). She describes consequences such as blackouts in restaurants, miserable relationships and one-night stands, drunk driving, and an unplanned pregnancy. Her stand-up career in ruins, she routinely performed so drunk that she held on to the microphone stand to keep the room from spinning (168). When she wrote a screenplay she thought would be her comeback, she instead encountered a producer who would work with her only if she slept with him, an offer that repulsed her. But rather than feeling anger at the sexist machineries of Hollywood production, Cho reports that she "felt like a failure. I couldn't even fuck my way to the top" (163). This wry remark suggests that Cho never loses her sense of humor about her darkest days, but it also demonstrates how, through an alcoholic lens, the odious behavior of other people gets processed as a continuation of her own personal shame.

Cho said the turning point was the recurrence of an incident that had happened before—waking up to discover she'd wet the bed—but this time she was with her boyfriend after a blackout and because the stain was in the middle, they couldn't figure out which of them had done it: "I thought, WHAT KIND OF FUCKED UP MÖTLEY CRÜE *BEHIND THE MUSIC* BULLSHIT IS THIS?!!!!" (195). Cho's reference is to the exposé of the heavy metal band Mötley Crüe on the VH1 television series *Behind the Music* (1997–2006); her identification with a group of musicians infamous for their debauchery is a grim joke about how loathsome her life had become. The horror of this particular low point jolted her into realizing she did not want to die, and despite a questionable boyfriend who was less serious about sobering up, Cho managed to give up drugs and alcohol. She discovered that "sobriety was wondrous" and that she was "funnier, more alive, happy" in her stand-up work when she was sober (196).

For the master narrative of recovery, this crucial turning point involves the discovery of a higher power, which is almost always described in traditional terms as God. Cho's narrative is far less conventional, although she occasionally uses language that suggests belief in a traditional Judeo-Christian deity.[8] But in describing her moment of spiritual awakening, Cho instead talks about encountering a specifically feminine energy during a yoga class: "I discovered that there was a goddess deep inside me. . . . I saw that whatever I had in front of me, I could use her strength, instead of mine, to lift it. She agreed to be my power plant, which was such a relief, as I had been running on empty for so long" (200). This is clearly recognition of a power outside of herself, but the following passage also indicates that it's a spiritual power available at the human level. In the supermarket on the way home, Cho finds herself weeping and being comforted by an old woman "in a plaid coat and snowy white hair" who offers Cho her ticket for the deli line. "How could I refuse a goddess?" Cho asks (200–201).

Describing her recovery in the remaining chapters of *I'm the One That I Want*, Cho emphasizes female power as her personal rendition of the spirituality that imbues traditional recovery narratives. Because her excessive drinking was a symptom of her self-loathing and shame about her body, Cho goes into detail about her new attitude toward her body and her weight following the huge shift in perspective that happened with sobriety. Once she rejected network television and mainstream popular culture as the higher power of her life, she realized she "didn't have to be thin to be acceptable" (205). Cho begins to speak in the plural about her new attitude. "Let's not hate ourselves," she writes. "We are all we have. We cannot do anything until we accept that. I cannot do this alone" (91). Cho's narrative in this way features what Warhol and Michie call the "collective protagonist" of the recovery story, the "we" that reiterates the twelve steps: "We admitted we were powerless over alcohol" (332). The reason the recovery story must be retold in endless variations by the entire recovery community is group identification.[9] Recovery from addiction is possible insofar as the individual addict can internalize her story as part of a much larger story by admitting what she has in common with other addicts.

The appeal to collective experience — "I cannot do this alone" — is an important aspect of the recovery process, but it's also a serious pitch Cho can't make in the comic mode of her stage performances, nor is it commensurate with the queer, raunchy, outrageous comedy for which she is best known. My point here is that by producing a book and a performance as her autobiographical come-back, Cho engages several modes of self-representation, from the introspective and didactic to the raucous and comic, and mobilizes multiple identities that include the recovering alcoholic in the same way she claims identity as Asian American while resisting it as final or absolute.[10]

Cho concludes her book with statements that efface the individual speaker and confirm larger truths of a master narrative about a great turnaround that made her life better and richer. She speaks of "the unseen strands of love that connect us all to each other" and tells a story about a gay couple, one of them dying of AIDS, who cherished her new CD. The story is important to her because, having renounced success on Hollywood's terms—the size 4 body, the appeal to white audiences—Cho says her new interpretation of success is the ability to touch the lives of others: "I never would have met them if I hadn't survived. I never would have made that CD if I hadn't stopped drinking" (211–212). This passage loops back to the beginning of her book in expressing gratitude for surviving and recovering. So although the recovery story engages only the last quarter of *I'm the One That I Want*, the memoir itself is the story enabled by the recovery.

FAG-HAG MANIFESTO

The film version of *I'm the One That I Want* came prior to the memoir, but I've discussed the memoir first because it details the process that made the performance film and Cho's comeback possible. These two autobiographical texts function as alternative versions of her story or—like a Möbius strip—as two sides of a continuous story narrated in different tones and modes. The differences are best exemplified in their concluding statements, which illustrate the rhetorical differences between the recovery story and the manifesto. The book's final sentences begin with collective identification: "When we are able to love ourselves, we open the door to more love. So much rushes in. So much rushes out. Never underestimate the power that you have in the world. After meeting such remarkable people, I know that I never will" (212). This visionary declaration of personal power taps the tone and discourse of the master narrative of recovery: direct address to the reader, affirmation, and big-picture generalizations. It is a contemplative way to summarize her battle with self-image and bodily shame, even though this is not the voice for which Cho is best known.

That voice—boisterous and confrontational—resonates in her conclusion to the concert film *I'm the One*, which delivers self-affirmation as defiance rather than didacticism and is laced with specific autobiographical details rather than the generalizations and collective-voiced conclusion of the book. While the book's conclusion shows that Cho has turned away from an alcoholic death, the film emphasizes that she has turned away from the deadliness of mainstream media ideals:

> I'm not going to die. I'm not going to die because my sitcom got cancelled. And I am not gonna die because some producer tried to take advantage of me. And I am not gonna die because some network executive thought I was fat. [*Applause*] It's so wrong that women are asked to live up to this skinny ideal that is totally unattainable. For me to be 10 pounds thinner is a full-time job, and I'm handing in my notice and walking out the door. [*Applause*] I'm not gonna die because I failed as someone else. I'm gonna succeed as myself, and I'm gonna stay here and hog the mic until the next Korean American, fag hag, shit starter, girl comic, trash talker comes out and takes my place. [*Uproarious applause*]

Delivering this conclusion, Cho's voice rises in crescendos with each sentence so that each statement is more forceful and dramatic than the last, and the crowd in turn roars its approval ever more loudly with each.

Most tellingly, her triumphant declaration is grounded in opposition and speaks for a larger cause, both of which are characteristics of the manifesto. Cho's final sentence positions her as belonging to an emerging line of defiant, marginalized, women comics whose queerness is adversarial — "fag hags, shit starters, trash talkers." Writing of the nature of a manifesto, Sidonie Smith emphasizes its push for an alternative public sphere and its challenge to the idea of a universal voice or experience. Cho makes this move with her ethical claim that "it's so wrong that women are asked to live up to this skinny ideal." The claim springs from material she performed in comic mode earlier in the film, the entire story of her wish for mainstream success, the failure of the show, the self-destructive behavior. Concluding with a generalization and a judgment, she has moved out of comedy and into a rhetorical stand, a call for social change. This is a very different agenda from the recovery story, which is by its nature an appeal for individual change, even though recovery stories have to be shared in a community. However, the recovery story dovetails here with the manifesto as autobiographical acts. Both are didactic and both posit the autobiographical subject in a highly significant relationship with the community.[11]

Cho's concert film demonstrates what autobiographical manifesto looks like as theater, with an impact that is physical as well as verbal.[12] As opposed to the canned laughter of the *All-American Girl* sitcom built around a body deemed acceptable to the television network, Cho evokes laughter on her own terms through the physical performance of the body she has declared as the one that she wants. A good example of Cho's theatrical performance of manifesto is her extended routine showing the martial arts stereotype as a primary marker of Asian identity. The routine begins with Cho relating her agent's remark that "the Asian thing" may not work for her as an entertainer. "What the fuck is 'the Asian thing'?" Cho asks. "Like it's some gimmick I pull out of my ass every couple of years, to jazz up my career." In the book version she uses the same sentences, minus the expletive, to describe her reaction, while in the film she performs a comic example of "the Asian thing" by mimicking a series of martial arts moves, the karate chops, kicks, and body spins that audiences know from films that, she says in her memoir, are more likely to star white than Asian actors.[13] This troubling of racial dynamics is part of Cho's manifesto, her renunciation of what white audiences "want" in order to assert the value of her body on her own terms.

Yet at other moments Cho emphasizes the specificity of her experience as Asian American, particularly as a body always already marked with racial difference. The confirmation of race suggests how autobiographical manifesto dovetails with Cho's comedy in its refusal of a universal subject. The traditional subject of autobiography is situated as an insider yet as universal, a position that "proffers authority, legitimacy, and readability. It also proffers membership in the community of the fully human," Sidonie Smith notes. The position of authoritative insider with a universal voice is particularly attractive to minorities—but at the cost of minority uniqueness. That is, the qualities of authority, legitimacy, and readability are presumed to be embodied as white, male, heterosexual. Smith is instead interested in "anti-'autobiographical' forms" or "out-law genres," which is where she places the autobiographical manifesto as a text that features the "unauthorized speaker" who, in claiming a story, challenges categories of the "natural" or "universal" (154–155).

Like traditional autobiography, comedy has often posited universal topics and audiences as white and male. In her essay on women's stand-up routines Allison Fraiberg notes a racial strategy Cho used even in her early 1990s comedy to disrupt the assumption of universal comedy and to underscore the importance of her Korean American identity. Cho often invokes a universal situation, Fraiberg says, that invites audience identification—rebelling against parents, being a difficult child. Cho then hones in on her particular circumstances that make the situation racially specific. For instance, she tells a story about the childhood embarrassment of being hauled off to a staid, middle-class department store every Saturday morning by her mother. It's a "cross-cultural moment" about parent-child conflict, Fraiberg argues, until Cho gets to the part when she does an imitation of her immigrant mother calling the kids to go to Montgomery Ward. Taking on a heavy accent and an exaggerated squint, Cho foregrounds the specificity of being the Korean American daughter hailed by an immigrant mother who is herself being hailed into assimilation by way of bourgeois commodities. The cultural and racial dynamics are what make the story funny but also mark "the end of the illusory universal moment" (324–325).[14] Fraiberg describes the trajectory of Cho's stand-up routines as a continual process of inclusion and foreclosure, with stories that invite the audience into identification and then remind them that the Korean American experience is, in fact, very specific. The overall effect is to "disturb the familiarity and assumed mass appeal" of Cho's persona and to destroy "the false collectivity of 'universal humor'" (326).

In the film *I'm the One That I Want* Cho uses the racial tactic cited by Fraiberg to remind viewers how the experience of racism is a constant in her life, as in her anecdote about how walking a dog is a chance to talk with strangers. But instead of encountering friendly dog-lovers, Cho is taunted by a man who calls out, "That dog gonna wind up in a pot of rice!"—a reminder that even an activity as prosaic as pet-walking can provoke a racist encounter. The joke caps Cho's long story about her visit to the animal shelter and her adoption of a dog, stories that Rachel Lee says seem to have "universal appeal." But given Cho's revelations about racism in culture and in the entertainment industry, Lee says, the wish for universality can only indicate "the pathetic nature of liberal ignorance" in the "disavowal of race" (124).

When Cho makes her climactic self-assertion at the film's conclusion, she incorporates race/ethnicity into a larger, adversarial identity of the Korean American trash talker, the queer identity at the heart of her manifesto. The performance of *I'm the One That I Want* begins on this queer note as well, with Cho's self-proclamation as a fag hag, an identity that challenges the traditional, male, "authorized" speaker of stand-up comedy and the concept of "female comic" as an essentialist category of gender.[15] Bacalzo points out the significance of this claim at the beginning of the concert. Despite her attention to her status as an Asian American artist later in the film, "Cho identifies with a marginalized community that is, significantly, not the Asian/American community" (43). In her memoir Cho devotes an entire chapter, "On Being a Fag Hag," to this particular queer identity, celebrating the "two derogatory terms, *fag* and *hag*," she writes, which together signify "the union of the world's most popular objects of scorn, homosexual and woman" (37). While her thoughts on being a fag hag are developed in the book in essay style, her announcement of fag-hag identity in the film is built up as campy comedy, with Cho drawing out the resonances of her outrageous statements for full dramatic effect. "Fags," she declares, beaming and pausing for emphasis. "I love the word 'faggot' because it describes my kind of guy." She pauses as the audience erupts in cheers. "I am a fag hag. Fag hags are the backbone of the gay community." More exuberant cheering follows.[16]

The declaration comes five minutes into the concert, setting the tone of manifesto, the public announcement that serves, Sidonie Smith writes, as a call "for a changed relationship to subjectivity, identity, and the body. We see this agenda in recent texts by women who pursue self-consciously political autobiographical acts, who issue calls for new subjects" (157). Cho gets a wildly enthusiastic response to her manifesto statement because the fag hag has historically been a highly maligned identity even within the gay community, an "object of scorn." Deborah Thompson, in an analysis of the meanings and cultural positions of the fag hag, claims that long after Stonewall the gay man–straight woman relationship remained a "love that dare not speak its name." Consequently, well into the twenty-first century there is no "respectable" word for the woman in this dynamic, Thompson says, given that both "fag" and "hag" are disparaging terms (40). When Cho reclaims the fag hag as a "new subject," she is contesting the contemptible status of this identity within the queer community while making an audacious claim for the legitimacy and value of an identity that, if acknowledged at all, is conventionally understood as a failed position within heteronormativity: the straight woman who can't get a straight man and instead substitutes attachment to a gay male friend.

This heterosexist definition denies the female pleasure of the relationship, according to Thompson; she argues for the importance of the fag hag as a queer identity that resists identity politics by focusing on binding relationships rather than individual autonomy. Conceding that the fag hag bears the weight of the stigmatized stereotype, Thompson uses Cho, Madonna, and the Grace character of *Will and Grace* to exemplify the "new" fag hag who, rather than being a figure of abjection, is "generally smart, sexy, sassy, and *happy*" (41) and looking to gay men not as substitutes for an erotic relationship but as family. Thompson pushes the latter point by stressing that the fag hag "is not simply a woman who has gay male friends" but rather one who is "hailed into the queer community early on, and that is her home. She does not just go there to visit; she lives there" (42).

I want to go back to this as a point of difference between Cho and Kathy Griffin, although some of Thompson's insights are relevant to both performers. In discussing Griffin's slippery identifications with gay men earlier, I drew on José Esteban Muñoz's term "disidentification," the "dissing" of a fixed identity, and on Roberta Mock's concept of the "heteroqueer," the straight woman who enjoys the gay male community as a respite from her role in heterosexist culture.[17] Thompson's argument for the fag hag is similar to both. In a move that parallels Muñoz's take on dissing, Thompson says the fag hag demonstrates the value of identifying "with" rather than "as" another, thus moving away from essentialism toward alliance and "cross-identity identifications" (45). And like Mock, Thompson is interested in how a straight woman's relationship to gay men "troubles the borders of 'queerness'" by revealing how powerfully a heterosexual woman can be emotionally invested in a relationship with no romantic or sexual returns. Thompson concludes that "committed fag hags (including heterosexual ones) *are* queer" (46).

Regarding Kathy Griffin's relationships with men, I have argued that Griffin's queerness resides in her pseudoromances and dates with inappropriate men, attention to her gays, dismissal of straight men in her audience, and identification as the sidekick rather than the romantic heroine. No doubt for all of these reasons Cho outs Griffin as a fag hag in a routine in *Beautiful* when she talks about the joys of "hanging out with some fucking fag hags: Kathy Griffin, fag hag. Major fag hag. Cindi Lauper, fag hag. And Olivia Newton-John, who is like the Dalai Lama of the fag hags." What she exhibits here is the powerful thrill of naming popular entertainers under the banner of a defamed identity recovered as an honor and a mark of prestige. And the agenda, the outing of queer identities and affinities, is part of Cho's manifesto style, an obstinate proclamation of a marginal and illegitimate relationship.

Yet I would differentiate among the varying politics and positionings of the entertainers Cho names here, especially in light of Thompson's distinction between women who have gay friends (and followers, I would add) and women for whom the queer community is home. Thompson talks about the fag hag's "accountability," a sense of responsibility "to gay men and the queer community at large" (46). Margaret Cho stakes out her position in this marginal territory as her primary point of reference. For one thing, her descriptions of her various sexual practices make it clear that queer culture is her everyday life. Cho began these descriptions in the film *I'm the One That I Want* with her story about taking a woman lover while she was on a gay cruise. "I went through this whole thing. Am I gay? Am I straight? And I realized I'm just slutty. Where's my parade?" Lee contends that this question about Cho's "liminal position between sexual identity categories" signals the larger question of "where to locate the space of Asian American queer citizenship" (125).

And this nonwhite queer citizenship forfeits the prestige of Kathy Griffin's Hollywood, which remains Griffin's home, her scene as insider/outsider. Griffin, too, performs on lesbian cruises, but there is never a doubt that she is there as the observer, not a participant in amorous affairs. In 2009 and 2010 Griffin organized rallies for gay marriage and the end of the Don't-ask-don't-tell policy in the military. Indeed, it is possible her activism got attention because she is perceived as a straight celebrity who is "gay friendly": she herself has nothing to gain from the policy and legal changes she is advocating. No matter how queer her presentation and skewed her relation to heterosexuality, Griffin's most prominent image is neither as fag hag nor as queer advocate but rather as the gossipy red-carpet wag, loud-mouthed expert on celebrity, and would-be Hollywood insider.

In contrast, since *I'm the One That I Want,* Cho has turned her back on mainstream audiences and has focused on the gay and queer community as home, a site where discussion of her fag-hag status is welcome. In her later concert films Cho draws on this status to demonstrate her resistance to concepts of natural gender behavior and cultural precepts about sexualities. In *Assassin* she asserts that her fag-hag power has queer-enhancing qualities for gay men and the power to make straight men gay. "I make every gay man infinitely more gay just by my presence," she boasts. "I am the nelly maker. I am the fag whisperer." However, she also jokes about the limitations of the fag-hag affiliation in that a primary aspect of the gay man's life is wholly outside the relationship with his hag. Describing herself in *Beautiful* as a "lifestyle fag hag," she talks about the pleasures of going to gay bars with her male friends "until it becomes dick o'clock." At that point, she says, anyone without a dick has no reason to be there, not even if it's "Judy Garland back from the dead."

This conflict built into the fag-hag friendship—the sexual priorities of gay men—is developed in more detail in the film Cho wrote and produced in 2005, *Bam Bam and Celeste.* In it she and comic Bruce Daniels play lifelong friends trapped in their dreary Midwestern hometown, where they had been the only queers—the fag hag and gay man—tormented by the high school "in crowd." To escape, they take a road trip to the queer paradise of New York City, where they hope to resettle. Celeste cheerfully stands by or waits out Bam Bam's sexual trysts along the way, at one point sitting on the hood of their car that bounces rhythmically as Bam Bam has fun with a young Amish man they'd passed on the road. But at a moment when she truly needs Bam Bam in New York, he's off on another tryst, and in their later heated argument about this, Celeste tearfully tells him that she's not his best friend at all: "Your best friend is your penis."

In the film's comic trajectory, their fight gets resolved like a lovers' quarrel in a romantic comedy in that each discovers how life had gotten much worse when they were apart: "I gained fifteen pounds!" "I got genital warts!" But the larger structure of the narrative is Celeste's discovery of her own beauty despite the lifelong mockery and torment she has suffered from "the beautiful people," the high school meanies who later became the owners of New York's most prestigious salon, that is, the arbiters of hegemonic taste. Throughout the film Bam Bam is the only one who has always believed Celeste is beautiful and tells her so consistently. The resolution of the narrative is Celeste's ability to see what Bam Bam has seen all along. The enduring bond of the relationship, the narrative suggests, is a way of seeing, and the bond persists despite moments when the woman's best interests are truly not a priority for the gay man. The acknowledgment of this conflict is another way Cho troubles the borders of queerness, insisting on the value of a relationship that includes contradictions about sexuality.

BODY/BAWDY COMEDY

In this book's survey of how women comedians have challenged the pretty versus funny tradition, Cho's comedy registers as the most radically defiant because of her celebratory embrace of queer identity. Cultural ideas about prettiness are relentlessly heterosexual despite the confounding nature of femme lesbianism. Prettiness is associated with the physically pleasing body and with the gender ideology of pleasing, accommodating femininity within a heterosexual framework. Cho's resistance to this concept of pretty is evident on the DVD cover of her performance film *Beautiful*, where her face is rendered into a painterly image of gorgeous androgyny and she wears the Liza Minnelli cabaret hat and mascara that are shorthand for campy performance. The cabaret bowler is usually black; in this image, its bone-whiteness matches the stylized whiteness of her skin and makes a striking contrast with her black hair, emphasizing the Asian twist to this queer icon. Especially because it's the cover for a comedy concert, the seriousness of Cho's expression is striking in its implications that this is not a pretty woman doing comedy. This woman is queer and beautiful.

After *I'm the One That I Want*, Cho maintained her primary allegiance to gay and queer audiences by focusing her comedy on topics that would offend or shock mainstream tastes and politics. Countering the racism and conservative discourses that became prevalent in the United States after 9/11, Cho aggressively developed her stage persona and routines around themes of political and antiracist critique and queer sexuality. As the artwork for *Beautiful* suggests, Cho's comedy foregrounds the outlaw status of her body, its desires and race, as well as its cultural histories and how others

In her 2009 concert film Beautiful, Margaret Cho appeals to audience members to find themselves beautiful as a way to resist narrow, mainstream concepts of beauty.

perceive it. Confirming her sexual difference, Cho's stand-up routines are often graphically explicit about sexual practices considered marginal. In *Notorious C.H.O.* she talks about eating pussy, being fisted, and experimenting with discipline and bondage, always with a comic edge. "Those S&M people are bossy," she complains. In *CHO Revolution* she does a comic rumination on the "weirdness" of monogamy, claiming that when she was living with a guy she felt like "a prostitute with really low rates: 'I'll do oral and anal if you take out the garbage.' 'I'll lick your balls if you open this jar.' 'Do I have to eat your ass to get you to mow the lawn?'" In *Assassin* she describes how she used strap-on dildos on straight men because "straight guys love it in the ass. The way to a man's heart is not through his stomach." And in *Beautiful* she talks about how she loves to "eat ass" even though "it's an acquired taste." Women comics doing raunchy and explicit sex talk have become commonplace since the 1990s, as seen in earlier discussions of Sarah Silverman, for example. But the political ramifications of Cho's graphic sex talk are central to her comedy of manifesto, the continual self-validation of subject positions deemed marginal, illegitimate, and unauthorized.

Reinforcing the political thrust of her sexual themes, Cho in 2009 wrote an autobiographical essay that served as the foreword to the feminist anthology *Yes Means Yes! Visions of Female Sexual Power and a World without Rape*. The anthology is a sex-positive approach to rape education that emphasizes female sexual agency and the right to pleasure, as opposed to the No-means-no approach that, the editors point out, ignores "how suppressing female sexual agency is a key element of rape culture" (Friedman and Valenti, 6). In her foreword to *Yes Means Yes!* Cho writes about how she was date-raped at fourteen. In her own memoir *I'm the One That I Want* she recalls conditions surrounding the incident: "We didn't call it rape back then. . . . We thought what happened was passion, romance, ravishment. It felt wrong to me, but I still defined it in those terms because those were all we had" (45–46). In the *Yes Means Yes!* foreword Cho expands on the rape by admitting that the narrow ways of thinking about forced sexual activity "back then" played out in her adult life: "I am surprised by how much sex I have had in my life that I didn't want to have" (2). She links her experience to the general message of the anthology, which in turn links self-respect with the right to pleasure. The essays in the volume, she tells readers, "encourage you to say yes to yourself, yes to your desires, and yes to the idea that you have a right to a joyful sex life, free from violence and shame" (4). The exhortation to female pleasure is yet another facet of Cho's manifesto agenda.

Cho insists on the Asian woman as an actively desiring subject as opposed to the stereotype of the quiet, docile, Asian female body. She frequently satirizes the pornographic version of that stereotype. Imitating the stock Asian whore, she does an impersonation in *Notorious C.H.O.*: "Sucky fucky two dollah. Me love you long time." And in an extended routine in *CHO Revolution* she imitates Bangkok street hawkers calling out come-ons for exotic sex shows: "Pussy eat banana! Pussy play ping pong! Pussy write letter!" The comedy lies in Cho's puzzled and skeptical facial expressions as she listens to these come-ons and tries to imagine how they could be enacted: "Really play on a table and stuff? How does it hold the paddle? What kind of letter is pussy going to write?" The punch of this routine is the Asian woman as critical thinker and subject listening to a description of Asian female sexuality objectified to the point of being surreal. In the larger context, when Cho speaks of her own sexual desires and pleasures, she is speaking back to the Bangkok sex-show hawker but also to the mainstream Hollywood scripts that give Asian women equally objectified roles. The street hawker's projection of the Asian woman as "pussy" is the vulgar version of the Asian woman who speaks only to say "Welcome to Japan, Mr. Bond."

Cho's marriage in 2003 to writer-artist Al Ridenour enhanced rather than negated her queer reputation through her insistence in interviews and in her stage acts that marriage can be queered, too. "The secret to a happy marriage," she says in *Beautiful*, "[is that] you have to fuck a lot of other people. It takes a village." In a 2010 interview for *New York Magazine* Cho describes her marriage by saying, "We've never had a monogamous relationship. I need the ability to be myself and do what I want" (in Calhoun). Speaking to a reporter for *The Advocate* two years earlier, Cho stopped short of calling it an "open marriage," saying instead that its "boundaries" are "all very unclear." In the same interview, though, she made some remarks that reframe the discussion of heterosexual relationships altogether by undermining the status of the male body as sexual partner. She said she is inclined toward relationships with female-to-male transsexuals. "I still love cock, all cock," she said. "Cock doesn't necessarily have to be cock to be cock. It can be a store-bought cock" (in Hensley). Her quip about cock in relation to pleasure rather than as an essentialist body or identity is a more radical version of Kathy Griffin's denial that straight men are present in her audiences.

Cho makes an unmistakable connection between queer sexuality and national politics by way of a satirical comment in *Beautiful* on promiscuity and xenophobia. After stating that she identifies as queer rather than gay or bi, she says that "queer . . . for me means, I don't care who you are, I want you to want me. . . . I used to fuck everybody, but you just can't do that anymore. No, not after 9/11." The joke is a turnaround of the usual cliché about the dangers of promiscuity after the emergence of AIDS and sexually transmitted diseases. But the joke also alludes to the ways in which nonwhite, non-Christian, noncompliant bodies became suspect after 9/11 when, under the 2001 Patriot Act, unauthorized surveillance was legitimized and all "suspicious" behavior and persons could be covertly investigated as a threat to "homeland security." By linking her queer sexuality to the ways people were cautioned to be distrustful in the era of homeland security, Cho demonstrates her keen awareness of how power operates through bodies, in the Foucauldian sense. She refuses to be a disciplined body, and her refusal entails describing in detail the sexual practices deemed marginal or, by the most conservative religious standards, immoral or even illegal.

Cho's awareness of the relation of disciplined bodies and political and economic power is evident in a manifesto speech she gave toward the end of her concert film *Notorious C.H.O.* Her traumatic experience with network television in the 1990s made clear to her the commodity value of the feminine ideal. For *All-American Girl* she was required to become the appropriate body for primetime television driven by advertisers that profit from products promising the ideal body. Thus when she winds up her *Notorious C.H.O.* concert with a long spiel on the importance of self-esteem, she drives home the warning that "self-esteem" is a value laden with commercial snares, "especially in women's culture and in gay male culture." If her audiences of women and gay men look in the mirror and find they are "too old, too fat, too ugly," she exhorts, what they are really seeing is "billions upon billions of dollars of advertising, magazines, movies, billboards geared to make you feel shitty about yourself so that you will take your hard-earned money and spend it at the mall and spend it on some turnaround cream that doesn't turn around shit." This is a didactic attack on the notion of pretty that is far more politically explicit than, for example, Silverman's song about pooping at the mall, which likewise targeted the role of consumer culture in producing practices like the child beauty pageant.

Cho instead picks up the notion of pretty as one of several marginalizing ideals by linking too fat, too old, too ugly to other positions outside the mainstream. She begins this segment of her performance by talking about the urgency of self-esteem for minorities and then recites a long, inclusive list of which groups are minorities: "If you're a woman, if you're a person of color, if you are gay, lesbian, bisexual, transgender; if you're a person of size, if you're a person of intelligence, if you're a person of integrity, then you are considered a minority in this world." The inclusiveness of the statement extends the scope of Cho's manifesto politics, satirically encompassing people of intelligence and integrity as political outlaws and acknowledging how her own experience of sexism and racism is not a personal issue but a larger cultural problem that can be politicized in popular culture.

REWRITING ALL-AMERICAN GIRL

My argument has been that Cho's traumatic experience with *All-American Girl* prompted her to rewrite the story of her failure into a manifesto about reclaiming herself and her body. In doing so she takes on the concept of pretty far more radically and politically than the other comedians discussed in this book because of her explicit self-identity as queer and feminist. So I conclude this chapter by illustrating how two of Cho's projects in the 2000s rewrote *All-American Girl* through these lenses. The 2005 movie *Bam Bam and Celeste* and Cho's 2008 reality TV series, *The Cho Show*, profoundly revise the representation of the Asian family that was heralded as innovative and progressive in 1994 and allow Cho to represent herself as a camp star and a diva, respectively. Though *All-American Girl* was supposedly based on Cho's life as the American daughter of immigrant Korean bookstore owners in San Francisco fictionalized as the Kim family, the show cleaned up or eliminated all references to gay culture, erased Cho's real-life experience as fag hag and outsider in high school, and was structured around a stock mother-daughter conflict as the basis of the show's comedy. The series erased any representation of racism and xenophobia that the fictional Kim family would have experienced. Sarah Moon Cassinelli says the series was modeled after the "minority sitcom formula of *The Cosby Show*," offering "a cohesive, nuclear family with strong values and just a little touch of comic mischief" (139). *All-American Girl* used the adversarial mother-daughter relationship as a way to reinforce a dangerous cliché about assimilation as an either-or choice between generations (132).

The first part of *Bam Bam and Celeste* shows Celeste as a high school student living at home, much like the main character Margaret Kim on *All-American Girl*. But Celeste, far from being a sweetly assimilated young student, is a fag hag with wildly pink-striped hair who wears a blood-stained bridal gown to the school prom — her date, of course, being the openly gay African American Bam Bam, who is regularly beaten up in the boys' bathroom at school. Celeste, too, is tormented for looking and being different. Taunted by her high school peers as "the ugliest girl we have ever seen," Celeste internalizes the criticism and truly believes she's fat and unattractive — as Cho herself did during the time she starred in *All-American Girl*.

Bam Bam and Celeste cuts out the fake jolly-immigrant family of the sitcom, instead having Celeste's "Mommie" played by Cho in her famous impersonation of her immigrant mother. Wholly unlike the glamourous, demanding mother on the sitcom series who harped constantly about the need for Margaret to have a Korean boyfriend, Mommie wears cheap, floppy vests and is delighted that Bam Bam is Margaret's date for the prom. Mommie doesn't seem to understand Bam Bam's sexual orientation, so she keeps reminding them to use condoms and is confused when she finds a large, pink dildo under Celeste's bed, a realistic reminder of how single young women are likely to find pleasure without a sexual partner. But Mommie is wholly supportive of Celeste, and the film makes clear that cultural conflict, far from being centered in the family, is more likely to emerge from racism and xenophobia from the outside. During their road adventures Bam Bam is nearly killed by Klan members who appear at a South Bend gas station, and Celeste is taunted as a "Chink" by the owner of the next gas station down the road. In her bedroom Celeste keeps as a reminder of everyday racism a poster from the internments of Japanese American citizens during World War II titled "Instruction to all persons of Japanese descent."

Bam Bam and Celeste targets the hegemonic ideals of prettiness that tormented Cho during her *All-American Girl* days and the racism of those ideals. The high school bullies who grow up to own a prestigious beauty salon are openly racist about who they hire and what can be considered beautiful. The climax of the film is the defeat of the stylist bullies during a makeover television show in which, despite the protests and insults of the stylists, Celeste proclaims herself beautiful. The diegetic audience members for the show are at first flummoxed, but then they too turn against the bullies when Celeste points to them and exclaims how beautiful they are. The rebellion against the makeover show is a manifesto of self-proclaimed value and esteem directly related to the manifesto on self-esteem at the end of *Notorious C.H.O.* However, the more subtle rebellion is the one against the economy that sponsors network shows like the makeover and sponsored *All-American Girl* only if Cho could lose enough weight so that her face wasn't "too big for the screen."

The Cho Show, Cho's 2008 VH1 seven-episode reality show, likewise focused on self-validations of the body and revision of standard notions of what is pretty by taking up the topics of beauty pageants, soft-porn music videos, and plastic surgery. *The Cho Show* was a scripted reality show with scenarios filled in by improvised dialogue along the lines of *Curb Your Enthusiasm* (2000–), Cho told a reporter (Mazey). Each episode covered a quirky backstage adventure of the star similar to the structure of Kathy Griffin's *Life on the D List*. Also similar to the *D List*, *The Cho Show* featured an entourage that made up a surrogate family and regular appearances by Cho's parents, who—one reviewer put it—were "incapable of artifice" no matter how staged the premise of the episodes (Lloyd). In a thoroughly different trajectory from Griffin's reality show, however, *The Cho Show* focused on the celebration of a queer diva, not the comic abjection of a would-be mainstream star. Cho told an interviewer she wanted to "make it a point to be naked in every episode" to display the body that ABC producers and tabloid journalists had deemed too fat in her sitcom days (Quinn). Cho is not nude in every episode, but she does manage to dress suggestively or with props barely covering intimate body parts as she poses in a painted-on dress, gets herself spray-tanned, and makes a soft-porn music video with a lot of chocolate ice cream. These are nearly identical to ploys and plot lines Griffin used on her *D List*, but *The Cho Show* also goes into bodily territory the more conservative Griffin would not approach. In one episode Cho gets a colonic and a "G shot," a collagen injection in the vagina to enhance orgasms. In another episode she considers plastic surgery but instead goes for anal bleaching as well as tattoos on her arms, chest, and back. Overall, this is a manifesto about the queer body and its pleasures, offering physical intimacy and the transgression of boundaries as the text of the diva star.

Given Cho's niche stardom, the series did not garner high enough ratings to sustain it for more than seven episodes.[18] Unlike the *All-American Girl* series, this show was no litmus test for the viability of Cho as a star, given that her popularity had been limited to gay and feminist fans for years. Cho's reality show can more productively be thought of as the sitcom parody version of *I'm the One That I Want*, developing the plots and characters Cho wants and a network sitcom could never accommodate, from anal bleaching to the gay and little-person co-stars. Didactic as well as campy, the series enabled Cho and her little-person assistant Selene to put on a beauty contest that everyone wins and let Cho feature her real-life loving relationship with Mommie, whose over-the-top comments need no script, as when she tells Margaret that her near-naked sprayed-on dress is "too Chinese." When *Boston Herald* reviewer Mark Perigard complained about Cho's continual references to the *All-American Girl* fiasco—"Time to get over it"—what he missed is that the network's 1994 sexism and racism were far from over; rather, they are typical of mainstream television, which continues to favor one narrow version of what is pretty—the fit, homogeneous bodies that can best support ads for products to make viewers slimmer and blonder. Cho's refusal to get over her network experience is the fuel that continues to inflame her material for comedy, reasserting her value as the one she wants.

In 2009 Cho took on a recurring minor role on the Lifetime summer-replacement comedy-drama series *Drop Dead Diva* (2009–), which focuses on body image and large bodies through the gimmick of an empty-headed size 0 model reincarnated in the plus-size body of a brilliant lawyer. A 2010 *New York Magazine* article notes that despite her presence on a sitcom and as a guest on ABC's *Dancing with the Stars* for a few weeks that year, "Cho retains her underground cred—which is to say, she's still niche-famous" (Calhoun). Indeed, her reappearance on ABC as a dancer sprang from a far less mainstream performance, *The Sensuous Woman*, a neoburlesque revue Cho headlined in New York in 2007 that featured a wide variety of dancing bodies in a celebration of diversity. Given Cho's childhood fantasy of grooming herself for the dance that she never got to—the fantasy of getting ready for her debut into white femininity—it is especially significant that Cho was invited to dance on a primetime television show and in a woman-centered burlesque venue in New York, finally arriving at the dance as the one that she wants and as herself—queer, Asian, and beautiful.

CHAPTER FIVE

"White People Are Looking at You!"

WANDA SYKES'S BLACK LOOKS

DANCING IN THE CAR

IN THE LAST MONTHS OF 2009 WANDA SYKES WAS "EVERY-where," as one reporter put it: as a supporting character on *The New Adventures of Old Christine* (2006–2010), an occasional guest star on *Curb Your Enthusiasm* (2000–2011), a cartoon voice on Nickelodeon's *Back at the Barnyard* (2007–2011), and a talk-show host beginning her own late-night gig on Fox, *The Wanda Sykes Show* (2009–2010), not to mention her status as "high on every talk show host's lists of favorite guests" (Fienberg). In November her HBO stand-up comedy special *I'ma Be Me* received rave reviews and was released as a DVD in early 2010, capping a decade in which Sykes developed into a highly visible, mainstream comic star.

Visibility is a major theme in Sykes's comedy, not the coveted celebrity prominence of being everywhere but rather the everyday hypervisibility of African Americans among whites. Sykes's recurring topics are the looks black people get, what black people look like to whites, and what the world looks like to a black woman. My argument in this book is that the female body and its looks become uproarious material for women comics who bridle against the loaded cultural expectations about feminine ideals. As we've seen, the racist underpinnings of those expectations fuel the comedy of Margaret Cho, whose failure to match the white, slim images on television nearly killed her before it inspired her passionate comedy celebrating alternative bodies. The comedy of Wanda Sykes is often likewise angry, evoking the racial stereotype of the angry black woman that in turn she excoriates with brilliant mimicry. The stereotype works in concert with the historical positioning of the black female body as the antithesis of white

With a confrontational comic style, Wanda Sykes often targets black hypervisibility in her work by lampooning the ways white people look at black bodies and offering her own oppositional look in return. Photo courtesy of Photofest.

femininity. As described earlier, femininity and prettiness in Western culture have been pictured and embodied as white, so for women comics of color the pretty/funny dynamic takes on a particularly bristly contour. Moreover, black female bodies are criminalized and pathologized as oversexed, so the black female body is seen not only as not pretty but as threatening. Sykes's comedy targets these racist ways of looking as well as the black self-policing of the body that results from this surveillance.

More than that, Sykes herself is offering her own look at the visual dynamics of race, echoing bell hooks's thoughts on "black looks" and the "oppositional black gaze." At one time in history, hooks points out, black people were punished for looking; the slave was not supposed to meet the eye of the master; the black man was not supposed to look at white women. Looking is powerful for blacks, hooks says, as a way to "both interrogate the gaze of the Other but also look back, and at one another, naming what we see. The 'gaze' has been and is a site of resistance for colonized black people globally" (116). Sykes's comedy is important because it does the political work described by hooks, interrogating and naming what she sees and exposing the practices of everyday racism.

A good example is Sykes's extended riff at the beginning of *I'ma Be Me* on how stereotypes are internalized. She starts with her tongue-in-cheek declaration that because of the 2008 election of Barack Obama, the first black president, black people can let their guard down about their public image. "We always gotta be so dignified," Sykes says, "cause if we fuck up, we set everybody else back a couple years." Sykes mischievously explains that with a black president who has banished the stereotypes, she can now do all the things she was too embarrassed to do before, like tap dancing, as she demonstrates with some exuberant onstage dance steps. Looking back on the ways stereotyped behavior was frowned upon within the black community, she remembers her mother forbidding her and her sisters from "dancing in the car," moving their bodies to radio music as they drove along. "My mother would stop the car. 'Do you wanna dance or do you wanna ride in the car?'" she'd demand. When Sykes and her sisters protested, their mother would hiss a warning: "White people are looking at you!"

Sykes does an impression of a childhood self shrugging off her mother's warning but then doing a double take and realizing, with alarm, that her mother was right. *I'ma Be Me* develops the white surveillance theme elaborately; Sykes describes how in trying to evade stereotypes she was intimidated about such acts as buying a whole watermelon. She mimics her covert behavior among other customers at the grocery store—"Look at all those white people looking at me!"—resulting in her unhappy retreat to the salad bar, where she could buy little pieces of watermelon and "cover them up with cantaloupe." But now, with a black president, she says triumphantly, she can even go to Popeye's for fried chicken. In fact, she says, she can go through the drive-in, eating watermelon and dancing in the car.

The watermelon and fried-chicken stereotypes are not gender-specific, but the dancing-in-the-car admonition suggests the way black femininity has been scrutinized due to suspicion of its uncontrollable sexuality; her mother's warning is rooted in the politics of respectability, the black middle-class reaction to the stereotype of the Jezebel and myths about primitive black sexuality. Given the stereotypes about the black female body, particularly in relation to femininity, I focus on two elements of Sykes's humor that most directly confront the prickly notions of pretty: black female sexuality and black female anger. Sykes's comedy resists the policing of the white gaze by successfully expressing both anger and sexuality—her own pleasure and, later, her lesbian identity—under the scrutiny of a spectatorship keyed to racist preconceptions about African American women. The titles of her comedy specials reflect her political consciousness through references to African American activists. *Sick and Tired* (2006) cites the famous quotation by civil rights activist Fannie Lou Hamer (1917–1977): "I am sick and tired of being sick and tired." And *Tongue Untied* (2003) without doubt refers to Marlon Riggs's *Tongues Untied* (1989), a documentary film defying and protesting silences around black gay identity.[1]

Sykes, born in 1964, graduated from historically black Hampton University in Virginia and worked for the federal government until 1992, when her success in Washington, D.C., comedy clubs prompted her to move to New York City. Her stand-up work in New York came to the attention of Chris Rock, who had risen from the requisite black-guy spot on *Saturday Night Live* to become a formidable presence on the comedy scene. Rock hired her as a writer for his HBO series *The Chris Rock Show* (1997–2000), where she earned three Emmy nominations and won the 1999 Emmy for Outstanding Writing for a Variety, Music, or Comedy Special. She also appeared on the show as a performer, leading to a half-hour special of her own on *Comedy Central Presents* in 1998. In her study of black comedians Bambi Haggins finds that Sykes's work with Chris Rock "positioned her within a black comedy elite" that gave her "a degree of cultural cachet and legitimacy with black audiences" (175). Sykes tapped that cachet in her occasional guest roles playing herself on *Curb Your Enthusiasm*. In the "Krazee Eyez Killa" episode she dates an intimidating black rapper, and in "The Bowtie" she accuses her friend Larry of having gotten a "racist dog" that attacks her no matter how often he sees her but is fine with white strangers. Sykes developed her persona of mouthy, kick-ass troublemaker in her 2003 sitcom *Wanda at Large*, for which she was both writer and star, playing a feisty investigative reporter and progressive political commentator on a television news show.

In her comedy specials Sykes's anger is sometimes explicitly directed at sexism and sexist political policies. In *Sick and Tired* she quips that in light of the policies of the George W. Bush presidency, with women's rights getting scarcer all the time, she had two abortions on the way to the performance "to stock up." The openly feminist themes of her comedy are evident in her 2004 book *Yeah, I Said It*, in which she disparages Bush's policies on women's reproductive rights (21), as well as blame-the-victim attitudes about rape: "If you get knocked out while at an ATM, nobody is saying, 'You know what you were asking for. You standing there, telling everybody, 'Hey, I got money'" (46).

At other times, her anger focuses on the everyday consequences of white surveillance. In *Tongue Untied* she argues that the "random" searches at the airport are actually coordinated to a Sherwin Williams paint sampler: "If your ass is darker than khaki, you gettin' searched." And for black women, she implies, the stereotypes of racism and sexism double up. When a black man murders a black woman, she writes in *Yeah, I Said It*, he's likely to get a life sentence instead of the death penalty "because judges are sympathetic. They know how a black woman can drive you to murder with all our 'attitude and sassiness'" (64).

"Sassy," in fact, is a flashpoint word for Sykes, summoning up the racism embedded in the stereotypes of the sassy black comic and the angry black woman, both of which dismiss or belittle what the black woman has to say. One episode of her 2003 sitcom *Wanda at Large* is about Wanda's fury at the white boss who compliments her sassiness ("Back to the Club"), and in a 2004 interview she pointed out that besides its racial associations—"No one calls Ellen DeGeneres sassy"—the word implies style instead of substance: "Sassy is all attitude and no content. And I've got something to say" (in J. Stein). Having something to say is the political thrust of her work. In *Sick and Tired* she says she is fed up with the racism, sexism, and lunacy "of all politicians across the board." In the cover photo of the DVD she stands outside a hospital emergency room scowling at the camera and wearing a hospital gown that says "SICK & TIRED."

I'ma Be Me's lampooning of the white gaze and of the consequent restraints on the black body cites a foundational concept in African American thought—W. E. B. Du Bois's description of "double consciousness" in his 1903 essay "The Souls of Black Folks." Du Bois describes this as a "sense of always looking at one's self through the eyes of others, of measuring one's soul by the tape of a world that looks on in amused contempt and pity" (869). Du Bois's insight captured the idea of the disciplinary gaze decades before Foucault theorized the dynamics of surveillance that replaced physical punishment as a means for restraining and controlling bodies in the modern state. For Michel Foucault the nineteenth-century prison design of the Panopticon epitomizes this dynamic; one wall of every prison cell is open for observation from a centralized tower, so the prisoners, not knowing when exactly they are being watched, are disciplined by a gaze that may or may not be literally present. The result, he writes in *Discipline and Punish*, is "a state of conscious and permanent visibility that assures the automatic functioning of power" (201). Connecting this dynamic to the practice of racial profiling, Karen Glover contends that race functions as the "marker of criminality and the permanent visibility induced by the Panopticon—always being under suspicion" (243), so "the panoptic effect also involves an awareness of oppression, similar in process to Du Bois's double-consciousness" (245). Glover's interest is the surveil-lance dynamic that makes all persons of color visible as potential criminals, but the examples Sykes gives in *I'ma Be Me* demonstrate how this dynamic makes even innocuous activities highly visible. Buying a watermelon and eating fried chicken are triggers for the automatic functioning of power and amused contempt and pity.

In *I'ma Be Me* Sykes fixes on the bodily discipline induced by white sur-veillance—the physical restraint of black girls who want to dance in the car, a black woman's detour to the salad bar. And she extends this idea into the theme of racial profiling, the suspicion of all blacks as potential crimi-nals, when she turns to President Obama as an example of black physical self-discipline. Sykes does an imitation of his confident, presidential stride across the White House lawn and compares this to his far more cautious way of walking while he was still campaigning. She imitates him counting out his steps, memorizing his moves, and keeping himself in check: "One, two, smile. One, two, smile. Whatever you do, do not touch your penis. Touch your dick, it's all over. Stop looking at Michelle's ass." The stereotype behind the comedy is Obama's presumed criminality as a black male who is implicitly a sexual threat to white women. The self-restraint imposed by a lifetime of surveillance teaches him to control his steps, his hands, even his eyes, which must be averted from his own wife's body.

The themes of white spectatorship and surveillance show up in the work of three black-studies scholars writing about black entertainment, all of whom extol Sykes as an exemplary comedian. Their contrasting per-spectives in significant publications from 2007 to 2010 are worth exam-ining because they demonstrate the variety of cultural burdens the black woman comedian carries. For media scholar Bambi Haggins in her book on black comics in "post-soul America," Sykes is the "diva-in-training," the promising heir-apparent to "crossover diva" Whoopi Goldberg, who was distinctive in the twentieth century as a black female comic able to achieve stardom in mainstream entertainment. "Crossover" is the key term here. Haggins argues that even more than Goldberg, Sykes has legitimacy with black audiences and the ability to convey confident black identity "across cultural boundaries" (175). While Haggins emphasizes the role of racial authenticity in Sykes's success, cultural critic Glenda Carpio emphasizes the riskiness of sex and gender stereotypes for Sykes and other black women comedians. Carpio says these comics deal with the "triple jeopardy" of race, gender, and sexuality in their self-presentations. Carpio contends that she admires Sykes's ability to convey her sexuality without making it her primary topic and identity (36); emphasizing their sexuality is a problem, she alleges, for performers like Mo'Nique who "reinforce stereotypes of black female sexuality by relying heavily on their own often sexualized personas" (34). In sharp contrast to Carpio's praise for Sykes's self-control, sociologist Shayne Lee, in her book *Erotic Revolutionaries* on black female entertainers, sees Sykes's sexual frankness as a pioneering effort leading to the even more sexualized and hence more politically significant personas of the same women comedians that Carpio criticizes. For Lee the transgressive value of black women comics is found precisely in "explicit sexual content that challenges the politics of respectability" (98).

It is worth noting that all three critics see black double consciousness— "White people are looking"—as the lens for how to interpret Wanda Sykes. For Haggins the issue is keeping African American authenticity while also keeping the attention of white audiences; Carpio is concerned with "the most persistent stereotypes of black femininity: the asexual Mammy and the slatternly Jezebel" (34). Lee is likewise troubled by black female stereotypes, but her perspective also takes in black women's internalizations of these stereotypes about sex—the "politics of respectability" rooted in American racial history. The observations of all three critics reveal racial problems that are distinct from the Asian stereotypes that afflict Margaret Cho and the ways Sarah Silverman draws on her Jewish identity among her shock tactics. In the racial hierarchies of contemporary American culture the black body is far more devalued than the Asian or Jewish body and certainly far more criminalized; its connotations as dirty and lower-class are rooted in the history of slavery, the demeaning practices of Jim Crow laws, and what Patricia Hill Collins calls "the new racism" evident in patterns of education, income, infant mortality, unemployment, HIV/AIDS, and housing (*Black Sexual Politics*, 5–8).

The triple jeopardy of the black woman comedian—in her race, gender, and sexuality—figures into the question of why Sykes has not had a long-running television show of her own despite her high visibility in mainstream venues. For its first season of six episodes, *Wanda at Large* drew Fox's fourth-highest ratings. The ratings dropped in the second season, which aired in autumn of the same year, 2003, and the show was cancelled. In 2004 Sykes produced a short-lived Comedy Central reality show, *Wanda Does It*, in which she tries out a number of different professions. Her late-night talk show on Fox, *The Wanda Sykes Show*, also lasted just one season, perhaps predictably, given its Saturday 11:30 p.m. slot against *Saturday Night Live*. Ironically, Sykes's most extended television role has been as the best friend, a sitcom role derided by Kathy Griffin and Sarah Silverman, on the critically acclaimed series *The New Adventures of Old Christine* (2006–2010). Sykes was not a writer on that show, but the scripts cleverly confronted some of the black best friend clichés by calling them out directly. When Christine (Julia Louis-Dreyfus) runs into a therapist who makes her "blurt out all these dark, intimate things I never knew I felt," she impulsively introduces the Sykes character as "my black friend Barb." Christine is horrified at her own gaffe, but Barb quips that it's okay because "it's been an unspoken thing between us for years" ("No Fault Divorce").

The relegation of Sykes to black friend Barb, even on a well-written show, suggests the limits of popular black female comics on both network and cable television. The only other highly visible black woman comedian on television to date has been Mo'Nique, who starred in her own sitcom on UPN, *The Parkers* (1999–2004). The show remains distinctive for its relatively long run in an era when television series centered on black women were hard to find. When journalists celebrated the surge of women comics heading their own shows in 2011–2012 — *Whitney*, *2 Broke Girls*, *Are You There, Chelsea*, *30 Rock*, *Parks and Recreation* — no one noted that the surge was strikingly white. This in turn reflects the relative scarcity of well-known African American women comics. In Haggins's book on black comics only one chapter focuses on women, discussing Whoopi Goldberg and comparing her to Moms Mabley and Pearl Bailey as predecessors and to Sykes as her likely crossover heir — in all, a scanty genealogy. The gender gap was evident again when *Ebony* magazine polled readers in 2011 for the "top twenty [black] comedians of all time," and Goldberg was the only woman named in the results (T. Glover) even though *Ebony* had devoted an extensive 2007 cover story to Mo'Nique and praised Sykes in the same issue for being "bold, daring, ribald, and politically incorrect" (Holloway).

Given the current popularity of stand-up comedy, its multiple venues on the Internet and on cable, and the trend of niche marketing, black women comics are slowly gaining visibility. During the later years of BET's *Comic View* (1992–2008) women appeared more regularly as performers, and the 2008 film *Queens of Comedy* documented stage performances by Mo'Nique, Sommore, Adele Givens, and Laura Hayes, a group that became known by the film's title. More recently, Issa Rae has come into prominence through her popular web comedy series, *The Mis-Adventures of Awkward Black Girl* (2011–), which began with videos that went viral. But overall, black women remain a minority within the minority of women stand-up comics, and in this context, Sykes's success at attaining mainstream visibility through film roles and in television series, short-lived though the latter may have been, makes her all the more remarkable.

I center my discussion of Sykes around the themes and routines of *I'ma Be Me* for several reasons, not the least of which is its dialect-inflected title, which highlights the racial implications of the pretty/funny dynamic for black women. It's the Sykes concert film that most directly targets the angry black woman stereotype and its effect, for black women, of being scrutinized for unfeminine—that is, not pretty—behavior. *I'ma Be Me* is also Sykes's first performance film after coming out as a lesbian in 2008, so that her lesbianism, marriage to a white woman, and motherhood of two children are topics of her comedy. As a married black lesbian whose children are white, Sykes asserts her hypervisibility and refuses to be disciplined by a gaze that would disapprove of her agency, pleasures, and desires. By the end of *I'ma Be Me* Sykes has subtly expanded the meanings and implications of "white people looking" to include multiple pressures on female bodies, but her citation of the racial and colonial gaze is central to the significance of her comedy. My discussion is guided by the issues put forward by Haggins, Carpio, and Lee as the jeopardies of the black female comic: an authentic black perspective that doesn't alienate white audiences; the pressure of stereotypes, from the mammy to the Sapphire and the angry black woman; and the politics of respectability that restrains representations of black female sexuality and desire. These jeopardies powerfully illustrate the historical resonance of Sykes's black looks.

BODIES AND HISTORIES

Sykes takes up contentious issues as part of her querulous comic persona who is sick and tired of sexism, racism, homophobia, and war. All three of her stand-up performances on DVD—*Tongue Untied, Sick and Tired,* and *I'ma Be Me*—teem with jokes about political topics ranging from Condoleezza Rice and Dick Cheney to the war in Iraq. *I'ma Be Me* is scathingly critical of Proposition 8, the 2008 California referendum that rescinded the right to gay marriage. Sykes refrains from the manifesto rhetoric deployed by Margaret Cho, and she is far less didactic than Cho in asserting the value of her race and sexuality in her performances. However, she is not averse to plainspoken political directive; in *Sick and Tired* her warning about reproductive rights is blunt: "They're after *us*, ladies, the whole abortion thing. The last two Supreme Court appointments— I'm nervous, man, I'm scared. Ladies, if you wanna protect your rights, you gotta get out there, gotta be heard." She follows this with a comic bit about how "pro-choice" doesn't mean women are casually having "abortion parties," but the satire doesn't backpedal on the political point she makes. Without naming this particular routine, reviewer Layla Merritt in the African American newspaper the *New York Amsterdam News* criticized *Sick and Tired* for bits that "can feel heavy like propaganda."

Indeed, Sykes is up-front and unapologetic about her left-wing politics; she relentlessly lampooned the George W. Bush administration in her stand-up work, and in her talk show, *The Wanda Sykes Show*, she fiercely attacked critics of the new Obama administration. It follows that her character on *Wanda at Large*, her sitcom, was a left-wing political pundit. Nor is Sykes averse to using her celebrity for didactic purposes. In 2009 she was a participant in the ThinkB4youspeak television campaign sponsored by the Gay, Lesbian, and Straight Education Network and aimed at making young people aware of the impact of homophobic language. In a public service announcement she confronts a group of teenage boys and explains—with humor but also with a tough edge to her voice—the problem with using the word "gay" to mean dumb or awful. "So knock it off," she concludes brusquely. Referring to her no-nonsense persona the sponsors commented, "When Wanda says 'knock it off' people listen" (GLSEN). Generally, as in the work of the other comedians covered in this book, the body politics of Sykes's comedy is linked to her critiques of conservative agendas.

Yet even in the larger context of Sykes's work, *I'ma Be Me* is striking for its themes of political visibility—black, female, and lesbian. It is also striking for its self-conscious positioning of overlapping histories—personal, racial, and national—encapsulated in the election of the first black president occurring just as Sykes came out as gay. The title *I'ma Be Me* pronounces an identity in dialect that confirms her credentials to African American audiences and establishes her minority perspective for others. And because *I'ma Be Me* begins with the theme of how black people can act in public after Obama's election, the entire performance is framed by the issue of public visibility for blacks and gays and the historical conditions that enable it: Sykes openly identifying as a black lesbian while doing stand-up in a highly prestigious concert hall in the nation's capital.

Locating itself at the intersection of the gay rights and civil rights movements, *I'ma Be Me* annotates the impact of those histories on one body and one personal history. Sykes links these identities by emphasizing that the day Obama was elected was also the day that Proposition 8 passed in California. "I was so hurt and so fuckin' pissed," she says. "That night was crazy. Black president—yay! Oh, Prop 8 passed. Oh shit, now I'm a second-class citizen. What the fuck!" She also emphasizes in this performance and in interviews that it was her anger about Proposition 8 that moved her to come out during an impromptu appearance at a post–Prop 8 event in Las Vegas. So *I'ma Be Me* is, in effect, the comic performance of her statement to *The Advocate* after her coming out: "I am proud to be a woman, I'm proud to be a black woman, and I'm proud to be gay." If those assertions of female, gay, black pride are clichés, her comedy animates them by inviting audiences of whatever race or ethnicity to enter into an upbeat conversation about these identities. In Haggins's descriptions of the cultural interracial work done by comedy she often returns to a quotation from Dick Gregory, "Comedy is friendly relations," summing up the successful dynamic of crossover comedy even when, as in Gregory's case, it entails "in-your-face social and political critique" (18). The same tone of friendly relations characterizes Sykes's impassioned political statements; her persona is often grumpy but also gleefully mischievous about her defiance.

In *I'ma Be Me* this gleeful mischief is evident in her recounting of her controversial Beltway appearance several months earlier, in May 2009. Sykes reminds the audience of her own intersection with national history when she "caused a little trouble" the last time she was in Washington, D.C. She had been invited by President Obama to perform at the White House Correspondents' Association Dinner, the first black woman and the first openly gay entertainer to do so. But afterward Sykes drew fire from the media for her jokes about conservative pundit Rush Limbaugh. In the early days of Obama's presidency Limbaugh got a great deal of attention by publicly proclaiming he hoped the president would fail. Many journalists, bloggers, and pundits protested that this hope for failure was unpatriotic, but Sykes went much further by characterizing Limbaugh as a traitor on the level of Osama bin Laden. Referring to Limbaugh's well-known treatment for addiction to prescription drugs, Sykes quipped that Limbaugh was the 9/11 hijacker who didn't show up because he was "so strung out on OxyContin he missed his flight."

While some journalists welcomed the Limbaugh jokes, others were deeply critical of Sykes and of President Obama because he was caught on camera laughing. Conservative commentators argued that to preserve the dignity of his position, a president shouldn't laugh at a joke that is in bad taste. However, this line of criticism calls to mind Mel Watkins's thoughts on African American laughter as "a dilemma, or, quite often, a source of irritation for mainstream Americans" (16). Watkins introduces his extended study of African American humor by noting the uneasy effect of black laughter on the white listener/audience/eavesdropper, illustrating how black humorists have traditionally developed two faces, one for the public white gaze and the other "reserved for interactions among themselves" (35). Significantly, then, when Sykes says in *I'ma Be Me* that she caused a little trouble at the correspondents' dinner, she is recalling the repercussions not only of edgy political comedy but of black laughter and its transgressive nature within institutions not known for racial diversity, namely, the government and the press.

Recounting the details of the correspondents' dinner, Sykes pushes the issue of black irreverent humor by explaining how, before the event, she was warned by White House personnel not to say the "f" word or the "n" word during her routine. Sykes first expresses outrage that the staffers felt they had to give her a warning: "I mean, it's the president of the United States! The First Lady is there, all these dignitaries are there. Did they really think I was gonna go in there and go 'Nigger! You're the fuckin' president! Nig-GAR [*drawing out the word*]! You're the motherfuckin' president!' . . . What the fuck! You gotta be one ignorant nigger to do some shit like that," she proclaims. She adds sheepishly, "So I had to rewrite my act in an hour." This is the first time she uses the word "nigger" in this performance, and her use of the term in relation to both herself and Obama is significant. On one level, Sykes's joke reinforces her point about the racial impact of Obama's election, claiming identification and even intimacy: she was prepared to use the word casually with the president of the United States as a sign that "one of us" was in the White House. In this way the word has an important differentiating effect on white audience members, who are not privy to its casual usage. Sykes has drawn a line and reminds viewers of that boundary. However, she also invites them to cross the line, to engage in transgressive behavior by laughing at her use of the word to describe herself and at the nervousness of the White House staff. In short, the joke is transgressive both in its crossing of a racial boundary and in its ridicule of white authority, suggesting the complications of African American humor as one of the histories informing Sykes's comedy and this particular set.

Given the subversive edginess of comedy, its "drive to level, disrupt, and destroy hierarchy," to use Rowe's description (101), racial and ethnic humor has long been a cultural and political means of resistance. Media scholar Omotayo Banjo finds that "ethnic humor in America is about power differentials," with oppressed groups confronting power by "owning" the degrading stereotypes and lampooning the social hierarchy (140). Scholars of black American comedy inevitably emphasize its roots in slavery and oppressive conditions that prompted ironic play with stereotypes and the undermining of white authority (Gordon, 256–258; Cooper, 224–227). The rhetorical devices of African American comedy—innuendo, cryptic reference, the trickster—are usually attributed to the double consciousness that resulted from the colonial structure that displaced Africans to another language and culture. Other devices, such as playing the dozens (ridicule of family or friends), have been traced to African culture and yet others (call and response) to African American church services (Watkins, 64–68). Certainly Sykes's comedy is indebted to these traditions. The strategy of the racially inflected trickster, for instance, is evident in her *I'ma Be Me* anecdote about how she has fun at Babies R Us stores by pretending to kidnap her two white children. She says she gets looks from the white people in the store when she shows up in a ball cap and wanders away from the rest of her family. She chooses her moment, she says, and then "I knock my wife out the way and take the stroller! Boy, they lock those doors quick."

While the strategies of the trickster and innuendo foreground the African American roots of Sykes's humor, her joke on herself as an "ignorant nigger" engages a more complicated history and audience dynamics. Watkins notes that the usage of the word among blacks is a "private alteration of public stereotypes" with a variety of meanings, including extensive uses in African American comedy (131–132). In 1942 Du Bois described the effectiveness of the word for black entertainers of black audiences: "The use of the word 'nigger,' which no white man must use, is coupled with innuendo and suggestion which brings irresistible gales of laughter." In an article on African American humor Gerald Early uses this quotation from Du Bois to make his point about the risks of misinterpretation of racial comedy. Early describes how during the 1970s Richard Pryor's use of the word in his routines drew harsh criticism from the black press, even though he was drawing on the tradition cited by Du Bois. Intriguingly, Early suggests that the disapproval of black journalists may have boosted Pryor's popularity among whites; Pryor offered the pleasures of language doubly verboten in that a black entertainer was being condemned by the black community for its usage (33).

Evan Cooper coined the term "culturally intimate humor" to describe the play with stereotypes that can be entertaining within one's own group but has inordinate cultural weight outside the group because of the relative scarcity of minority representation. After all, he says, white audiences are not embarrassed by the foolishness of the Three Stooges or Adam Sandler (246). But even the hippest comedy that draws on any African American stereotype can be misread as representative of "real" black culture. Dave Chappelle famously cancelled his popular television series that often caricatured blacks because, he says, he became uncomfortable with the way a white spectator was laughing at a sketch that involved inflammatory stereotypes (Farley).[2]

Because of the riskiness in acting out a racist stereotype, Sykes's most ambitious routine in *I'ma Be Me* is her extended riff on Michelle Obama, which draws on the image of the Sapphire and the more general cultural figure of the angry black woman, a typology that haunted the First Lady from the earliest days of her husband's presidential campaign.[3] Although the stereotypes overlap, the Sapphire has a specific history that originated in the nineteenth century as the nagging, scornful, black woman pictured in relation to the black man she dominates (Jewell, 45). While the Jezebel is primarily a seductress, the Sapphire is primarily an emasculator. As the evil alternative to the nurturing mammy, the Sapphire is perpetuated in television and film roles as the sharp-tongued woman who can be a comic character but whose bitterness can also lead to violence (Springer, "Waiting," 175–178). The angry black woman, in contrast, is a more nebulous figure, a rhetorical trope more than a consistently pictured image, but a stereotype, nevertheless, that can silence a voice of protest as mere emotion or noise. The dynamic is evident in a June 14, 2008, *Fox News Watch* segment when conservative political writer Cal Thomas used the angry black woman image against Michelle Obama. At the time it appeared likely that her husband could become the Democratic presidential nominee. "Look at the image of angry black women on television," Thomas said, citing Congresswomen Cynthia McKinney and Maxine Waters as examples. "And who are the black women you see on the local news at night in cities all over the country? They're usually angry about something," he proclaims. This characterization of black women trivializes their grievances by implying that their motivations are primarily emotional. D. Soyini Madison contends that this particular stereotype is a deliberate misrepresentation of the "political and purposeful" anger of black women that has energized social change, "from black women in welfare lines to picket lines, and from black women poets to university professors" (323). In short, outspoken black women who engage in social critique run up against a critical white gaze dismissing them as always angry about something.

Sykes's routine about Michelle Obama is exceptionally rich because it is framed with citations of black double consciousness and the power of the white gaze to restrain the black female body. The theme begins with her story about dancing in the car and ends with the fantasy of Obama's mother-in-law trying to contain a marital spat that has spilled out onto the White House lawn, in each case "making a spectacle" that white people will judge as contemptible and representative of the race. Sykes begins by commenting on the media buzz that immediately followed Obama's inauguration. "Gotta get used to having a new First Lady," she says. "That's why we had all those articles when he first got into office: 'Who is the real Michelle Obama?' 'When will we see the real Michelle Obama?' You know what they're saying: When are we gonna see *this*" — and here she explodes into a manic physical performance of confrontational rage, her head wagging in fury, one hand on her hip, the other frantically waving and mimicking a kiss-my-ass gesture, and concluding with a fierce "cut eye" and a series of theatrical arm thrusts signaling "talk to the hand." It's a caricature that embodies the angry black woman, her temper out of control, and the Sapphire, nagging and relentless. Stepping out of the mimicry and drawing herself up with dignity, Sykes says, "Well, you're not gonna see *that* from Michelle Obama," adding a little more defensively, "and we all don't do *that*." The raucous laughter from the audience demonstrates the familiarity of both the stereotype and the denial.

The Sapphire stereotype embodies two qualities that are especially resonant in this satire of preconceptions about Ms. Obama. First, the Sapphire is inevitably portrayed in relationship to the man she is dominating. Given Ms. Obama's professional standing as a Harvard-trained lawyer, there was considerable curiosity about how she would take on her role as First Lady, especially in light of Hillary Clinton's active political use of that role. However, the wariness about Ms. Obama in relation to her husband had distinctly racial overtones. During the presidential campaign she was often cast in the media as "a symbol of her husband's Otherness," as writer Ta-Nehisi Coates said in *The Atlantic*. Ms. Obama's public comment that his nomination made her proud of her country "for the first time" was criticized as proof of her bitterness and racial resentment. A Fox News commentator described her as "Stokely Carmichael in a dress," and the *New Yorker* cover of July 21, 2008, facetiously responded to the inflamed discourse surrounding her and her husband's loyalties: the cover illustration depicts them fist-bumping—him in presumably Arab dress, her wearing combat fatigues, a machine gun on her shoulder, and an Afro hairstyle reminiscent of Angela Davis in the Black Panther days. Analyzing this cover image, Lakesia Johnson notes that it sums up long-standing fears about black women as "domineering, unpatriotic, militant, and dangerous" and connects Ms. Obama with "images of revolutionary black women from the seventies" (110–112). Even a *New York Times* overview of media criticisms of Ms. Obama seemed to justify the critique by saying that she "sometimes speaks with a passion unusual for a potential first lady" (Powell and Kantor). When Sykes acts out a comical rendition of Michelle Obama's passion she is satirizing the anxiety that the "real" First Lady is capable of overpowering and humiliating her husband and that a dangerous—in fact, a specifically un-American—black fury is ensconced in the White House. Madison argues about Ms. Obama's image that "projecting her as angry and then casting her anger as irrational, rootless, unjustified and, of course, gendered and racialized is the perfect discursive precursor for the characterization of ungrateful and unpatriotic" (323).

Second, the Sapphire stereotype is related to class, and this is the quality that is imbricated in concepts of black women as "unfeminine." When Ms. Obama was being painted as a dangerous black radical during the 2008 campaign, *Salon* writer Erin Aubry Kaplan summed up the class implications: Michelle Obama was being portrayed as "angry, obstinate, mouthy—a stereotypical harpy lurking in all black women ... [suggesting] an old racist sentiment that you can take the girl out of the ghetto, but you can never take the ghetto out of the girl." The conduct spoofed by Sykes is ghetto behavior, at odds with the dignity and poise that are middle-class markers of femininity. And while Kaplan accurately pinpoints the white anxieties that construct the stereotypical harpy lurking in all black women, the flip side of that anxiety is its presence in the African American community as well. For black women and girls the Sapphire is a powerful cautionary figure, Kimberly Springer argues, because of her potential violence and obstruction to upward mobility. Such women are scorned by some in the black community for their lack of "home training" that should have taught them "about being well mannered in public, being a lady, and being middle class" so that "talking back and running one's mouth are verboten activities" ("Waiting," 176–177). Later I discuss the politics of respectability in more detail regarding its sexual implications, but the black imperative for home training is another version of the internalized white gaze; under its surveillance black women who are well mannered possibly have access to but no guarantee of middle-class privilege.

In Sykes's routine about Ms. Obama she continues the satire by assuring viewers that they're not going to see *that*, the furious ghetto behavior: "I happen to know for a fact that during the campaign, she had rods inserted in her neck, so she is incapable of doing *that*. You see sometimes she wants to, but she can't." Here Sykes does an imitation of a woman in perfect control of her rigid body; a strong emotion begins to appear on her face, but she successfully squelches it. "Everybody's just waitin' for one of those rods to snap," Sykes concludes, "and she'll get pissed one night and throw all his shit onto the White House lawn. 'Fuck you, Barack, you ain't shit!'" Sykes imagines Michelle's mother coming to the door and urgently whispering the same kind of advice Sykes's own mother had offered: "Please, Michelle, you gonna get that boy impeached! Get in the house, get in the house! White people are lookin' at you!" The elegance of the routine lies in its clever twist on the Sapphire and angry black woman images by delineating the white perspective that has created them and the deployment of that perspective in the home training by vigilant mothers. And the metaphor of the internalized white gaze as a rod inserted into a woman's neck powerfully dramatizes that gaze as a palpable, physical, material force.

The question, then, is how Sykes herself has successfully side-stepped the limitations of the Sapphire and angry black woman stereotypes to sustain her ongoing political critique as mainstream comedy. A 2003 *New Yorker* piece describes her as a comic with "an oversized and combative personality" (Franklin), and in 2009 a journalist described her in *The Advocate* as "the angry loudmouth, hilariously outraged at the injustices of the world" (Karpel, 54). Indeed, Sykes's fearless, outspoken style has remained central to her persona, as flagged in the title of her book, *Yeah, I Said It*. Her political stance is likewise stated in the book's introduction: "I love my country. So please don't pull that Dixie Chicks scare tactic of labeling me 'anti-American.' Although in America you have the freedom to do so, just like I have the freedom to tell you to kiss my red, white, and blue ass" (6). Sykes refers to the popular country-western trio that drew controversy and boycotts when in the wake of 9/11 they criticized the policies of President George W. Bush. Unlike the Dixie Chicks, Sykes has the rhetorical advantage of comedy as a traditional platform for the outsider, the iconoclast, and the aggressive satirist. "Comedy should always be on that very fine line of going too far," Joan Rivers has said (in Clarke, 85). And while Sykes draws on the tradition of African American humor "as an expression of anger and even rage" (Gordon, 259), my argument here is that Sykes also draws on a number of comic strategies and rhetorics that allow her to maintain her persona as the angry loudmouth but also her mainstream standing.

Haggins admires Sykes's crossover appeal and argues that she has been more successful at this than Whoopi Goldberg, whose work is similarly imbued with leftist politics. Wary of Goldberg's ambiguous status in the black community, Haggins claims that Goldberg has ended up being "simultaneously trapped and empowered by her personae, her personal politics, and the public perception of them both" (168).[4] In contrast, she says, Sykes "has the edginess of Goldberg's early work," but her "ease of delivery" is more persuasive: "Capturing the nuances and inflections of black vernacular speech, Sykes's voice, often brassy and a bit curt, speaks across cultural boundaries without seeming to make an effort to do so. Sykes emits a comfortable sexuality and self-assurance that shows no signs of either self-deprecation or self-denigration—neither too grateful to be in front of an audience nor too haughty to play to the crowd" (175). The description by negation is grounded in Haggins's comparative methodology that situates black female comedy in relation to the conditions and traditions that make this comedy possible. Thus she positions Goldberg as the heir of twentieth-century comics Moms Mabley and Pearl Bailey and Sykes as the "diva in training" or successor to Goldberg. For Haggins, it is particularly important that Sykes avoids the mistakes of Goldberg ("too haughty") and the exaggerated poses of Mabley and Bailey ("self-deprecating," "self-denigrating"), though she notes that Sykes echoes Mabley's self-positioning as "truth teller." Her point is that these stances and comic strategies were developed by the comics within the constraints of their historical eras and audience expectations. And her explanation of Sykes's success opens several questions: How, exactly, does one speak across cultural boundaries without seeming to make an effort, especially in a voice that shows ease of delivery but is often brassy and a bit curt? What exactly does it mean to emit a comfortable sexuality and self-assurance, and how are these qualities related to Sykes's political critiques?

Sykes's routine on Michelle Obama in *I'ma Be Me* is particularly self-reflexive in its take on black female anger, but in the broader range of her work Sykes has also developed a persona that can engage in comedy as friendly relations at the same time that it engages in satirical and sometimes outright angry critique. The shaping of this persona is evident in Sykes's early material and her first extended performances for a national audience, her 1998 special on *Comedy Central Presents* (in which, before her divorce, she was Wanda Sykes-Hill) and her sitcom *Wanda at Large*. In the Comedy Central performance (included on the DVD *Tongue Untied*) Sykes introduces herself through two routines that position her against the humorlessness of feminism and politically correct African Americanism. The first story is about performing at a feminist benefit where no one got her jokes about having to get home to give her man oral sex "by 9:45." She assured them she was just joking: "He likes oral sex anytime." Nor did they like her jokes about President Clinton, she says, because they were all Clinton supporters: "I like Clinton, too, but he's an idiot: he's on TV apologizing for getting oral sex." By describing herself as a speaker at a feminist conference Sykes allies herself with feminism even as she makes fun of the feminists who didn't laugh, making a shrewd distinction between political alliance and pious ideological rigor about what's funny. In her later sitcom, *Wanda at Large*, Sykes expands this routine into an entire narrative segment that further emphasizes the whiteness of the feminists and their cluelessness about black women. The title of that episode, "Clowns to the Left of Me," is a quotation from the Stealers Wheel song "Stuck in the Middle with You"; the episode is a witty encapsulation of the position of black women in relation to feminism.[5] So while Sykes later incorporates feminist concerns into her routines through topics such as rape and reproductive rights, she maintains her wariness about some aspects of feminism as well. The wariness can be traced, historically, to the whiteness of equality feminism and academic feminism of the Second Wave; Third Wave feminism has scrambled to be more inclusive, though the image of feminism as well-meaning but white persists.

In the Comedy Central performance Sykes links guardedness about feminism to her own lack of political correctness about race, given that she doesn't like to be called "African American" and doesn't care about Africa, even if it's where "we all" came from, because "not once did they come over and try to get us back." However, her next set of jokes is about how Tiger Woods is portrayed in the media as progressively whiter the more successful he becomes. But if he gets into trouble, she predicts (presciently, as it turns out), "the headline will be 'Black golfer arrested.'" So in this introductory performance, Sykes distances herself from ideologies perceived as humorless but establishes herself as a satirist with sharp perceptions about race and the whiteness of the media.

By the time Sykes pitched her sitcom *Wanda at Large* she had amassed a following for her skits as an irreverent field correspondent on HBO's *Inside the NFL* from 2001 to 2003 as well as for her guest appearances on *Curb Your Enthusiasm* playing herself and usually intimidating or arguing with Larry David, also playing a tongue-in-cheek version of himself. Sykes told *Jet* writer Scotty Ballard that the reporter skits on *Inside the NFL* inspired her to develop her sitcom journalist character, Wanda Hawkins. Like the Margaret Cho character in *All-American Girl*, the Wanda Hawkins character in *Wanda at Large* is a stand-up comic but with a twist: she can't make a living doing comedy, so she gets a job as an investigative reporter for a Washington, D.C., television station doing "Wanda at Large" exposés and political commentary on its Sunday-morning talk show. In this way, topical and political satire is built into the story line, as is the cantankerous persona, given that Wanda's job is to be controversial. Both the sitcom and the talk show within it open with a clip of Wanda doing an on-the-scene report in one of her "Wanda at Large" news segments about a provocative topic that she unfailingly presents satirically: school vouchers, television censorship, a country club that doesn't admit women, tax policies about marriage. One of her investigations takes on the touchy topic of African Americans demanding reparations for slavery ("Wanda and Bradley"). Wanda takes her adding machine into the streets and approaches a white man. "Hi, I'm black. You owe me fifteen dollars and thirteen cents," she tells him. At the end of the segment she ends up in a cemetery digging up the grave of a slaveholder in an attempt to take whatever's left. For her investigation of the sexist country club in the episode "King Rat," Wanda infiltrates by dressing up as a cleaning woman and going out onto the golf range with her clubs disguised as mops and brooms hidden inside a janitor's cart, a witty comment on the "place" of women and the invisibility of the black woman janitor in a white male space. The comic strategy here is the freedom of the prankster and the clown that allows Wanda to dress up in costumes and disguises for her undercover reporting. But these trickster strategies target the racist and sexist practices of everyday life: black women janitors are invisible to white men, so that's a way to enjoy a game of golf at their expense.

The comedy of the trickster generally ameliorates the edginess of the Wanda Hawkins character and of Sykes's stand-up persona, as seen in the joke about pretending to kidnap her white children, a subtle jab at white suspicions about black criminality. Along the same lines, she has a routine in *Sick and Tired* describing how she does a number on white men in fancy cars who pull up beside her in traffic. She'll stare at a guy until he looks back, she says, and then she locks the door. "How *you* like it?" she asks him. In *Wanda at Large*, Wanda Hawkins uses trickery in the episode "Hurricane Hawkins," in which she is infuriated by the television executive who flatters her by calling her "sassy." Wanda snaps back at him and refuses to apologize for her angry words, a move that has punitive repercussions for the entire talk show and eventually forces her to quit her job. But as one of the characters remarks about her, Wanda is not one to back down and certainly not one to play by the rules. Rules, Wanda says, "are just those things that somebody and an army made up." Accused of disrespecting the network executive, she replies, "I show everybody the same disrespect, no matter race, creed, color, or parking space." However, Wanda Hawkins does want her job back, so she plays a trick on the executive by getting one of her comedian friends, a man who does voice impersonations, to phone him and apologize. Technically, she hasn't backed down, but the executive hears an apology and she's able to go back to work. A joke is being played on the white man, but the audience is in on the joke and on Wanda's side in it because the plot positions viewers to sympathize with Wanda's anger about the insult.

Generally the Wanda Hawkins character is far more prickly than most sitcom heroines. Nancy Franklin wrote about the character in the *New Yorker* that "Sykes delivers her zingers with a coy, winning smile. . . . But if there is a heart of gold under her crankiness she's slow to let it show." Franklin cites an episode in which Wanda angrily walks out of her surprise birthday party. With other sitcoms, Franklin notes, it's inevitable that the character will come back and enjoy the party, as does happen in this episode, "but with Wanda you're not sure." For Franklin, the show's problem wasn't Sykes's crankiness but rather the series's exclusive focus on its star:

This promotional shot for the sitcom Wanda at Large *demonstrates how Wanda Sykes's investigative-reporter character was a version of her own quarrelsome, hard-hitting stage persona. Photo courtesy of Photofest.*

"Sitcoms that highlight big personalities to the exclusion of the other characters tend to have short lives." It's impossible to know if it was Sykes's big personality, its Friday-night time slot, or the lack of good supporting characters that led to the ratings decline and eventual cancellation of *Wanda at Large*.

Given the contrasting success of Sykes's similarly assertive supporting character on *The New Adventures of Old Christine*, it's possible that for a big personality—in particular, the persona of the combative, disrespectful, black, woman comic—the role of sitcom heroine is particularly difficult to negotiate. Women comics have been fiercely critical about the kinds of roles they've found on television in traditional narratives. Sykes adds the further racial implications of this problem when in *Tongue Untied* she talks about how her agent tried to pitch a show for her in which she would play a family maid who wins the lottery but who loves her white family so much she stays on to work for them. In her book Sykes tells this story with her retort to the agent: "Set it up. I want to meet these people [the producers]. So I can slap the shit out of them" (241). She recounts another pitch for a sitcom about "a single mother with twelve children. All fathered by different men" (242). In short, racism compounds the problem of networks imagining a strong, funny sitcom heroine who is not wife, mother, girlfriend, or—in the case of women of color—domestic help.

Nevertheless, the narrative structure of *Wanda at Large* reveals in detail at least two other strategies that allow Sykes's persona as the angry loudmouth—and more pointedly, the black angry loudmouth—to sustain mainstream popularity. First, in terms of comic discourses, Sykes draws on African American comedy traditions of critique that maintain her ties to the black community but also invite crossover enjoyment. Second, she draws on the license for comic subversion, showing everybody the same disrespect, through the coding of the hip, cool, and authoritative black outsider. This is the black hipness that white rappers aspire to, a code that is attractive to both white and black audiences.

When Sykes as stand-up comic or as Wanda Hawkins takes on the voice of righteous moral authority speaking back to institutional power, she works in the tradition of the black "truthsayer" that Haggins connects to the work of Moms Mabley, who "made clear her willingness to speak her mind regardless of whether her particular stance was popular with her audience" (149). As her stage name suggests, Mabley drew on the authority of the granny—albeit, in her case, a bawdy granny—to speak out about civil rights and social injustice in the 1960s and 1970s. Haggins emphasizes the centrality of truth-telling also to the groundbreaking comedy of Richard Pryor, who is acknowledged as the founding voice of "post-soul" comedy fueled by pride, anger, and confrontational swagger. Drawing on material ranging from black folklore to the black urban drug scene, Pryor mimicked multiple characters and voices, such as his famous "crazy nigger" character that proved to be especially marketable as a basis for some of his film characters (10). Pryor's comic genius is often described as his gift for theatricality and authenticity. In his autobiography Pryor himself emphasizes uncomfortable truth as the basis of good comedy. His philosophy of comedy, he says, is "telling the truth. . . . The truth is gonna be funny but it is gonna scare the shit outta folks" (in Haggins, 54). Pryor's historical significance, Haggins argues, was his ability to convey the anger and the truth about racism through comedy that spoke to black and white audiences, thus enabling the crossover popularity of later comics such as Eddie Murphy, Chris Rock, Dave Chappelle, and, I would add, Wanda Sykes. When Sykes impersonates the "ignorant" comedian who would hail President Obama with "Nigger! You're the fuckin' president!" she is not only citing Pryor's "crazy nigger" character but also drawing on this post-1960s tradition of the streetwise black comic whose routines call out racist practices, cite and play with stereotypes, and use comedy for pointed, often angry social critique.

Wanda at Large enabled entire episodes to be built around Wanda's insistence on telling the truth and speaking bluntly, no matter what the consequences. In the episode about her refusal to apologize to the network executive, Wanda stubbornly endures the wrath of her co-workers when the entire talk show is punished by having the time slot and taping changed to a predawn hour. In "Death of a Councilman," Wanda is furious when her exposé about a crooked politician gets edited after his death to make it look like a respectful tribute. And in "The Favor" she targets network censorship as the enemy of social truth and comedy. In addition, her deadpan quips are frequently rooted in her arch awareness of racial injustice. So when her conservative colleague on the talk show complains about government farm policies and says, "You can't force someone to farm," Wanda gives him a sharp look and retorts, "It's been done" ("They Shoot Reporters"). Likewise, when the news crew gets the scoop about Rush Limbaugh's drug problems, Wanda says she's "glad he admitted he's addicted to painkillers and racism" ("Clowns").

My point here is that the prototype for Sykes's sitcom character and stand-up persona—the black troublemaker and blunt, outspoken critic— has circulated as mainstream comedy for decades, beginning with Pryor's breakthrough portrayal of "the way black people joked among themselves when most critical of America" (Watkins, 562). If her candidness is a legacy of both Mabley and Pryor, so is Sykes's speaking style. Watkins says Pryor in particular brought to mainstream audiences the uniquely African American "off-color vernacular speech . . . insistently down-to-earth and bluntly realistic," incorporating the "explicit obscenity and hyperbole of urban street folks" and the "guileful misdirection of rural blacks" (561). In *Wanda at Large*, Sykes's character comes across as more likable than that of her conservative black colleague Bradley in part because of her use of vernacular speech in comparison to his more proper English. Certainly Bradley's character is deliberately set up as Wanda's nemesis; he's uptight, petty, and bombastic, making her liberal inclinations look all the more sympathetic. But Wanda's use of black vernacular works as a marker of her authenticity so that her political point of view is positioned as more real than his conservative one.

And this cultural figuration—Wanda Hawkins as the cool, critical, black outsider—allows her to express anger about racist practices and stereotypes but to maintain her likability. Scholars have shown that the fascination of white Americans for the hip African American is entangled in fantasies that are not necessarily progressive. Musicologist Ingrid Monson, analyzing the impact of black music in the early twentieth century, describes the fantasy of "African Americans as a symbol of social conscience, sexual freedom, and resistance to the dominant order in the imagination of liberal white Americans." The concept of true blackness as transgression romanticizes black resistance to "bourgeois pretensions" but "paradoxically, buys into the historical legacy of primitivism and its concomitant exoticism of the 'Other'" (398).[6] The emergence and popularity of hip-hop in the past thirty years has further complicated white appropriations of black transgression, even as hip-hop has enabled the mainstream popularity of edgy black comedy. Haggins sums up the dynamic of the appeal to white audiences when she describes the varieties of subversive material that black comics have been able to offer on primetime television since the 1970s, providing viewers with "a degree of cultural cachet as a reward for being 'down'—meaning hip to the sociological positioning of black language, style, music, and humor embedded in the texts" (207).

On *Wanda at Large* the Sykes persona of hip black outsider to white culture is part of the sitcom's basic premise: Wanda's family consists of her widowed, white sister-in-law and biracial niece and nephew. As opposed to the uptight white mother, Aunt Wanda is the cool, single, fun-loving, black aunt who's "down" with the kids. The episode "Don't Take Your Daughter to Work Day" explicitly spells out the unsuitability of Aunt Wanda for motherhood—she's neglectful, distracted, unmindful of consequences—although it also underscores that the young niece would much rather have a black, fun mother than a relatively uninteresting white one. Wanda Hawkins is divorced and dating, but she is not interested in another marriage. Sykes's character is a partier, frequently shown with her buddies at a bar, and though it's not portrayed, she's a casual user of marijuana. Told that having a child would "mellow her out," she retorts, "So does weed, and it's more fun to take to the zoo" ("Wanda's Party"). The series regularly associates Wanda with cool black culture: she's the one who takes the kids to see a black rap band in concert, where they're dismayed that the audience is mostly white college kids and Larry King ("The Un-Natural"). Furthering Wanda's connections to this culture, her ex-husband shows up for one episode and is played by Dave Chappelle ("The Favor"). And on her job,

Wanda Hawkins torments the prim, white producer of her talk show, who is continually staggered by her shocking opinions. Asked how to solve unemployment, she suggests making everything legal: murder, prostitution, drug dealing. "We're all good at something," she quips ("The Favor").

Sykes deploys the authority of black hipness in her stand-up comedy as well. In *Tongue Untied* and *Sick and Tired*, her withering routines on the policies of President George W. Bush and the war in Iraq are juxtaposed with jokes about her fondness for alcohol ("Drinking will make you feel like a sexy twenty-six-year-old"), her visit to a strip club, and her love of porn. As was true of her Wanda Hawkins character, the Sykes persona is a partier. In 2012 one of her recurring jokes on talk shows was framed by her sympathy for President Obama's overwhelming problems; referring to the First Lady's highly publicized gardening, Sykes quipped that she hoped Michelle Obama was growing weed. Her language in her stand-up routines is graphic and colorful, and Sykes looks the part of the hip, black player in her television specials and on her own talk show; chic and slightly masculinized, she wears slacks with snug suede or leather jackets that emphasize her trim, full-busted figure without fetishizing it.

The leather, the blue language, the devastating wit, the sharp political critique, the black vernacular—these are the codes that Haggins describes as intrinsic to the savvy, black performer that the liberal, white audience is inclined to embrace in the hope of being down. And they are specifically male codes, Haggins points out, a comic tradition of candid anger, graphic sexuality, and attitude that runs from Pryor and Dick Gregory through Eddie Murphy and Chris Rock (232, 242). If this line of comedy is traditionally male, then the sexual explicitness of Wanda Sykes's comedy, her embrace of topics from rape and porn to faked orgasms, complicates this tradition and demonstrates a decidedly gendered resistance to white surveillance.

RESISTING RESPECTABILITY

A core theme of *I'ma Be Me* is the physically restraining impact of the white gaze, on black men, too, as seen in her joke about President Obama's cautious pre-election walk. However, her recurring topic is the restraint of the black female body, from the joke about rods implanted in the First Lady's neck to a sly insinuation that female bodies on television are carefully tailored for white people's looking. Sykes's defiance of this restraint evokes a troubling history of the politics of respectability and the policing of black female bodies in public. Springer asserts that, given the history of black female sexuality as either exploited or policed, "there is little discussion of what it sounds like to speak *for* black sexuality in progressive, liberating ways." Springer is interested in expressions of black female sexual subjectivity, which she defines as those "that permit black women to speak on their own terms about who they are as sexual beings, which sexual acts they enjoy (doing and having done), how they relate to their bodies, and myriad expressions that fall within the bounds of sexuality" ("Policing," paragraphs 1, 5). *I'ma Be Me* is explicitly framed by critique of the white surveillance that inhibits these expressions, but Sykes's previous stand-up comedy also demonstrates resistance to the policing that Springer and others have documented as a significant factor in black women's cultural history.

The politics of respectability refers in the broadest sense to the pressures for public decorum placed on African Americans who migrated to northern cities in the early twentieth century and sought privileges of class and citizenship (Higginbotham). The public behavior of black women, especially single black women in cities, attracted special scrutiny, Hazel Carby reports. Both black and white institutions, she argues, were complicit in positing these women as a threat to racial relations, urban morality, the establishment of a black middle class, and the status of black urban men (741). Given this suspicion and surveillance and the history of slavery that had cast black female sexuality as excessive and seductive, the politics of respectability influenced generations of African American women to repress expressions of sexuality in order to avoid the lascivious stereotypes and additional exploitation. In the 1950s and 1960s, leaders of the civil rights movement escalated this dynamic with their concern about protesters being seen as worthy of white respect. Black lesbians, queers, and women considered unruly in their looks or behavior were excised from public visibility and later from official histories of the movement (Berg). Even after mainstream representations of sexuality became more liberal in the 1970s, black women aiming for middle-class status continued to feel many of the same constraints about sexual expression in light of continued representations of the sleazy Jezebel and the hypersexual black female body as object or décor (Springer, "Policing"; P. Collins, *Black Feminist Thought*, 124–125). Because femininity and attractiveness are intrinsic to concepts of female sexuality, the history of abjection and shame suggests black women's complicated relation to notions of pretty; it also suggests the racial tension implicit in Sykes's comic strategy of funniness aimed at these notions.

Emerging from this history is the complicated fallout, for black women, of white people looking: objectification, internalized surveillance, and the erasure of black female sexual expression and agency. Scholars have indicated how the pressure for favorable images skewed self-representation of black female sexuality throughout the twentieth century, resulting in emphasis on book-club culture and the "black lady" as acceptable middlebrow tropes. With the exception of sexually explicit female blues singers, black women often have resorted to silence and dissemblance about their own desires, and their contemporary efforts to reverse this trend are frequently encumbered by religious and governmental censure.[7] Discussing cultural repression of black female sexuality, Shayne Lee argues that more than the politics of representation is at stake here: "Through rigid self-surveillance and careful policing of each other's bodies, many black women continue to hold each other accountable to middle-class sexual decorum" (x). In *I'ma Be Me* the joke about dancing in the car registers this self-surveillance as well as this much longer history of scrutiny and self-consciousness, an emphatically sexed and gendered version of double consciousness.

Nevertheless, black women performers and artists have a counterhistory of resistance to this policing, and Lee's project is the foregrounding of the counterhistory in which Wanda Sykes and other black women comics figure prominently. Lee's case is that despite the internal and external prohibitions about sexual expression, recent popular culture has been the site of an "erotic revolution" of black women writers and performers whose work offers "nuggets of empowerment . . . asserting discourses of sexual agency and autonomy" (xiii). For Lee, stand-up comedy is unique in its ability to offer black women a venue "to experiment with provocative discourse" and to "valorize sexuality" in explicit ways (111); she is especially interested in the work of the young black women on BET's *Comic View* and performers Sheryl Underwood, Mo'Nique, and Sommore, for all of whom sexual material—and the sexual appeal and status of their own bodies— is central to their acts. Lee lauds Whoopi Goldberg and Wanda Sykes as "elder stateswomen" to this "younger breed" of performers that "takes even more liberties in lacing sets with explicit sexual content that challenges the politics of respectability" (98). So in the war against the history of restraint Lee sees a generational divide (although Sykes, Mo'Nique, Underwood, and Sommore were all born between 1963 and 1967) of younger comics taking "even more liberties" in what they say, act out, and mimic about sexual acts and their own needs and desires.

While for Lee this is a matter of more or less sexual explicitness, the distinction she draws between Sykes and these other comics serves my purpose here of sorting out how exactly Sykes stands up to the politics of respectability in order to express her sexual subjectivity in the terms laid out by Springer—the ability to speak of pleasure, identity, and her relationship to her own body. For Whoopi Goldberg and Wanda Sykes, for instance, sexual material is part of but not central to their work, which instead contains considerable political critique, far more than the other comics discussed by Shayne Lee. Also, Lee's comparison with these other comics suggests how Sykes engages in sexual patter and jokes without in fact being provocative or offering herself as a sexual object. There is nothing coy or flirtatious about her speaking style; her leather-jacket ensembles are sexy without being sexualized. Carpio says Sykes "moves on the stage in a manner that marks her as a sexual being without making that sexuality the defining characteristic of her identity" (36).

Sykes herself makes a similar point in an interview about how she made the decision to come out as a lesbian. She calculated that the effect on her career would be minimal because, she says, "People really don't think of me in a sexual context. . . . They don't look at Wanda Sykes and think sex" (in Karpel). Instead, Sykes positions herself in her routines as the amused observer about sex, so even when she jokes about her sexual experiences, her own body is not the main point of the comedy. This allows her to play within a heterosexual framework, in her pre-2009 performances, without the effect that she is herself personally invested in heterosexuality. She was divorced in 1998, and in her comic routines she uses that status to maintain a cynical detachment about men. The cageyness of the strategy may be apparent only in retrospect following her coming out, but in a 2009 interview Sykes talked about the effect of her self-disclosure on her performances: "Now I don't have to dance around anything. I don't have to think 'Well, if I say that, they're going to figure this out and that's going to lead to this'" (in Carter).

Sykes's ironic distancing from heterosexuality allows her to emphasize sexual autonomy. In *Tongue Untied* she does a long riff about the differences between men and women in terms of sexual behavior and ends with a joke about masturbation as a better bet for women than sex with a man. "For men, sex is like going to a restaurant," she says, "and no matter what you order, you love it." But at the restaurant, what a woman gets isn't necessarily what she wanted: "Sometimes it's good, sometimes you gotta send it back." This, she says, leads women to realize, "You know, I think I'm gonna cook for myself today. Something about the way I cook, it's always filling . . . and I'm a fast cook. The time it takes you to make one meal, I can make three." In *Sick and Tired* Sykes is even more open about how she enjoys staying in hotels while she's traveling alone because she can watch porn, masturbate, and even take on two loud voices of encouragement and bliss: "You work that shit, you bitch! Come on, fuck it like that!" and "Yes! I'm good, I'm good!" In all, this exemplifies Springer's ideal of allowing women to speak of their desires and bodies "on their own terms."

While Sykes graphically acts out sexual satisfaction in this routine, the point is autonomy; the best sex is solo sex. For the Sykes comic persona, sexual poses and foibles are the topics of her sets: the preening exhibitionists on a gay male cruise (*I'ma Be Me*), faking an orgasm as "time management" late at night (*Tongue Untied*), the wish for a "detachable pussy" that would protect women from misunderstandings on a date (*Sick and Tired*). In her stand-up acts Sykes often throws her body into elaborate mimicries in her routines about sex, but these performances enact comedy rather than sexiness. In *Tongue Untied* and *Sick and Tired* she imitates strippers giving lap dances or displaying their crotches, for example, and in the latter, she mimics a very old stripper, Ethel, forced to work because of cuts in Social Security. The exaggerated postures and gyrations of all these routines play on the thin line between sexiness and absurdity.

Even when Sykes's jokes about her experiences she stops short of sensationalizing her own body as an object of provocation for the audience. An example is her routine that pokes fun at the fetishization of breasts. "If titties are identical, they're fake," she says in *Sick and Tired*, explaining that her right breast is "nicer" than the left because she's right-handed and her breast on that side gets more workouts. "When I get undressed, I always pull the left one out first, cause that's the appetizer. . . . 'You like that, baby? Wait till you see—BOOM!'" Her phrasing "When I get undressed" glosses over what the rest of the joke makes clear, that she's undressing for a lover. By erasing the sexual partner, the emphasis falls on the funny conviction that one breast is nicer than the other. And because of this the context of the joke as heterosexual or lesbian is far less important. Attitudes toward breasts, her own and others', are also the butt of a routine about going with male colleagues to a strip club. Sykes describes her outrage about being asked to pay a cover charge, given that she has her own "titties"; "BYOT," she says, and adds that she can look at them or even play with them any time she wants "for free." Demonstrating this, Sykes gives each of her nipples a defiant pinch, comically demystifying the act. Continuing the story of her experience at the strip club she says, "Once I saw those triple G's and stuff, I went back and paid. Now I see. These are professional titties. . . . I guess if your titties are as big as your head, you can pay some bills with that" (*Tongue Untied*). By conventional standards, Sykes is a well-endowed woman, but this demystification draws attention away from her own body to the carnivalization of bodies in strip clubs, turning upside down traditional American attitudes toward large breasts.

Sykes's use of raunchy material is very different from the sexual comedy of Sarah Silverman, who embraces taboos with the aim of confronting the ways the female body is abjected. For Silverman, her own body and its Jewishness—doubly abjected—are what is most at stake. In contrast, Sykes's sexual comedy engages in neither abjection nor self-preoccupation, embodying instead what Haggins describes as "comfortable sexuality and self-assurance." In this way, it is very different from the sexual comedy of Mo'Nique and the other Queens of Comedy, who embrace sexuality with the aim of defying the cultural disdain for the black female body. As mentioned previously, Carpio criticizes the latter comics with the argument that with their "overly sexualized personas" they "reinforce stereotypes of black female sexuality" (34). Given that Shayne Lee lionizes these same performers and privileges them as more explicit and thus more groundbreaking than Sykes, one can see how profoundly the politics of respectability informs critical discussion of black women performers. It was, after all, a sensitivity to overly sexualized stereotypes that shaped the internal surveillance of respectability. Springer finds that this policing is grounded in and proliferates contempt for black female sexuality as excessive, hypersexual, and always available ("Policing," paragraph 29). When the Queens of Comedy proudly promote and glamourize bodies that have been culturally dismissed as too large and too black, they are celebrating an explicitly racialized unruly woman, a figure that makes Carpio uncomfortable in its brush with stereotypes. In contrast, Carpio says, Sykes "manipulates stereotypes of race and gender without making her own body bear the burden of that manipulation" (36).

My point here has been that Sykes shifts this burden by focusing on sexuality and the black female body in broader racial and cultural themes: she demystifies topics such as porn, masturbation, and breast size; she sends up sexual obsessions and fetishizations; and she mimics black stereotypes. In *I'ma Be Me* she satirizes the politics of respectability as the consequence of white surveillance. Her most raucous sexual comedy, in fact, is part of her routine about white surveillance on the Obamas and the constraints they have felt on their bodies. She recounts that she met them at the White House Correspondents' Association Dinner and picked up on the "energy" between them. "They fuckin'," she says frankly. "There's some fuckin' goin' on at 1600 Pennsylvania Avenue. They should put a sign out on the White House lawn—'Don't come a-knockin' when the White House is rockin.'" With this she performs a bawdy mimicry of wild, ass-slapping sex. "Oh, you want my stimulus package?!" the lusty president cries out. Because the performance crowns the long routine about black cautiousness under white surveillance, it celebrates uncontained, unashamed black sexual energy and bodies.

Given the emphasis on visibility and the restraining gaze in *I'ma Be Me*, one of this set's key moments is when Sykes shifts to the topic of her own coming out as a lesbian and her marriage to a French woman—"'French' sounds nicer than 'white,'" she says. Shayne Lee notes this as the first time a major black female comic has made her lesbian status a topic for her performance (98). Significant, too, is the way Sykes positions and jokes about lesbianism in this set, first of all distancing it from the explicit sexual material in the routine about the Obamas. Unlike Sykes's earlier concert films in which her sexual experiences are topics for jokes or satire—masturbation, faking orgasms, the wish for a "detachable pussy"—the graphic sexual material in *I'ma Be Me* is limited to the heterosexuality to which she can remain the wry observer, her imagining of sex in the White House and a routine about the devastating effect of Viagra for older wives who thought their sex lives were blissfully over. For any man over seventy-eight, Sykes says, a Viagra prescription should be given only with "a note from three women who want to fuck you."

As opposed to these bawdy routines, Sykes's material on lesbianism focuses on racial rather than sexual issues, reflecting a concern that showed up often in her 2008–2009 interviews when she talked about homophobia in the black community. She was particularly disappointed, she often said in those interviews, that black voters and black churches played an important role in the passing of Proposition 8 (in Karpel, Anderson-Minshall, Hope). As noted earlier, the politics of respectability has always been grounded by African American religious and social establishments anxious to establish black middle-class credibility. Black homophobia illustrates the effectiveness of sexual policing that cuts across male and female populations marked as sexually deviant, particularly by black churches, which remain a significant influence on all segments of the black population (Ward, 494–495; P. Collins, *Black Sexual Politics* 11–12, 107–109). In particular the policing of black gay men has produced the "down low" strategy of the secret double life that sometimes leads to wives and girlfriends becoming infected with the HIV virus. Citing this problem, Sykes told *Advocate* reporter Ari Karpel, "There's such a stigma about being gay," as seen in this particular circulation of HIV, that "we're literally killing ourselves over this fear of homosexuality."

While anxiety about male homosexuality has been attributed to black investment in hypermasculinity, bias against lesbians is also a problem in the black community. Barbara Smith finds that lesbians threaten heterosexual status as one of the few privileges—as opposed to racial or class privilege—black women have been able to enjoy. She cites the politics of respectability, specifying that the risk of coming out as a black lesbian is that of losing "any claim to the crumbs of 'tolerance' that nonthreatening 'ladylike' Black women are sometimes fed" (20).[8] Given this context, it is understandable that Shayne Lee lauds Sykes's coming-out material as revolutionary in the struggle against the politics of respectability, not for its sexual explicitness but rather for its radical claim to black female public identity. Tellingly, the joke Sykes makes about the black response to her lesbianism targets the responses of other black women—the fear Smith points out—rather than the larger problem of black homophobia or policing by black churches. The joke is based on race rather than sexuality; it diverts the question of homophobia into a focus on Sykes and her wife as an interracial couple. "The only group that's been fuckin' with us is black straight women," she says. "What the hell. You're straight! It's not like you lost one. 'Look at the white girls. Takin' all our good black dykes. Just can't keep a good black dyke.'" While the setup is a comment on black women's homophobia, the twist is that black lesbians are put in the position of black men who date or marry white women, so black men and black lesbians are paralleled as prizes for white and black women. It's a savvy move in that it calls attention to the problem Smith cites, the threat of lesbians to black heterosexual female privilege, but it frames the issue with the claim about the scarcity of black men as heterosexual partners, diplomatically satirizing one kind of threat by citing another.

Sykes's other commentary about coming out as a lesbian in *I'ma Be Me* addresses the question of how race complicates the metaphor of the closet, with its images of containment versus visibility, given that the visible black body is already considered aberrant, excessive, and outside the norm. Marlon B. Ross, among others, has critiqued the "racial normativity" inherent in Sedgwick's "epistemology of the closet" and Foucault's "invention" of homosexuality, contending that both concepts rely on a "normal" body that is racially unmarked.[9] Sykes alludes to this problem by parodying coming out as a racial rather than a sexual issue. Being gay is harder than being black, she says, because at least she didn't have to come out as black. She enacts this absurdity by staging a racial coming-out confrontation with her mother, who attributes the aberrant condition to bad parenting or her daughter's choice of friends: "Oh God, not black! Anything but black! . . . I knew I shouldn't have let you watch *Soul Train*! . . . You've been hangin' around black people, and they have you thinkin' you black." The routine parodies the standard responses of a horrified parent to a gay child, but it also foregrounds homosexuality and blackness as conditions considered aberrant. The routine illustrates Marlon Ross's concern for the way coming out is complicated for African Americans who must "uncloset their sexuality *within* the context of a racial status already marked as an abnormal site" (183).

While Sykes's material about coming out is more inflected by concerns about race than about sexuality, she devotes equal time about her new lifestyle on the ostensibly far less controversial topic of domestic life with a wife and twins, taking care of a perpetually wailing baby or quarreling about exposing the babies to television. The gist of her comedy is that family life with two small children is so exhausting that sex is neither appealing nor even practical. If she was ever caught in another woman's bed, she says, she'd be there to get some sleep. Arguing for the revolutionary sexuality of Sykes's comedy, Shayne Lee finds these details most transgressive: Sykes's casual chatter about her family, she says, is "a discursive slam dunk on heteronormativity" (98). This slam dunk scores against the heterosexist politics of respectability and those of stand-up comedy. Family life, with all its absurdities, stresses, and bedlam, is often the theme of stand-up comics who can draw on heterosexual privilege to cite a common ground with audience members. So when Sykes uses family and parenthood humor as a connection, a citation of human experience, while at the same time asserting the decidedly nonmainstream nature of her family, she is taking up a transgressive stand against multiple norms.

More than heteronormativity is involved here because Sykes takes great pains to emphasize the whiteness of her wife and children, and several of her jokes foreground their visible differences as a family group—how she could never claim her children if they got lost at Disney World, for instance. The visible differences are fodder for comedy that in turn defies the challenge of "white people looking" and of a black disapproving gaze that would pass judgment on this lesbian couple in an interracial, multilingual family. In short, by treating these domestic topics as everyday, noncontroversial ones, Sykes is queering the way terms like "family" and "parenting" are usually used. In this way Sykes participates in what Jennifer Reed describes as the unique work done by queer comics like Paula Poundstone and Lily Tomlin who perform for mainstream audiences and "create personae that encourage spectators to identify with a queer subject positioning" ("Sexual Outlaws," 766). To be sure, Sykes's audiences for her stand-up shows are self-chosen—a liberal audience open to comedy performed by a leftist, black lesbian. But because she is also a mainstream celebrity, likely to show up on afternoon and late-night talk shows, she shares this queered family structure with a much larger national audience.[10] When on *Ellen* she jokes about her spouse and twin toddlers, the material is everyday life, but she is referring to a scenario that implicitly challenges the racial, sexual, and cultural norms involved in what "everyday life" usually means on daytime network television. For Reed, comedy provides an opening that makes this subversion of norms possible so that "we see the structures and forms, which we have often taken as natural, to be arbitrary" and can laugh at the "shared experience of incoherence as part of being human" ("Sexual Outlaws," 774, 776). Moreover, when Sykes attains a national audience by appearing on *Ellen*, her jokes about domestic life occur in the context of another queered family-friendly space — Ellen DeGeneres as all-American girl and soft-butch lesbian married to a glamourous woman — and this space, too, is made possible by comedy.

In *I'ma Be Me*, Sykes's final joke about the white gaze makes a stinging jab that exposes television glamour as another apparatus of whiteness. It opens up the set's "white people looking" framework to acknowledge the way whiteness operates as the unspoken but assumed element constituting fashion, good taste, and the representable body. In short, the joke suggests the ambitious scope of *I'ma Be Me* as a multilevel commentary on race and the body. In this segment of the performance Sykes makes a series of jokes that come directly from the pretty/funny tradition of satirizing the ideal female body. Her topic is the aging female body, her own, as unreliable, porous, and lumpy, a discourse that also participates in the lower-body comedy described by Bakhtin. Sykes says the roll of fat around her stomach has become such a familiar and permanent fixture that she's named it Esther. She says Esther loves bread and alcohol, and when Sykes is driving, Esther is apt to take control of the steering wheel to direct the car to the Cheesecake Factory. And Esther has a voice of her own, a low growl that makes rude demands: "Fuck you, I like bread! Give me a drink!" The only way to keep Esther in check, says Sykes, is to "put her in the Spanx," the brand name of the popular girdle-like "shapewear" that promises to give the stomach and hips a firm, slimming look. Esther hates the Spanx, Sykes confides, but she herself has no choice about using them for important things like appearing on TV.

The Esther routine returns *I'ma Be Me* to its earlier themes of the unruly body being disciplined by looks and expectations and restrained by an imaginary rod implanted in the neck. In this case, the restraint for the body is a familiar commodity. Even the brand name, Spanx, connotes physical discipline under the larger cultural gaze: women and men alike pay money for an uncomfortable garment that allows them to fit, literally, into a norm and stand up to a judgmental gaze. Sykes leads up to her punch line about Esther by telling the story of how, when Sykes was appearing on *The Tonight Show with Jay Leno*, Esther became fed up with her cramped quarters and decided that she, too, wanted to be on TV. To her horror, she says, Esther "began to crawl out of the Spanx." Appalled, Sykes chastised her: "No one wants to see your fat ass on TV!" But it was too late. Esther had crawled out and popped up to say "Hi" to Jay.

Sykes says that, wholly ashamed, she hissed at Esther the ultimate admonition: "White people are lookin' at you!" On one level, the joke is a sly comment on the presumed audience for Leno's bland, middlebrow show, a sharp contrast to the white audience members for Sykes who want to be down with her hip persona and frame of reference. But the refrain also pinpoints white people looking as the source of mainstream conventions of attractiveness. The punch line exposes whiteness as the appraising gaze that disciplines bodies into restrictive shapewear for them to be acceptable; it acknowledges whiteness as the bourgeois code of appearance and behavior that would implant rods into the necks of unruly women. And it confirms the white nature of prettiness in the comedy of women who find the conventions of attractiveness funny.

CHAPTER SIX

Ellen DeGeneres

PRETTY FUNNY BUTCH
AS GIRL NEXT DOOR

COVER GIRL

THIS BOOK BEGAN WITH THE QUESTION OF HOW POPU-
lar culture has pictured women in comedy. The traditional
placement divides them into the pretty ones, cast in perky romantic comedies, and the funny ones, the female comedians Hollywood has been reluctant to picture in the most popular stories of heterosexuality and romance. In the previous chapters I have argued that many women comics
draw on mainstream notions of pretty as material for their comedy, seen
in Tina Fey's smart-aleck *Bossypants* cover photo, for instance, and complicated in the cover-girl histories of Fey and Sarah Silverman, whose conventional good looks confound the usual pretty-or-funny way of thinking
about women entertainers. Kathy Griffin's comic D list satirizes and grudg-
ingly acknowledges the power of the cover girl and feminine ideals, while
Margaret Cho and Wanda Sykes ferociously expose the whiteness of those
ideals and the dynamics of spectatorship, of white people looking.

Pretty/Funny concludes with Ellen DeGeneres, whose looks and the
question of how she is looked at open alternative ways of thinking about
women and comedy, as can be glimpsed in her famous breakthrough performance in 1986. The occasion was her guest spot on *The Tonight Show
Starring Johnny Carson* (1962–1992), her first network television appearance. Born in Metairie, Louisiana, in 1958, DeGeneres had been doing
stand-up comedy for four years when she was spotted by Jay Leno and referred to Carson. Clips of that performance, easily available on the Internet, show the young DeGeneres in sneakers, a bad haircut, baggy slacks,
and a loose polyester top, a careless look that matches her low-key patter about innocuous topics—family, petrified wood, fleas. In hindsight, it

would be easy to read the sneakers and oversize clothes as signs of the butch lesbian, but it would be just as easy to read her as funny as opposed to the glamourous women who usually appeared on *The Tonight Show*.

DeGeneres made history with her *Tonight Show* spot: she was the first female comic ever to be invited by Carson to join him at his desk, after her routine, for a follow-up chat. The coveted invitation to Carson's desk after a first-time appearance, signaling approval by one of the most influential men on television, was every comic's dream; it meant invitations to high-profile venues and more television talk shows, as in fact happened with De-Generes. Carson's history of favoring male rather than female comics for this star-making gesture followed from his famous assertions that women aren't funny, despite his own help with the career of Joan Rivers. In his casual chat with DeGeneres after her debut on his show, the topic was gender, with Carson and DeGeneres agreeing that stand-up comedy is tougher for women because audiences can accept aggression from men more easily. DeGeneres's routine was hardly aggressive, but the aggression and hence presumed masculinity of stand-up comedy is the act itself and its authority to make an audience laugh. Carson's invitation to the desk and his comment about gender and aggression acknowledged that DeGeneres was good enough to be one of the boys, befitting a comedian who did not dress or coif or primp herself to look the way women looked on 1980s television, the era of Heather Locklear and Victoria Principal.

The masculine slant to DeGeneres's image throughout her career heightens the irony in DeGeneres's significant appearances as a cover girl. In 1997 she made television and pop-culture history by appearing on the April 14 cover of *Time* magazine with the headline "Yep, I'm Gay," followed a few weeks later by the much-publicized coming out of Ellen Morgan, the character she played on her sitcom *Ellen* (1994–1998), making that series the first to feature a gay leading character. But the *Time* magazine debut was not the only surprising turn in DeGeneres's cover-girl career. By 2010 she had become such a popular and beloved celebrity that she regularly appeared on covers of women's magazines, from *Redbook* to *Ladies Home Journal*, cast as the wholesome girl next door. And in the previous year, the CoverGirl cosmetics corporation asked her to become a spokesperson and model, the first time in history a self-identified butch lesbian became the face of a major beauty-product line. Margaret Cho proclaimed herself beautiful as a manifesto of queer defiance, but CoverGirl was betting that Ellen DeGeneres could sell beauty to mainstream, white, American women.

Clearly this is prime material for thoughts on the pretty versus funny binary and the body politics of women comics. However, this chapter on

Ellen DeGeneres differs in method and approach from the treatment of the other comedians in this book. My focus here is more on DeGeneres herself than her comedy, and my interest is in how her popularity invites rethinking of questions about comedy and the body for the next surge of critical conversations on this topic. DeGeneres's body, its visibility and politics, are intrinsic to her cultural significance. Scholars have done extensive analyses of her television sitcoms, especially *Ellen*, given its groundbreaking representation of lesbianism. Nevertheless, the work that made her a mainstream star and a much-loved celebrity, CoverGirl model, and host of numerous award shows was not her sitcoms but rather her role as host of the daytime talk show *The Ellen DeGeneres Show* (2003–). As a talk-show host, DeGeneres has staked out a popular following and everyday presence far larger than that of Griffin, Fey, Silverman, Cho, or Sykes. And she has done so while abjuring the mainstays of Hollywood success for women—femininity and heterosexuality. DeGeneres sometimes dresses up in a fitted blazer and vest for her show, but she also makes television appearances wearing baggy trousers and tennis shoes, minimal makeup, and a careless look that defies Hollywood and television ideals of femininity. When as a joke she wears a dress for Photoshopped video gags or makeover-by-the-audience skits on her talk show, it's clear that she's in drag. Likewise, when she asks a guest like Paris Hilton to teach her how to do runway poses, DeGeneres's mimicry is comic because it exposes femininity itself as a pose and affectation. In short, she is highly visible, but she is also visibly butch lesbian in her appearance as well as in her occasional teasing on television about her sexual orientation.

Generally, though, DeGeneres's talk-show comedy is low-key and apolitical—goofy, often slapstick, bantering but never malicious. Her jokes are far more likely to be about an experience at the dry cleaners than her experience as a gay woman in Hollywood. In fact, queer critics have accused her of selling out to the feel-good milieu of middlebrow daytime television. My own claim here is that the radical nature of her talk show is not in its comedy but rather in the public identity and visibility of its host, who has been accepted by mainstream audiences as a tomboy version of America's sweetheart. Her political impact is substantial even if her style and presence are very different from the edgier comics treated in this book. In their skepticism or outright critique of gender expectations, Griffin, Fey, Silverman, Cho, and Sykes rely on caustic wit, scathing satire, and humor that is sometimes risqué, angry, or even crude. In the previous chapters, I have emphasized how their bodies are read and judged by conventional standards and how they themselves talk back to those readings and judgments. Although their bodies are, in one sense, the text of their comedy, my study

When Ellen DeGeneres mimics femininity, the comic effect emphasizes her own status as a kind of body rarely represented on network television, as seen in this shot with Paris Hilton on The Ellen DeGeneres Show. *Photo courtesy of Photofest.*

has been their comedy texts, the skits, jokes, sitcom narratives, and stand-up spiels in which they convey their cultural critiques.

For DeGeneres, though, my focus is the star herself, her public presence and her popularity in a culture still underwritten by homophobic practices and politics. In this I follow a point made by Jennifer Reed in her essay on the impact of queer comics Lily Tomlin, Margaret Cho, and Paula Poundstone. In the history they have created, Reed says, their importance "is not found so much in one joke, or a series of jokes . . . but in a body of work over an extended period of time that creates a queer public presence" ("Sexual Outlaws," 767). Along the same lines, my emphasis in this chapter is the queer public presence of DeGeneres, particularly her comeback from sitcom failure to overwhelming success in daytime television. So while my topic is DeGeneres's comedy, I am moving away from comedy as a series of jokes or skits in order to talk about it as a mode that has enabled DeGeneres to develop a generous, feel-good, tousle-haired, lesbian persona with broad appeal. I refer to some of DeGeneres's gags and routines, but I am more interested in the impact of her presence, the comic presence of the lesbian body, its legibility, its mobility through multiple contexts, its resistance to social and sexual categories, and its blond whiteness that enables this versatility.

Most of all, I am interested in how the comic body of DeGeneres connects with her audiences and fans. Susan Bordo has written elegantly about the visceral and emotional impact of bodies in representation, arguing that the bodies seen on television or in magazines are never "just pictures" registered only intellectually or visually. Bordo argues for the way these bodies "*speak* to us" in visceral and dynamic ways as objects of pleasure and desire: "We are drawn to what the desired body evokes for us and in us . . . to the meanings they carry for us" (124). Richard Dyer's take on stardom in *Heavenly Bodies* shares this interest in the body as locus of psychological and social meanings. For Bordo and Dyer, the bodies of stars, models, and celebrities are never merely good images or bad images; instead, they have emotional impact. They provoke desire, incite imitation or inspiration, and can make viewers feel connected or understood. This approach to media bodies is my starting point for thinking about the comic body of Ellen DeGeneres, the lanky, funny, soft-butch, slapstick-prone body that has projected such a comfortable presence that it has won over huge audiences and many fans. I conclude by speculating on the theoretical approach of Gilles Deleuze, specifically as interpreted by contemporary feminist cultural critics, to think about the contradictions around DeGeneres's image not as binary options but as keys to the multiple ways DeGeneres has attracted a large following. This approach offers a way to rethink the pretty/funny binary and invite a broader discussion about women comics in that vein.

PICTURING ELLEN

Visibility—literally, the various ways she is seen and interpreted—is an issue for DeGeneres more than for any other comic treated in this book. The 1990s outings of herself and her sitcom character required audiences to reread and rethink what they had been seeing for years. And another shift of public visibility occurred when DeGeneres moved from controversial celebrity to a major cultural presence as a daytime talk-show host. The pilot episode of DeGeneres's first and groundbreaking sitcom, *Ellen*, was built around a joke about what Ellen Morgan/Ellen DeGeneres looks like and how viewers can picture her. The plot is about Ellen's driver's license photo, which is especially terrible even for the genre of Department of Motor Vehicle photos because the photographer has asked her to smile like a "pretty girl." Exasperated with this request, Ellen grimaces, resulting in a photo apparently so awful that when she later hands her license to a cashier asking for ID, the cashier asks if it's a photo of her husband. While we never see the photo, the joke is that it's singularly grotesque or unflattering. But given that some segment of the audience already knew about DeGeneres's lesbianism—not officially revealed until three years into the series—the crack about the husband is doubly funny in implying that the photo has captured DeGeneres's butch identity. The photo joke operates in the "double voice" that critic Marusya Bociurkiw attributes to the *Ellen* sitcom in its early years, delivering an obvious meaning for mainstream viewers and a queer meaning available for fans in the know (180).

For the purposes of my own reading, the joke is an especially self-conscious play with how DeGeneres is not the pretty girl expected on a network sitcom, not because of her facial features but because she doesn't participate in the codes of dress, hair, cosmetics, and accessories coded as traditionally feminine. This is made clear in a scene when Ellen decides to turn herself into the pretty girl the photographer had requested. She pretends to lose her driver's license so she can have a better photo taken. But when she dresses in conventionally pretty ways, wearing makeup, a low-cut top, and large earrings, she looks hilariously clownish. The effect is especially funny for some viewers because the woman behind her in the line is coded as butch, making Ellen's appearance all the more obvious as drag or femme masquerade.

The sitcom *Ellen* was designed along the *Seinfeld* model, also seen in Cho's *All-American Girl*, to showcase a comic playing a thinly disguised version of herself. Helene Shugart demonstrates that the controversy and media drama that erupted around the coming-out events indicate that mainstream audiences had interpreted both DeGeneres and her sitcom character as heterosexual, and the series frequently deployed heteronormative devices allowing Ellen Morgan as well as Ellen DeGeneres to pass as straight. The series often used the disastrous date plot, for example, or crazy foil characters who made Ellen Morgan seem normal (36–42). These heteronormative frameworks glossed over what the audience saw regarding Ellen Morgan's body and dress, for "neither [DeGeneres] nor her character conformed to established norms of feminine beauty in the entertainment industry," Shugart writes. Instead, the physical appearance of the actor and character "was notably androgynous by conventional standards" and lacked traditional feminine charm: "Both were characterized by their chronic lack of social adroitness and outright goofiness" (35). Shugart's point is that Ellen Morgan could pass as straight through strategies that distanced her from heterosexuality without actually suggesting lesbianism.

However, I want to emphasize that the pretty/funny convention of comedy itself allowed for the androgynous looks and dress that would otherwise be obvious as butch. Audiences were predisposed to interpret Ellen Morgan/DeGeneres's awkwardness as a funny version of pretty, if "pretty" is the shorthand for the heterosexual femininity typically seen on sitcoms. Ellen's awkwardness could also be interpreted within the comic framework of comedians from Fanny Brice to Phyllis Diller who have played the failure of femininity for laughs. So both the heterosexist logic of the sitcom and the tradition of the female clown as inept woman allowed a reading of Ellen Morgan/Ellen DeGeneres as a heterosexual despite the queer semiotics.

Nevertheless, some audiences and fans already viewed Ellen Morgan as a lesbian whose passing as straight produced entertaining queer comedy. Rachel Giese argues that Ellen Morgan was far more interesting before she came out because her looks and "her disdain for the conventions of heterosexuality" provided "a sly critique of straight TV properties—in which women must be obsessed with men and traditionally pretty" (in Bociurkiw, 179). Jennifer Reed contends that the queerness of the series was not just readable for gay audiences but was instead "hard to miss by any reader" ("Ellen DeGeneres," 28). Reed's point is supported by Suzanne Moore, who remarks in *The New Statesman* that the coming-out event was "somewhat perplexing" because the semiotics seemed obvious: "What, I wonder, were we supposed to think Ellen was before? A heterosexual? Puh-lease. She never wore skirts, she didn't have breast implants, she covered up her body in 'sweats' and she never participated in that staple of American comedy and indeed American life: dating" (47). The indication that Moore doesn't remember the disastrous-date episodes suggests what critics have pointed out as the series's lack of narrative tension about romance, the dynamic that usually drives sitcoms about straight singles.[1] But Moore's remark also suggests that for those who noticed Ellen Morgan's obvious differences from other women on network television, the body spoke more strongly than the narratives or the comic convention of failed femininity. And finally, this same body's capacity to pass as straight for many viewers points to the unsettling queer potential of that very convention, similar to Kathy Griffin's queer sidekick character on *Suddenly Susan*.

The historic coming out of DeGeneres and her character in 1997 illustrates how strongly DeGeneres's career has been tied to questions of perception, interpretation, and legibility not only by various audiences but by scholars who have debated its politics and meanings for queer representation.[2] The ABC network and DeGeneres's publicists began a media campaign about her sexuality months before the actual coming out, and DeGeneres began to make teasing references about it on talk shows. When the much-publicized coming-out episode of *Ellen* finally aired, it broke ratings records for ABC's entire season. The wave of titillating publicity continued after DeGeneres revealed her romantic relationship with Anne Heche, an actor who previously had identified as straight. Their public appearances together, including an emotional tell-all on *The Oprah Winfrey Show*, inaugurated a new kind of media event featuring the visibility of a celebrity gay couple. DeGeneres was not the first comedian to come out as a lesbian; Lea DeLaria, Suzanne Westenhoefer, and Kate Clinton, among others, had been doing stand-up lesbian comedy for years, and Westenhoefer was the first to make such an appearance on network television. But DeGeneres was the first mainstream television star who outed herself, and *Ellen* was the first network series featuring a main character who was gay, unquestionably making a historical impact on gay representation.

The actual effects of this impact are much contested. Bonnie Dow argues that DeGeneres's friendly "poster-child" lesbianism depoliticized homosexuality by turning it into a personal rather than social issue ("Ellen"), while Becca Cragin contends that *Ellen* triggered more political heat than DeGeneres intended and more than her goofy-kid persona on the series could withstand (200–203). Indeed, my larger question is the multiple and often contradictory effects of DeGeneres's visibility and later celebrity, and though my focus is her later career as a talk-show host, it's clear that her career is—more than any other comic covered in this book—characterized by its own "leakiness," to borrow the Bakhtinian term, its slippages out of categories and definitions.

In 1997 the triumph of the personal and sitcom outings was soon trumped by controversy, backlash, and fierce media scrutiny of DeGeneres's television show and her relationship with Heche. The fierceness of the backlash startlingly demonstrates what it meant for a mainstream star to come out as gay in 1997. Conservative and religious critics denounced the series and picketed ABC, which in turn slapped a parental guidance warning on episodes in which the Ellen character is affectionate with her girlfriend, even though their affection is represented in a fashion that would easily have been given a "G" film rating if the characters had been straight. Gay-rights advocate Chastity (later Chaz) Bono was quoted as saying the show was "too gay," and even though Bono later insisted the remark was taken out of context, it contributed to network uneasiness about the series. Nor were mainstream media entirely comfortable with representations of gay celebrity. In an editorial titled "Ellen and 'Ellen' Come Out," the other-wise sympathetic *New York Times* tsk-tsked DeGeneres for putting her arm around Heche for photos at a White House dinner, calling it an "ostenta-tious display of affection with her lover in front of President Clinton."

Within a year the sitcom's ratings fell, the series was cancelled, and the relationship with Heche faltered. For the next two years DeGeneres's work was limited to a few small film roles and an appearance as a charac-ter in the television drama *If These Walls Could Talk 2* (2000), for which she was also a producer. In 2001 she attempted another sitcom, *The Ellen Show*, which lasted only eighteen episodes. Its premise was the hometown return of a character who just happens to be gay in a determinedly hetero-normative world. The appeal to middlebrow safety fell flat, and the series was likewise a huge disappointment for queer fans hoping for the more imaginative sitcom plots of the final, gay season of *Ellen*. In the meantime DeGeneres demonstrated that her comic abilities were far more suited to good-natured joshing with live audiences than to the formulas of sitcom narratives, at least as they were imagined at that time. In 2000 she prepared a Broadway stand-up show, *The Beginning*, which was taped for an HBO special and distributed as a DVD performance film. It earned solid reviews and reminded producers that her rambling, naive comic style remained enormously appealing.

Her comfortable style got DeGeneres a role that was arguably the turn-ing point in her return to network television and mainstream popularity: hosting the 2001 Emmy awards broadcast.[3] The Emmys are usually awarded in September but had been cancelled twice because of the 9/11 catastro-phe. Making people feel at ease, both the live and television audiences, was crucial for the Emmys host because of the timing. The ceremony was finally scheduled for November, and DeGeneres won widespread respect for her ability to handle the show gracefully. She opened with a monologue joking about the heightened security and the nervousness of stars too in-timidated to show up. However, the joke that got the greatest audience response and later circulation referred to the public discourse about ter-rorism and to her own identity as a lesbian. At the time, the United States was at war in Afghanistan against the Taliban. Because the Taliban were infamous for suppressing all Western commodities and media, one strand of patriotic discourse encouraged Americans to carry on as usual to prove the terrorists did not win, and President George W. Bush famously encouraged Americans to go shopping to prove it. Also during this time the concept of women's rights was being exploited by hawks as a reason to invade Afghanistan; the Taliban's oppression of women quickly became a cause célèbre and call to arms, even though the Feminist Majority Foundation's Campaign to Stop Gender Apartheid in Afghanistan had been active since 1997 without rousing much attention from Washington. So DeGeneres slyly appropriated the pieties about minority rights and the right to enjoy entertainment but with a personalized and transgessive twist. Appearing onstage in a satin-collared, black tuxedo and addressing the front rows of television producers, she gave the usual pitch about the need to continue the business of entertainment: "What would bug the Taliban more than seeing a gay woman in a suit surrounded by Jews?"

Widely quoted, the joke encapsulates many issues of DeGeneres's visibility and affect, including the precariousness in the ways she made audiences comfortable. Certainly its cleverness lies in its recruitment of Jewish and Hollywood liberalism as well as the expression of homosexuality as signs of patriotism. However, like Republicans' sudden sympathy for Afghan women, DeGeneres's joke may have provoked a knee-jerk response decrying homophobia and anti-Semitism as a way to distinguish "us" from "them." It works in other conservative ways as well, by positing an elite and self-selected space where a gay woman in a suit can be welcome. The space is characterized as one inhabited by Jews, another often-maligned minority that nonetheless wields some clout. Also, the space is distinctly upscale, as was DeGeneres's appearance. Her Céline tuxedo sparkled with an opulence that was reinforced by DeGeneres's whiteness: this was the blond female whom Hollywood Jews had glamourized in movies since the silent era.

Yet DeGeneres is decidedly not that blond, glamourous Hollywood body. Her demeanor was unmistakably butch, not femme, and her friendly kidding with the producers and the audience had no traces of flirtation or glamourous posing. Nor was she performing only in the space of liberal, wealthy Jews. This event was considered a significant post-9/11 moment for television's representation of itself as an industry responding to the tragedy. The broadcast was given a special introduction by that stalwart figure of Americana, former anchorman Walter Cronkite, who seemed to be granting permission for the show to go on in solemnly announcing that "entertainment can help us heal." Thus it was positioned as a national moment with impact beyond handing out the annual Emmy awards, and it drew more than 17 million viewers.

DeGeneres's joke, calling attention to her body and her clothing, offered her sexual difference as citizenship. In this way she specified American citizenship as a safe harbor for homosexuality, purely an act of trust and hope. Just four years earlier the response to her outing on *Ellen* entailed viewer boycotts, blacked-out episodes by some affiliate stations, and picketing of ABC by religious groups. So the joke was at once sentimental, appropriating any mark of diversity as a patriotic affront to the Taliban, and political, the declaration of citizenship for a minority that, for many Americans, was still controversial and morally suspect. Nor was she offering as the lesbian body a feminine one that could pass but rather an attractive version of a masculinized body in a suit. Even if the joke merged with patriotic sentiment, it was nevertheless an act of transgression. In short, when DeGeneres used her lesbianism as the icebreaker at a moment of television and national anxiety, she was doing more than representing gays and lesbians. She was claiming citizenship. My point here is that she was functioning not simply as a likable image or even a controversial one but as a propelling force that created enormous goodwill, at least for that event and its follow-up discourses. For some segment of the American population, she was no doubt still the morally dubious or sinful "Ellen Degenerate," although her career over ensuing years would prove that sentiment to be in decline.

DANCING

The year before the Emmy event, DeGeneres had launched her comedy stand-up comeback with a dance, her introductory routine for her Broadway show *The Beginning*, as seen in the DVD concert film. Her choice to begin with a dance points to her own instinct that her body speaks to audiences through an immediate and likable comic mode. The image of DeGeneres dancing, mobile and in action, was especially significant because, as she tells the crowd at this show, her personal and professional life had declined into what she called a "scary place, very dark." DeGeneres tells the audience that this comeback show is "a very emotional night," given her journey since her coming out, and that she wasn't sure what to say about that journey. So, she concludes, "I feel it would be best expressed through interpretive dance." The pretentiousness of the last phrase draws appreciative laughter in anticipation of the dancing, which begins with DeGeneres's famous physical unwieldiness—stilted 1970s disco moves—followed by expansive and joyous free-style dancing in bright lights. Then the lights grow dimmer, the music becomes menacing, and her dance morphs into a pantomime of being attacked, tugged in different directions, under siege, and finally on the run. At the end of the attack, she's sitting in a crouch, her arms crossed over her knees, her head down in sadness or shame, until the music picks up and she's able to raise her head, smile, look around, stretch, and stand up straight, arms extended, ready for whatever's next. "So that's what happened," she says.

Over the next ten years, as DeGeneres made a turnaround into one of the most successful and prominent entertainers on television, dancing would become her trademark, not as a pantomime but as a performance of unself-conscious pleasure—energetic, unpolished, precariously balanced between agility and silliness. Ellen had often danced on her 1990s sitcom, and in her first book, *My Point . . . and I Do Have One* (1995), DeGeneres declares that she considers herself "blessed in this area" and born with "a sense of rhythm," evidence of which is her eagerness to teach readers "a simple yet hip dance" of her own invention called the Ellie-Gellie (135). As this implies, neither her dancing skills nor the Ellie-Gellie are meant to be taken seriously, but on her weekday talk show the fun of her dancing looks infectious. As part of her opening routine on each show, DeGeneres has her DJ cue up some pop, rock, R&B, or reggae music to which she dances, first on stage and then up and down the aisles, prompting the entire audience to get up and dance as well. The invitation to dance is an invitation to loosen up and join DeGeneres's comfort with her own body and the talk-show format, the venue that quickly became her niche for performance and interaction.

Indeed, when DeGeneres created *The Ellen DeGeneres Show* for NBC in 2003, she found the vehicle that would make her, as Reed puts it, "the most visible, the most famous, and the most loved lesbian in America" ("Ellen DeGeneres," 23). Comics frequently turn to talk-show venues to draw on their skills of chat, wit, and improvisation, as seen in the careers of Joan Rivers, Jenny Jones, and Joy Behar, for example, although talk-show momentum is also notoriously difficult to sustain. Popular celebrities from Cybill Shepherd and Candace Bergen to Queen Latifah have initiated shows that soon wilted (Fonseca, "New Queen"). In contrast, DeGeneres's talk show drew in audiences from the start and continued to win audience shares and thirty-two daytime Emmy awards as of 2012, quickly positioning itself as a formidable rival to *The Oprah Winfrey Show* (1986–2011).[4] Critics praised *The Ellen DeGeneres Show* as an upbeat party, the conversations light, the jokes never mean, and the humor silly and inclined toward pranks. The show features a stream of high-profile celebrity guests, games, and lavish gift giveaways for the audiences, as on *Oprah* but without the latter's melodramatic, therapy-laden interviews or discussions. When in 2010 Oprah Winfrey announced the end of her long-running talk show, journalists pointed to DeGeneres as her successor as the most powerful woman on television (Rice), a spot that seemed to be confirmed by her 2009–2010 stint as a judge on the popular talent show *American Idol* (2002–). Citing her presence on two popular series, daytime and prime-time, the latter associated with the music world, a writer for *Entertainment Weekly* remarked in 2010 that "the woman whose ABC sitcom was dumped in 1998 and who could hardly find work a decade ago has become the Queen of All Media" (Karger). Popular journalism loves a good comeback story and the hype of a royal succession like Oprah handing off the scepter to Ellen, but the turnaround in DeGeneres's career is truly remarkable in light of the nastiness of the 1998 controversy and DeGeneres's openness about her sexual orientation.

Critics have claimed that DeGeneres's success came at the expense of her political impact as a lesbian (Bociurkiw; Dow, "Ellen"). It would be easy to make that argument, especially because her daytime television persona is overwhelmingly identified with niceness, a trait easily interpreted as a compromise or effacement of lesbianism or sexual politics. So it is worth exploring exactly what this niceness entails and why it is commonly understood as the buffer or erasure of her lesbianism. Her reputation for being nice is generated by the warmth and kindness evident in DeGeneres's interactions with the guests on her talk show, which one journalist described as "a safe harbor in a craggy television landscape . . . a feel-good environment" (Steinberg). When she was chosen to replace Paula Abdul as a judge on *American Idol*, the January 15, 2010, cover of *Entertainment Weekly* featured DeGeneres with Simon Cowell and the headline "Nice vs. Nasty." A *New York Times* article ruminating on DeGeneres's presence on that show was titled "Ellen, 'Idol,' and the Power of Niceness" (Stanley). There are occasional reports of DeGeneres as a brisk, aloof person offstage (Berman; Griffin, *Official Book Club*, 107–108), but niceness is the element popular journalists emphasize in their stories and the one DeGeneres herself feeds to interviewers. The 2009 *Ladies Home Journal* issue in which she debuted as a CoverGirl model had an essay emphasizing her personal benevolence. "Most days, she says, the thing she strives for is not to be funny or fabulous but to simply be 'a good person . . . and to treat people with kindness'" (Newman, "Ellen Enchanted," 119). In her interview for a 2007 cover story in *W*, DeGeneres said she would never have Kathy Griffin on her show— "Very mean"—and dismissed nasty comedy as "easy" (Foley).

The niceness factor differentiates DeGeneres from contemporary women comics famous for their aggressiveness and acerbic style—Wanda Sykes, Sarah Silverman, Margaret Cho—but also from Tina Fey, the only other woman comic in DeGeneres's league as a star in network television. Fey is famous for the bite of her wit; Rebecca Traister calls her "one of the chilliest, prickliest celebrities around," a female star who doesn't "conform to expectations for cuddliness" ("Tina Fey Backlash"). For DeGeneres, in contrast, "cuddly" informs the entire star package. In 2008 a writer for the gay and lesbian news magazine *The Advocate* argued that DeGeneres's identity as a "friendly, cute, funny" celebrity had become more important than her identity as a lesbian. DeGeneres had "become one of those people who transcends common notions about gender or sexuality, much as a Bill Cosby or Tiger Woods seems to rise above common racial prejudices. She's so damn friendly, cute, funny—dare we say normal?—that the everyday Americans have seamlessly incorporated—and accepted—her sexual orientation as a part of who she is. No questions asked" (Kort, 46). But given my larger questions about the political impact of women's comedy, this is precisely what I find most intriguing: How exactly does DeGeneres's butch identity function in relationship to the popular perception of her niceness and hence to her mainstream popularity? And how does her comedy make this relationship possible? My larger argument about this is that DeGeneres's multiple positionings and the potential of the comic body can be better understood by shifting out of binary thinking that requires separating meanings from the body itself. But the overview of DeGeneres's evolving public image that I present here suggests the ways comedy itself has enabled DeGeneres's mainstream popularity as well as her frankness about her sexuality.

In the years since her historic coming out, the inflections of DeGeneres's lesbian visibility have shifted considerably, as have her own attitudes about it. DeGeneres at first resisted being seen as a spokesperson for gays and shirked from using the word "lesbian." In interviews she tended to use the word "they" in speaking of gays, distancing herself from gay identity at the very moment she was embracing it (Cragin, 202). However, by 2003 DeGeneres was far more at ease in incorporating her sexual identity into her comedy, as seen in her HBO special that year, *Here and Now*, when she teases the audience members by asking if they're all gay. "I have to say something gay," she says, "otherwise people would say, 'She's not our leader!' Seriously, if you're here tonight, you're probably gay."

For the first several years of her daytime talk show, DeGeneres carefully avoided mentioning her personal life in monologues and interactions with guests. But her visibility as a high-profile lesbian spiked in the media blitz around her much-publicized wedding to actor Portia de Rossi in 2008. On the cover of *People* magazine and in photos and footage on *The Oprah*

Winfrey Show, DeGeneres was the high-fashion butch, dressed in an elegant white shirt, trousers, and vest, next to her gorgeous, femme bride. The images are simultaneously transgressive and, in their romantic frothiness, utterly bourgeois. The latter mode is what's most often channeled on her daytime talk show when DeGeneres coos over babies, animals, and celebrities with equal enthusiasm. The lanky, butch image plays perfectly well as tomboy next door, which in turn plays ideally in her comic persona as clown, imposter, prankster, and "endearingly inept host," as Bociurkiw puts it (180).

The mainstream public image of endearing goofiness, pristinely excised from issues of sexual politics, was confirmed in 2004 when she was tapped for television ads for the American Express credit card, in which she performed her signature free-style dancing. But the commercialization of her image took on far more gendered meanings with her appearances as a CoverGirl cosmetics model in 2009. Here was one of the world's best-known lesbians in medium close-ups in television commercials and magazine ads, wearing glossy lipstick, dramatic eye makeup, and an upscale hairstyle. The first television ads were wholly without irony, though the later ones became more playful, pairing DeGeneres with traditionally glamourous actors such as Sofia Vergara for an impish pretty versus funny dynamic. The cleverness of these pairings, however, was the implication that not everyone can be as drop-dead gorgeous as Sofia Vergara, but everyone can be as attractive as Ellen DeGeneres: on the one hand, a reasonable tactic that everyone would like to look like a pretty-funny celebrity; on the other hand, a sign that CoverGirl put its money on the popularity of this pretty-funny celebrity trumping homophobia. In the meantime, DeGeneres frequently mocked her CoverGirl model status on her talk-show episodes with hilarious mimicries of the more serious "cover girl" poses, reminding viewers that she plays in several tonalities at once. The flip side of the chic cover girl is the roguish butch.

DeGeneres's mischievous persona was likewise recruited by J. C. Penney for a series of 2012 television ads in which DeGeneres plays the Average Shopper bewildered by standard retail practices (such as listings at $14.99 instead of $15.00). Penney's willingness to stake its advertising dollars on DeGeneres's popularity would seem to be another sign of how deeply she has been appropriated into middlebrow culture. A Penney's executive emphasized her drawing power as someone consumers can "trust": "She's lovable, likable, honest and funny, but at her soul, we trust her" (Wong). The choice of words here indicates intimacy—the public knows DeGeneres "at her soul"—as is often the case with talk show hosts who simulate what crit-

DOES YOUR **MAKEUP**
MAKE YOU LOOK OLDER?

Ellen looks simply amazing in Ivory.

By selecting DeGeneres as a model and spokesperson, CoverGirl cosmetics put its money on the appeal of her good-natured celebrity trumping homophobia.

ics call a "parasocial" relationship with a television audience that believes they know the "real" host-celebrity personally (Horton and Wohl). The curious use of the qualification — "*but* at her soul, we trust her" — suggests a defensiveness that in fact was prescient because the liminal edginess of De-Generes's celebrity quickly emerged. A much-publicized boycott against J. C. Penney was threatened by the American Family Association's spin-off group One Million Moms, self-described on the website as women who "want our children to have the best chance possible of living in a moral society." When news of the boycott surfaced, the One Million Moms Facebook page had to be dismantled because it was overrun by protesters. Meanwhile, J. C. Penney never swerved in standing by DeGeneres as a spokesperson, and six weeks later, the boycott was dropped. In the end, the protest appeared to come from a noisy but small minority; news reports estimated that the "one million moms" were closer to 50,000. Neverthe-less, the protest illustrates the controversial component of a gay celebrity who — unlike Margaret Cho — has been welcomed into the wholly bour-geois retail world of children's school clothes and vacuum cleaners — someone we trust "at her soul" who is also someone decidedly unlike most of the women buying vacuum cleaners at the mall.

The J. C. Penney ads themselves wittily push DeGeneres's butch per-sona. In one, she wears Victorian-lady garb, sporting a huge My Fair Lady hat with feathers, so that the overall effect is outrageous femme drag, funny precisely because it winks at audience knowledge about DeGeneres's lack of conventional femininity. Another ad puts her into a black and white *I Love Lucy*–style bedroom where Lucy and Desi look-alikes are waking up in their prim single beds. The joke is that DeGeneres is waking up in a third single bed in the same room, underscoring her distance from heteronormativity but also wittily painting it as a quaint 1950s idea. The ad shrewdly implies sexual differences among women — for DeGeneres is pointedly unlike the 1950s woman who is part of the couple — but also makes that difference comically disarming. Finding cuddly Ellen in the heterosexual bedroom is absurdly funny without being creepy, risqué, or objectionable. Granted the argument that DeGeneres has become a "user-friendly lesbian" with diminishing political effect (Dow, "Ellen," 268"), the subtle subversiveness of the J. C. Penney ads also attests to the political work being done in the mainstreaming of a lesbian whose "soul" is trusted. Intrinsic to that trust is DeGeneres's role as primarily comic and her enact-ment of comedy through a body that can't be mistaken for anything other than butch — hardly a mainstream representation, even if it has gradually become a more acceptable one.

The question is no longer whether to read DeGeneres as a lesbian but rather how to read this lesbian body: soft butch in her baggy trousers, groundbreaking gay role model, wholesome talk-show host, middle-age female superstar, spokesperson for CoverGirl cosmetics—that is, "pretty"—and for J. C. Penney, a trustworthy version of the average shopper. Some critics have argued that she is most legible as gay in her dancing, which has been interpreted as her queer signature, a repeated gesture of self-outing. Candace Moore persuasively links DeGeneres's dancing to the physical comedy on her sitcoms and her "discursive skirting" as evidence of how she performs her sexuality "as multiple self-outings" (20). The "dance with herself," Moore says, is "a daily declaration of queer identity" (23). After her 2008 wedding DeGeneres began more openly to dance around her sexual identity with jokes and allusions on her talk show and in other television venues as well. The references are indirect, relying on audience acknowledgment of what's unsaid. For example, in the episode when she hosts Mormon "sister-wives" from the reality show of the same title, DeGeneres describes in her monologue how the four women live together, sharing the household work as well as the husband. DeGeneres says she has several questions for the women, including "Why do you need a husband?"—playing on audience knowledge about DeGeneres without directly citing it. Along the same lines, in a talk-show skit in 2011 she Photoshops herself into a scene from the movie *The Fighter* (2010) so that she becomes the Mark Wahlberg character, who was supposed to yell at his brother Dicky. DeGeneres changes the dialogue, explaining, "I'm not saying 'Dicky, I want you.' It's not gonna happen."

This type of joking about sexual orientation derives from DeGeneres's comic style of digression, evasion, and equivocation. Describing her work as a judge on *American Idol*, Alessandra Stanley notes that DeGeneres "finds a way to remind audiences of her sexual status on almost every episode." Stanley cites a moment when DeGeneres teases a young male contestant about his good looks, telling him that "for most women, their hearts are going to start racing just looking at you, right, but then, for people like *me* . . ." The audience began to laugh, but DeGeneres held the beat a moment longer before her punch line: "blonds" ("Ellen"). Like her interpretive dance and her refusal to say she wants Dicky, the joke depends on what's not said, which Candace Moore would characterize as "discursive skirting."[5] It is also a joke that refers, directly and indirectly, back to Ellen's body, its sexuality, and its blondness. It is a reminder of her difference from the other, more traditionally feminine female bodies on *Idol* so that her punch line, "blonds," not only reverses expectations but makes an ironic contrast to what "blondness" as glamour usually means on television. And because white blondness is the iconic identity of the girl next door, the gag sums up the contradictory components of DeGeneres's celebrity.

These contradictions play out in a 2010 article by chick-lit novelist Jennifer Weiner. The article was the cover story for *Shape* magazine, and as *Shape*'s cover girl, DeGeneres was being held up as a healthy role model. Weiner's assignment was to fill in the details of that ideal. DeGeneres is an updated version of "Hollywood's girl next door," she writes, "blond-haired and blue-eyed . . . cute instead of sexy," even though she dresses in "a wardrobe of men's vests and ties that Doris Day would have immediately handed off to her brother" (59). The reference to Doris Day is telling, given that Day was unwittingly the beard for Rock Hudson, one of the most famous closeted gay men of the twentieth century. DeGeneres's stardom uncannily combines both poles of that iconic 1950s romantic couple: Day's identity as all-American girl, Hudson's yet undisclosed identity as gay. For Weiner, the latter is abject, the element that gets discounted in the all-American body being promoted by *Shape*. Weiner may also have forgotten or overlooked Doris Day's own status as a lesbian icon, further queering her appearances with Hudson. Thus in Weiner's list of the attributes that make DeGeneres likable and hip, the lesbian marriage is a footnote: "With a vegan diet, a dedication to yoga, a vocabulary salted with self-help buzzwords, and, lest we forget, a wife instead of a husband, Ellen embodies the modern version of everyone's neighbor and friend" (59). The vegan, yoga, self-help snapshot guarantees DeGeneres's credentials as white and upper class, making it easier for her to be, lest we forget, a lesbian in a marriage that a majority of California voters in 2008 regarded as illegal with the passing of Proposition 8 six months after DeGeneres's wedding. The political antipathy toward gay marriage appeared again in 2011 when several Republican candidates for the presidency apparently believed they would be more attractive to voters if they signed a pledge by the National Organization for Marriage vowing to push a federal constitutional amendment outlawing same-sex marriage. For the 2011 Iowa caucuses, a group named the Family Leader offered an even more stringent pledge it called the Marriage Vow and succeeded in having a few candidates sign.

Given these signals of continued homophobia and controversy about gay rights, the question remains what an article like Weiner's contributes to the construction of a "post-gay" DeGeneres persona, a return to the 2001 sitcom character who just happened to be gay in a world that did not need to acknowledge it. Academic discussions around DeGeneres's lesbian presence are often polarized around the question of whether she performs as homonormative, a lesbian presence careful not to disrupt conservative, heterosexist structures and thinking.[6] Her associations with American Express, CoverGirl cosmetics, and J. C. Penney seem to confirm the consumability of her gayness as "commodity lesbianism," a strategy that makes sexual diversity another consumerist choice or a colorful lifestyle option. However, my argument here is that DeGeneres maintains popular interest and succeeds as a comic by resisting those binary options of complicity/subversion and that she does so precisely by drawing attention to a body that as a comic body agile enough to bend the rules and open the boundaries is a comfortable presence, as seen at the 2001 Emmy awards broadcast.

In her influential 2001 essay on the relative consumability of certain lesbian images, Ann Ciasullo asserts that the butch creates an uneasiness that makes her less "consumable" for mainstream representation than a femme lesbian, who can be the object of multiple identifications and desires. The butch not only defies straight male desire but presents a threat that needs to be disavowed, for she has "the capacity to disrupt the notion that masculinity is an inherently male attribute" (604). Ciasullo emphasizes the supposed "ugliness" of the butch lesbian as an undesirable working-class stereotype. With her short hair and identification with the "tool-belt crowd ... the butch's perceived unattractiveness renders her invisible in an image-based culture," Ciasullo writes (602). Her primary argument is that the "lesbian chic" trend that emerged in the 1990s enabled only one kind of visibility, the consumer-friendly femme, and continued the ongoing invisibility of the butch in mainstream representations.

Ciasullo is one of several critics who claim that DeGeneres's popularity has been enabled by her ability to eschew working-class associations and take on the more attractive class and femme qualities of the consumable lesbian in popular culture. Looking at DeGeneres's famous *Time* magazine cover photo in which the comic wears a fashionable, low-cut, black shirt and subtle diamond on a necklace, Ciasullo argues that "*this* lesbian body—comfortable and comforting—doesn't look anything like the stereotypical lesbian body, the 'mannish,' makeup-less butch in boots and flannel so often associated with lesbianism. Here, Ellen is attractive (nice smile, light but appealing makeup), feminine (low-cut shirt—unusual for DeGeneres—and diamonds?), and inviting" (584). Ciasullo makes an important point about DeGeneres's attractiveness and its class and feminine markers in the cover photo. But especially since DeGeneres's talk-show debut in 2003 she has often veered closer to the stereotypical lesbian body in her self-presentations, never unattractive but never far from a soft-butch identity. She is likely to show up without makeup or jewelry, wearing loose-fitting slacks and her signature sneakers, when she makes a guest appearance on *The David Letterman Show* (1980–) or *So You Think You Can Dance* (2005–). She has maintained the image of a butch body that is comfortable and comforting but still decidedly lesbian, an affect that propels her mainstream popularity.

As popular as well as scholarly critics have noted, DeGeneres's whiteness, blondness, and associated signs of middle- to upper-class privilege are pivotal to the public comfort with her image. Bociurkiw argues that these factors were the very grounds of DeGeneres's public coming out on television; in the season following her coming out on the sitcom *Ellen*, the Ellen character's upward mobility was literalized in a subplot about buying her own home, so that coming out and buying real estate "were narratively presented as inextricable" (179). Bociurkiw emphasizes how DeGeneres relied on racial metaphors to talk about her sexuality during the months-long coming-out saga, comparing herself to Rosa Parks and using Oprah Winfrey on the coming-out episode to make the point about parallel oppressions (177–179). More than a decade later, when it was clear that DeGeneres had become one of the most powerful women on television, *Esquire* writer A. J. Jacobs went back to the Rosa Parks comparison to note that the NAACP had been exceedingly cautious about who could be fronted as the icon for the seat-on-the-bus protest. A black teenager who was arrested for that very crime was considered too risky because she later became pregnant, and civil rights leaders "waited for Rosa Parks, the amiable middle-aged woman." Ellen DeGeneres is gay culture's Rosa Parks, Jacobs says, not so much for her bravery but for her safe fit with middle-class ideals (63). Ironically, then, DeGeneres is most Rosa Parksish in being blond and white.

However, DeGeneres's popularity as a talk-show host may be better described in terms of audience comfort not with a butch lesbian but with a woman who is herself comfortable in her own body. It is true that her vegan diet since 2008 has slimmed DeGeneres down into magazine-model parameters and accentuated her cheekbones. But neither DeGeneres nor the show has fetishized or flaunted this development of a gradually healthier body, as opposed to the sensationalized weight fluctuations of Oprah Winfrey, who once wheeled onstage a wagon of fat to show how much weight she'd lost. Winfrey was frank in her discussions about her disappointments and anxieties regarding her weight, and given the health issues involved, this was a serious concern. But it was also a concern about appearance, as seen in Winfrey's use of tight jeans, for example, to emphasize her diet successes in the 1980s. My point here is that these anxieties about bodily appearance are simply not present on DeGeneres's talk show. One current of

DeGeneres found her television niche in the talk-show format that allows her to be the feel-good host and pop-culture fan, wholly comfortable with herself and her guests. DeGeneres is pictured here in 2003 on The Ellen DeGeneres Show *with rapper-songwriter Eve (Jihan Jeffers). Photo courtesy of Photofest.*

response to DeGeneres may indeed be the simplistic one that because she's butch, her appearance doesn't matter to her or anyone else. But because she engages the audience on many different levels, as a lesbian (which still matters deeply to many gay followers) and as a sweet-tempered host, a silly comic, a music fan, a feel-good entertainer, the effects of her bodily presence cannot be easily dismissed.

Film scholarship has long emphasized the star's body as central to the effects and meanings of stardom and posited the body as a text readable through codes of culture, sex, race, gender, and class. This is the semiotic approach to stardom largely shaped by Richard Dyer's influential 1979 study of "the structured polysemy" of cinema stars, "the multiple but finite meanings and effects that a star image signifies" (*Stars*, 63). Dyer's approach is often adapted precisely because it accounts for the paradoxes and multiple meanings of the star. Stardom rarely signifies a single, unified meaning, says Dyer, but instead most often involves contradictory elements such as Angelina Jolie's family-centered maternity versus her edgy glamour. The star image may "negotiate, reconcile, or mask" these contradictions "or else simply hold them in tension" (64). Dyer's methodology traces the social and cultural codings of the star's body, film texts, images, and media discourses and analyzes the slippages and disruptions of the social meanings, providing rich examples of the significance of stardom as registers of social conflict and change. Dyer's explanation of why stars matter is particularly relevant in the case of DeGeneres because of her everyday presence on daytime television as a friendly, accessible comedian, famous for her niceness with celebrities and fans alike. Stars "enact ways of making sense of the experience of being a person in a particular kind of social production," Dyer says. Stars are "embodiments of the social categories in which people are placed and through which they have to make sense of their lives" (*Heavenly Bodies*, 15, 16.). J. C. Penney tapped DeGeneres as a celebrity with whom women shoppers could identify as being in the same social category—the everywoman consumer trying to make sense of retail practices. Remarkably, even while representing J. C. Penney, DeGeneres never hid or effaced the social category of butch lesbian prioritized by One Million Moms as the only important one. For Dyer, this type of contradiction is one of the major tensions constituting stardom.

Yet while semiotics has amply described the importance of contradiction in the star image, what it doesn't account for are the elements of affect and desire that mobilize these meanings, frequently across or in spite of social categories. Affect and desire have instead been central to reception studies such as Jackie Stacey's interviews with women spectators and fans and their intensive investment in particular stars. For Stacey, their emotional investments are explained in psychoanalytic terms of identification, fantasy, and pleasure; she documents the reactions as "devotion" (138), "adoration" (138–142), and "losing oneself" in the star (145). That is, reception theory posits that stars create forceful feelings and trigger emotional responses. So for semiotics and reception studies, the star's body points to "something else," a move that distinguishes between the star body and what it signifies or prompts as responses.

Rather than discussing DeGeneres's body as a code or sign of something else, I would like to conclude by considering what her body does and how it works in process among various social registers at the same time. Susan Bordo's concept of how bodies speak, how they make an impact that is visceral, emotional, affective, is particularly relevant to the female stand-up comic, who offers her body for scrutiny in a visual dynamic that is traditionally male. Certainly in a predominantly white culture, the raced bodies of comics such as Margaret Cho and Wanda Sykes have an immediate impact in their difference, but DeGeneres's body attests to the plurality of sexualities among women, a less culturally obvious difference than race. The difference is physical, thus the "unnatural" effect that occurs when she wears feminine clothes, and cultural, an embodiment of historical meanings of the butch lesbian. This is a body that provokes specific currents of desire and anxiety, an anxiety immediately dismissed by her self-deprecating comedy and her persona of niceness, that is, the willingness to accommodate and make others feel comfortable despite the explicit queerness of the persona. As a talk-show host and previously as a closeted and then open lesbian on her sitcoms, DeGeneres acts as a relay point for multiple, often contradictory social desires evoked by her meanings as clown, celebrity, outsider, butch, blond, CoverGirl model, and groom to a femme bride.

STARDOM, BODIES OF COMEDY, AND DELEUZE

In framing the materiality of Ellen DeGeneres's comic persona and stardom, I am drawing on the thought of Gilles Deleuze and specifically on the Deleuzian approach to the body, which has had a growing impact on cultural and media studies since the 1990s.[7] A developed Deleuzian approach to women's comedy is outside the scope of this book, but I want to suggest that further studies of comedy and comedians could well benefit from Deleuzian thought, which has been deployed by scholars to focus on stardom as a process and ongoing event rather than a set of texts or codes. I offer the following discussion as a way to rethink not just the contradictions of DeGeneres's popular status but the larger contradictions of the pretty/funny binary that has structured pop culture's ideas about women and comedy as well as female comedians' responses and resistances to it. Deleuzian thought offers a way to consider the comedian's body, physical performance, and verbal jokes not as separate registers but as a force with multiple effects.

Scholars who have used Deleuze to discuss stardom are interested, like Dyer and Stacey, in the multiple registers of the star's impact on fans and spectators. But rather than understanding stardom in terms of what the star represents or means, a Deleuzian approach emphasizes stardom as an interactive, ongoing experience in which the desires of audiences create new energies in the encounters with the star's body and performance. Kathy Griffin's D-list stand-up comedy is a good example of a performance and fan interaction that has created a new kind of energy, exemplified in her campy dismissal of straight men in the audience. Fey's Liz Lemon and the stand-up personas of Sykes, Cho, and Silverman became popular because they generated a force, not simply a fan base or even a discourse so much as a rallying of desire. The desire is for identification, recognition of frustrations, confirmation about tastes or suspicions, celebration of the triumph of wit and comedy over marginalization or contempt for less-than-ideal bodies. People buy tickets to see a particular comedian not simply because they desire to laugh; they desire something the comedians make them feel and respond to. Margaret Cho's fans clearly desire her moments of manifesto and defiance; Silverman's fans desire her edginess, her ability to transgress the boundaries of taste and decency. Tina Fey's female fans so strongly desired a smart, funny, feminist voice on television that some were furious that Fey isn't feminist enough in their eyes. Obviously, any pop-culture success depends on the ability to fire up, create, and sustain desire.

Deleuze sees desire not as a response to lack, as Oedipal theories do, but as a force that makes things happen. In Deleuze's groundbreaking work with Felix Guattari, desire is reconceived as the basis of the life force and its flow: "Desire constantly couples continuous flows. . . . Desire causes the current to flow, itself flows in turn, and breaks the flows" (*Anti-Oedipus*, 5). Throughout this book I have been describing performances in which things happen by virtue of a comic and charismatic performance; concepts of the dominant and the marginal shift and take another shape, such as when the D list becomes more interesting than the A list; perspectives get re-focused, as when white audiences experience what white people looking feels like; assumptions like Hollywood success and the ideal of pretty are challenged. These shifts occur because desire is mobilized and the very pro-cess of laughter shakes viewers, listeners, readers out of complacency and passivity about what passes for the norm.

The body, too, is an ongoing process of becoming, shaped by desires, an interplay or relay point of forces, evident in audience responses to success-ful stand-up performances. More dramatically, the body can be conceived as a process of connections to other bodies and other processes as well as to multiple affects, as discussed by feminist scholars following Deleuze's thought.[8] The celebrity body of DeGeneres is an especially apt example of this process because of its multiple commodifications, political meanings, and appropriations, not all of which are favorable, given that she will always be a dangerous entity to the One Million Moms promoting a "moral so-ciety."[9] Cinema scholar Elena del Rio begins with a concept of the body "as a site of anarchic creativity" to analyze film performances for their "bodily and affective immediacy" (11). From the perspective of Deleuzian thought, the star body onscreen is not a representation but rather a force that sets other forces into motion; it is a relay point of multiple streams of desires—sexual, political, racial, cultural.

Del Rio suggests this dynamic way to think of the interaction between the spectator and the star as a model of spectatorship that foregrounds the immediate, intense, affective engagement of the spectator with the performer. Successful stand-up comedy, a performance in which interplay with the audience snaps with connection and response, is a prime example of such engagement. Writing of stardom through this lens, Susan Hayward argues that spectators encounter "the star body as material force, as vibration, resonance, and movement" in a meeting of "two distinct bodies," those of the spectator and the star (52). Their encounter is a linking up or becoming of something new, a connection that carries its own force. The star body is not a text that carries traces of meanings but is rather a dynamic element experienced "as a series of intensities, rhythms, and flows" that will differ in each encounter: "Each time we view the star body neither our presence nor the star body's is the same" (53). Deleuzian cinema scholars are particularly interested in how this framework "restores to the body the dimension of intensity lost in the representational paradigm," as del Rio puts it (3). That is, thinking of Ellen DeGeneres only as an image or a representation of a butch lesbian misses her meanings as an active, in-process entity stimulating new responses and interacting with new events and other stars.

The dynamic nature of encounters with stars and celebrities is grounded in the nomadic or unfixed nature of all subjectivity, in Deleuzian terms. Because this slippery, unstable subjectivity is dangerous in its creative potential, a tendency arises to "territorialize" the incessant flows of experience into categories and systems, shutting down connections that are inconvenient, puzzling, or uncomfortable. At its worst, Klaus Theweleit has persuasively demonstrated, a conservative politics works toward the damming and channeling of the flux, flow, streams, and messiness of life forces, directing them into the controllable boundaries exemplified by fascism. If DeGeneres is truly not funny to One Million Moms, it is because the dynamic of conservative politics works hard to channel all entertainment into moral versus immoral classifications. Indeed, pop culture is especially dangerous to right-wing ideologies because of the subversive potential of any performance or performer with intense emotional appeal that opens up channels of desire, welcoming contradiction and incoherency, as seen in the phenomenon of Lady Gaga. DeGeneres, with her firm footing in the middlebrow world of J. C. Penney and CoverGirl, is certainly not as unpredictable and wild as Gaga, but DeGeneres's predictable wholesomeness and upbeat nature are indeed disturbing elements for a conservative audience that would prefer to make butch lesbianism invisible or at least abjected. DeGeneres instead makes lesbianism itself incoherent for such a worldview.

This is a very different perspective on the question of why stardom addresses contradiction; stars and celebrities demonstrate, in a life writ large by extensive media coverage, the disparate, multiple ways social categories are experienced. A Deleuzian perspective encompasses social, physical, narrative, cultural, and biological forces operating simultaneously through the body. Comic celebrity DeGeneres can be seen not as an identity or even a bundle of conflicting or contradictory identities but as a site of becoming; the dancing, clowning, performing Ellen DeGeneres animates multiple narratives and images, from slapstick comedian and animal lover to queer icon and media scion. From a Deleuzian view DeGeneres may be embedded in simultaneous and contradictory power relations such that she simultaneously resists and complies with the status quo. In Deleuzian terms she "deterritorializes" desires, freeing them from their conventional contexts; a butch DeGeneres as middle America's talk-show host is a good example. However, her image is available for far more conservative ends, as some of the girl-next-door discourse around her stardom demonstrates. Deleuzian thought provides a way to talk about how the star body is in play among many desires and social narratives, in this case the varying legibility of DeGeneres's sexuality, the various degrees to which she has been read as queer or lesbian before and after her coming out. And finally, it provides a framework to describe the in-process nature of DeGeneres's persona, epitomized by her trademark dancing but also by her verbal comedy of skirting as well as by her physical slapstick and clowning.

In addition, a Deleuzian framework encompasses the niceness of DeGeneres's public image not as a diminishment or disavowal of her butch appearance but rather as a powerful force that has impact through her butch-style body. Standard scholarship on stardom would argue that the contradictions of DeGeneres's persona—perky girl next door and lesbian with a gorgeous wife—are reconciled or negotiated by her trademark niceness, implying that something has been traded off or exchanged. A similar binary perspective is demonstrated in Bociurkiw's argument that on her talk show DeGeneres "speaks in a double voice," her lesbian identity so deeply coded that she has effectively "gone back into the closet." Yet Bociurkiw admits that perhaps "codedness produces better queer TV" (180). In fact, queerness is based on a refusal of stable or monolithic identity, a concept essential to Deleuzian thought. The appeal of DeGeneres's talk show is precisely not a double voice that bifurcates her celebrity into two opposing elements but rather DeGeneres's comic, queer, ongoing play with multiple voices, tones, and interpellations by various audiences.

Feminist scholar Rosi Braidotti has been prominent in proposing a Deleuzian feminism of "metamorphosis" that celebrates the in-process body as the basis of social change. For Braidotti, popular culture is a key site in picturing and circulating the in-process body. She is particularly interested in stardom and celebrity. Certain celebrity bodies, she argues—Princess Diana, Michael Jackson, Dolly Parton, Elizabeth Taylor—compel attention with their mutability, their fusion of nature and artifice, and their contradictory meanings; they fascinate because they serve as a "crossroads" of intensities concerning race, sexuality, wealth, excess, grotesquery.[10] Some star bodies like these are far more subversive than others in exemplifying nomadic subjectivity, located in many or changing sites, unattached to single, fixed identities. Braidotti's work on celebrity bodies intriguingly overlaps theories of the grotesque and carnivalesque I used in the chapters on Silverman and Griffin in this book. For instance, Braidotti speaks of Princess Diana's conventionally beautiful body as being nevertheless "a leaky body, a less-than-perfect image," given her associations with bulimia and AIDS patients that disrupted her iconicity as fashion model and superstar. Her body and subjectivity continue to be an "event" that "simultaneously inhabits and challenges or disrupts the many facets of her social identity as princess/mother/wife/celebrity/sexualized female flesh/bulimic/desiring subject/single woman/philanthropist and so on" (108). Braidotti argues for the importance of Diana's celebrity in its disruptive energy and contradictory meanings. Her image has been appropriated as "hyper-inflated femininity" but also as abjected, "thus causing great turmoil in the register of representation" (109). For Braidotti, the disruption is the main point; Diana's meanings resist being fixed, so as a dynamic, contested site of meaning, her celebrity undermines dominant power relations. Diana can be claimed and remembered as a white, wholly commodified fashion icon, but not entirely; what cannot be unremembered is her embrace of abjection, literally, in her embraces of AIDS patients, lepers, and drug addicts but also in her acknowledgment of her own bulimia.

Ellen DeGeneres is a parallel case in that no matter how bourgeois and consumable some of her images may be, such as clowning with Justin Bieber on her talk show, it is impossible to unremember more transgressive images, such as posing with her bride on the cover of *People* magazine. One can think of DeGeneres's celebrity body as leaky, like that of Princess Diana's, far messier and less organized than a model of star elements that are negotiated or in tension. Leakiness is a function of the disruptiveness and disorder of comedy, its basic thrust of anti-authoritarianism, as

Northrup Frye has described it; comedy aims at the overthrow of hierarchy. Bakhtin's concept of the carnivalesque provides the example of the comic body that celebrates messiness, as opposed to the classic, ideal body that maintains itself in the neat, rigid boundaries and symmetrical forms of the beauty, the athlete, the fashion model. Shifting into Deleuzian thought, the classic body has dammed up its flows and limited its meanings, while the leaky body of the comic is open to creative possibility. The comic body resists territorialization, making its meanings more interesting and dangerous because they incline toward disorder and disruption. CoverGirl-model Ellen in *Ladies Home Journal* is the flip side of drag-queen Ellen femmed up for a joke lunch with the women from *The Real Housewives*.

A Deleuzian slant to the messy, disorderly, comic body offers a way around the binary thinking that has characterized scholarship on comedy in which it is often laid out as a linear movement toward or away from subversion. In the traditional way of thinking, comedy is a discrete wild zone outside of law and authority. The stand-up performance is a special event audiences attend or view, but part of its pleasure is its escape from the order and hierarchies of real life. Thus scholars have debated the political impact of the Medieval carnival described by Bakhtin, speculating whether the comic high-low reversals can be read as mechanisms that allowed the powerful to remain powerful by venting resistance through a liminal event that had no lasting consequences. Another reason to doubt the political power of comedy is that while the comic body is subversive, it is also disposable and marginalized; the bodies of the clown, the loser, and the schlep are inherently less valued in hierarchical social norms. And comic narratives, the sitcom or the comedy film, usually end with order restored, the madcap comedian's chaos staved off once again.

For Deleuze, however, the boundaries of performance are not entirely discrete, nor can the generated energy of performances completely dissipate. From this perspective the carnivalesque aesthetic becomes a powerful precursor of the Renaissance rejection of hierarchy. The disruptions and anti-authoritarianism of comedy, moreover, allow the narrative forms themselves to refuse closure. Comedians discussed in this book have transformed or undermined the sitcom formula, for instance, by reimagining its scope (*Wanda at Large*), parodying the formula (*The Sarah Silverman Program*), or turning the authority of the medium itself into comic material (*30 Rock*). Comic disorder is not wholly resolved in these sitcoms but is rather the point of the series; there is no linear return to the status quo. In Deleuzian terms these sitcoms open possibilities and streams of creativity rather than damming them up into predictable units of meaning.

The comic bodies of these performers likewise generate palpable energy and presence that defy categories and stereotypes and, by virtue of their mainstream stardom, likewise defy dismissal. Throughout this book I have emphasized the ways women comedians have challenged, satirized, and often savaged the pretty versus funny dynamic that has dominated traditional comedy. They have culled out what is funny about prettiness and have colonized funny as a place where the stories are more interesting than the place where only pretty bodies have a story, the story of romantic comedy. The comic body—unpredictable, leaky—is particularly apt at keeping the meanings of prettiness up for grabs and not necessarily at the disposal of conventional stories, as seen in corporate CoverGirl model Ellen DeGeneres, who cannot stop being a queer icon. Comedy itself defies dismissal because of the bonding power of laughter, which in Deleuzian terms is a force, both physical and psychological, that can make things happen for better or for worse—the racist and homophobic comedy that shores up hatred but also the queer and feminist comedy that opens up the flow of the possible.

Notes

1. Queer theory in its broadest terms rejects both sex and gender categories, pointing away from an identity politics and toward the continual undoing of normative identities, including that of gays and lesbians. Although queer theory critiques the gender-based identifications of feminism, Third Wave feminists like Margaret Cho push toward a diversity politics that celebrates both queer deconstruction of identity and more traditional sex and gender identifications. For an early articulation of queer theory, see Michael Warner. Judith Butler's "Against Proper Objects" and her interview with Rosi Braidotti, "Feminism by Any Other Name," stake out the intersections of feminism and queer theory.

2. For the tenets of Third Wave feminism, see Baumgardner and Richards as well as Rebecca Walker's influential 1992 article in *Ms.*

3. See, for example, Showden's essay, which analyzes the political effectiveness of the various feminisms associated with the Third Wave as well as the relationship between Third Wave feminism and postfeminism. For an extended overview and analysis of feminisms since the 1990s, see Coleman. Also see Harris for discussion of the ways these feminisms shape discourses among young women who do not call themselves feminists.

4. The most theoretically developed argument is that of Rowe, who draws on feminist revisions of Bakhtin as well as the work of Natalie Zemon Davis (1–49). Also see Mellencamp's use of Freud to theorize the subversive comedy of Lucille Ball and Gracie Allen in the 1950s. Other arguments about the feminist potential of women's comedy include Gray, 19–37; Barreca, *They Used to Call Me Snow White*, 171–192; and Banks and Swift. Also see Fraiberg's argument that focuses on women's stand-up comedy and Gillooly's review essay. The exception to this argument about feminist comedy is Joanne Gilbert, who argues that women's comedy can be subversive but not feminist because humor is about hierarchy—someone laughing at someone else—but also because feminism is about social change,

and "the very nature of humor is antithetical to action" (172). Reed's reply to this points out the heteronormative basis of Gilbert's argument (that feminism is about women versus men) and that comedy can be a community experience that in fact has social effects ("Sexual Outlaws," 764–765).

5. Mulvey's groundbreaking essay "Visual Pleasure and Narrative Cinema" introduced the concept of "the male gaze" as structured into the very apparatus of cinema, but the phrase has been widely used outside of apparatus theory to describe norms in visual culture. Mulvey describes the "to-be-looked-at-ness" of women in cinema as part of the wider binary in which men are positioned in narrative as controlling agents while women are positioned as passive objects of male desire. Her Lacanian analysis comes to a similar conclusion as Berger's social analysis, which he sums up as "*men act* and *women appear*" (47).

6. The woman "comes to consider the surveyor and the surveyed within her as the two constituent yet always distinct elements of her identity as a woman," writes Berger. ". . . [H]ow she appears to others, and ultimately how she appears to men, is of crucial importance for what is normally thought of as the success of her life" (46).

7. Limon's framework is Lacanian, but he situates his analyses in specific cultural histories such as the predominance of Jewish stand-up comics in the 1960s, positioned as outsiders to the rapidly developing suburban ideals. Limon claims that the body itself is the abject in comedy, the material grossness that wrongly defines and limits us as humans. The social implications are that "the black body, the homosexual body, and the female body . . . signify the body itself" (7) and thus are key to stand-up comedy. Limon published his study in 2000, just before the ascendancy of women stand-up comics, so he saw in the 1990s work of Paula Poundstone and Ellen DeGeneres a negation of the body itself—"the evacuation of the star's body at the moment it is evoked" (108)—rather than the assertion of the queer, dancing body that later defined DeGeneres's daytime talk-show persona.

8. Reed, in her essay on Lily Tomlin, Margaret Cho, and Paula Poundstone, notes that in the past thirty years "a relatively large proportion of women comedians in U.S. mainstream comedy . . . work outside of the terms of heteronormativity in a variety of ways" ("Sexual Outlaws," 762).

9. Fischer, in her 1991 essay "Sometimes I Feel Like a Motherless Child: Comedy and Matricide," was among the earliest to analyze the position of women in mainstream comedy through feminist theory; her observations about the absences of women in Hollywood comedy and the hostility toward female bodies, particularly maternal bodies, in comedy films remain sadly relevant.

10. For extended histories of women comics in the twentieth century, see Gray, 41–185; Nancy Walker; Sochen; Martin and Segrave; Banks and Swift; and Joanne Gilbert's summaries of women in stand-up, 73–128. Also see Kohen's oral history that covers American women comics since the 1950s.

1. The Ulmer Scale calibrates the bankability of film stars as their ability to draw audiences for a film based on their stardom. Gareth Palmer emphasizes the murky status of D-listers who attain public attention on television shows such as *Big Brother* or *Survivor* but fail to comprehend their actual place in the "celebrity pecking order" (38) and "their true economic value in the system" (40). As a result, their short-lived star careers inevitably barrel them toward inappropriate behavior, embarrassment, humiliating treatment by the media, and scorn. Palmer calls these would-be celebrities "the undead" because they blunder forward, not understanding they no longer have a viable "life" but instead occupy the "space between the unknown mass of ordinary people and the celebrity," which Palmer claims as the definition of the D list (41). Palmer emphasizes the D list's liminality and transgression, key elements in Griffin's comedic appropriation of this slippery site.

2. For Kristeva, the disavowal of abjection is a key to the becoming of the subject. John Limon draws on this concept in his study of stand-up comedy as "a psychic worrying of those aspects of oneself that one cannot be rid of, that seem, but are not quite, alienable—for example, blood, urine, feces, nails, and the corpse" (4). This concept of abjection as the dangerous, threatening space-where-I-am-not is relevant to the D list as the necessary grounds of the A list in Griffin's comedy.

3. In the episode "Kathy's Smear Campaign" in season 6, after Griffin was far more established in her stardom, her Madison Square Garden tickets sell out only after Griffin and her entourage mount a publicity blitz in New York just prior to the shows, and even then she's unable to sell the 600 copies of her book that had been ordered at a local Barnes and Noble. She and her staff take to the sidewalk with stacks of books in their hands, calling out for customers like hot-dog vendors.

4. On the one hand, Negra and Holmes argue, successful women celebrities are poised in a "waiting game" for the moment their precarious balance of stardom and personal relationships will collapse. On the other hand, "celebrities who are famous for 'nothing'" are almost always female as well. In both cases sexual excess is the guarantor of continued media coverage.

5. In a 2006 interview Griffin admitted that she was slowly "bringing the lesbians around. Tougher customers, lesbians" (in S. Smith, 70). Lesbians are not excluded from Griffin's comedy or from *My Life on the D List*, which documents how her friend Rosie O'Donnell recruits Griffin to perform on a lesbian cruise. However, Griffin's nervousness about lesbians is evident in the *D List* episode "Kathy with a Z," which documents her guest appearance as a lesbian activist on *Law and Order: Special Victims Unit* (1999–). The scene that made her most nervous, she says, is one in which she kisses Mariska Hargatay, a scene later cut. In contrast, she camps up her kissing scene with Hargatay's male co-star, Chris Meloni. In a remarkable queer performance for her *D List* audience, Griffin plays the Meloni kiss for comedy, calling out to gay men that she's kissing "the dreamy, the sexy, triple X Chris Meloni."

6. Douglas Crimp and Michael Warner, commenting on Madonna's usage of

gay men in *Sex*, remark that Madonna's celebrity is profoundly heterosexual no matter how she may appropriate gay imagery: "She can be as queer as she wants to, but only because we know she's not" (95).

7. Jenkins's analyses of film comedy of the late 1920s and early 1930s makes a persuasive case for popular comedy as a register of cultural changes in entertainment media, vaudeville to cinema, and in social and economic relations. Contentions about new kinds of comedy, he argues, were pressure points for much wider and more serious contentions about "industrialization, urbanization, immigration, unionization, women's suffrage, and generational conflicts" (41).

8. Turner is interested in the special occasions that express creativity and potential in opposition to the more rigid social structures where power resides. He calls this creative and moral force "communitas." While usages of Turner by cultural scholars are often critiqued as the "universalizing" of specific African cultural descriptions, Turner himself extends these descriptions of "subjunctive" activities to the work of artists and philosophers (128) as well as to "hippies" and "teeny-boppers" of the 1960s (112–113), claiming that liminality and communitas "are to be found at all stages and levels of culture and society" (113).

9. Roof finds that the comic female second works out cultural threats of the independent woman by making light of her dangerous status, even though this character suggests "a broader vision of what women can do and how they can do it" (16).

10. By continuing this dynamic in her reality show Griffin diverged from the route taken by other television sidekicks who go on to their own shows as stars. Long before *My Life on the D List*, Roof noted that in spin-offs, "a secondary type cannot be a star unless the show exploits the secondary qualities for their own sake" (167).

11. In her analysis of popular postfeminism, see Negra's discussion of fertility represented as the "ticking clock" crisis as well as "celebrity momism," righteous motherhood, and the glorification of pregnancy (50–70).

12. This is a different kind of failure as a woman than the Lucille Ball tradition cited by Osborne-Thompson and different from *Fat Actress* (2005) and *The Comeback* (2005), the other reality shows she discusses. For while Griffin fails with the mainstream audience at a couples' resort or corporate convention, she very much connects with the alternative audience that has sought her out, gets her humor, and responds enthusiastically.

13. Scholars have asserted that within the African American community, gay male identity is complicated by specific cultural anxieties about manhood and masculinity as well as by strong religious pressures (Brown, 30–32). Also see my discussion of this issue in the chapter on Wanda Sykes.

14. Leo Bersani identifies "the femininity glamorized by movie stars" as the prime target of camp parody for gay men who expose that version of "femininity as mindless, asexual, and hysterically bitchy." Bersani claims this representation should produce "a violently antimimetic reaction in any female spectator" and could help "deconstruct that image for women themselves" (208).

15. Ernesto Javier Martínez uses Robertson and Muñoz in a similar way to discuss Margaret Cho's camp comedy in her alliance with gay men (139–141).

16. Fabio Cleto contends that even such a "non-dogmatic" definition glosses over the most salient debates about camp as a politics, aesthetic, interpretive grid, or pop-culture fashion (4–5). For an overview of these debates, see Cleto, 1–36, and Cohan, 1–19. For the argument that camp is a specifically gay male aesthetic and politics, see Medhurst, 291. Also see Moe Meyer, who argues that camp is a primary characteristic of male homosexual identity traceable to Oscar Wilde's "transgressive reinscription of bourgeois masculinity" (105).

17. See Cleto, 356–359; Richardson, 164–165; Robertson, 11–13.

CHAPTER TWO

1. For a time, Fey's mimicry and funny lines were actually incorporated into the rhetoric and primary discourses of the presidential campaign. "In October [2008], it seemed that Tina Fey *was* the campaign, with journalists writing that she had 'swift-butted' Palin and derailed her future," wrote Washington insider Maureen Dowd in *Vanity Fair*. The reference is to the "Swift-boating" of presidential candidate John Kerry in the 2004 election, when a rumor about his service in Vietnam overwhelmed the campaign. It would be difficult to argue that Fey's comedy had the same damaging effect, given the urgency of the economic issues during the weeks before the election, and certainly there was no derailing of Palin's future in politics. But the Palin routines turned Fey's career "from red- to white-hot," Dowd wrote, and for a time boosted the ratings for *30 Rock*.

2. See Masugi. Palin's comments about Russia were made in an interview with ABC's Charles Gibson on September 11, 2008: "They're our next-door neighbors and you can actually see Russia from land here in Alaska, from an island in Alaska" (Palin).

3. News commentators noticed that Fey's shout-out may have had an immediate effect on Clinton's campaign, which began to be more aggressive in ads against Obama. In an interview a few weeks later Fey claimed that she didn't want to make "an endorsement" so much as protest the sexism that had hounded Clinton's campaign with jokes and slights on her looks and her age. "I just thought, 'Oh, that's gonna be me—someday people are gonna be like, 'Get out of here, we want some young male comedian instead!'" (in J. Armstrong, "No. 2," 36). Fey's satirical fictionalization of this fear showed up in the pilot episode of *30 Rock* two years previously when the older, female comic performer Jenna is displaced by the hipper black comic Tracy Jordan (Tracy Morgan).

4. Hilary Radner makes the argument that feminism needs to deal with femininity not as a "pathology" but as "one dimension in the play of gender and identity" in order to address the distrust of feminism and the proliferation of neoliberal ideas about gender (197).

5. In an interview Fey cited *The Mary Tyler Moore Show* as an important break-

through because the plots didn't focus on dating or Mary Richards's problems with men but instead "were about work friendships and relationships, which is what I feel my adult life has mostly been about" (in S. Armstrong).

6. The theme song of *The Mary Tyler Moore Show* begins, "Who can turn the world on with her smile?" The lyrics to the 30 *Rock* parody likewise pose a coy question: "Who's that kickin' it down the street / Causing a stir / Who's that, I know that you're wondering / That's her, that's her, that's her."

7. MTM Enterprises was the independent television production company responsible for *The Mary Tyler Moore Show* and critically acclaimed series such as *Hill Street Blues* (1981–1987) and *The Lou Grant Show* (1977–1982), garnering its reputation for quality television; see Feuer, Kerr, and Vahimagi.

8. See McEwan, Doyle, Dailey, and *Around the Sphere*.

9. Projansky describes several categories of postfeminist discourses producing these signifiers (*Watching Rape*, 66–89). Also see Negra's summary of the postfeminist imagery and narratives widely circulated in popular culture (2–7). For an overview of the major tenets of feminist critique of postfeminism, see Tasker and Negra, "Introduction." A different interpretation of postfeminism is offered by Radner, who argues that postfeminism is neither a rejection nor a reaction to feminism but rather a philosophy of consumerism, femininity, and independence that can be traced to Helen Gurley Brown's "Cosmo Girl" (2–25).

10. This use of a fictional character, Projansky notes, signals the importance of the media in the construction of postfeminism as well as the way feminism and postfeminism were represented and often continue to be represented as the story of white, middle-class, heterosexual women (*Watching Rape*, 68–70).

11. The widespread circulation of the baby-panic discourse explains the impact of Sylvia Ann Hewlett's 2002 book, *Creating a Life: Professional Women and the Quest for Children*, which engendered a blitz of media attention with its claim that women's chances of marriage and having families declined significantly with their success in the workplace. *Time* and *New York Magazine* featured Hewlett's book and "Baby Panic" on their covers, and Maureen Dowd made it the topic of two columns in the *New York Times*. See Franke-Ruta on the context and reception of Hewlett's book. Fey wrote and performed an *SNL* skit about the baby panic the book incited—"I can hear my ovaries curling up!"—and 30 *Rock* continued the satire with Liz's disastrous attempts at having or adopting a baby.

12. Kathleen Rowe Karlyn analyzes this mother-daughter metaphor in feminism and postfeminism as a continuation of her work on the unruly woman figure in popular culture; see *Unruly Girls*, 9–12, 17–20, and 28–35.

13. For a fuller discussion of "Rosemary's Baby," see my essay "Feminism, Postfeminism," paragraphs 15–25.

1. See Cuomo's discussion of the lesbian as outlaw as well as Munt, 95–131. Munt emphasizes the two poles of outlaw identity: a superior, heroic sense of self but also a shamed, abjected self, constituting the insider/outsider status of the lesbian subject in heteronormative culture.

2. The point of grotesque realism, says Bakhtin, is "degradation, that is, the lowering of all that is high, spiritual, ideal, abstract" (19). Bakhtin's larger argument is that the acknowledgment of the lower stratum of the body was an important turning point against the Medieval hierarchy that situated God and the Church as the upper cosmos and the human body as the lower cosmos. For the new Renaissance thinker who rejected this hierarchy, "the higher and lower stratum became relative" (363), making it possible to situate the human body as "the historic, progressing body of mankind" (367).

3. One of Bakhtin's most intriguing examples is the carnivalesque depiction of "old hags" who give birth and "combine a senile, decaying and deformed flesh with the flesh of new life," an image of contradiction he calls "precisely the grotesque concept of the body" (25–26). Russo notes that Bakhtin makes this claim without comment on the "connotations of fear and loathing around the biological process of reproduction and of aging," an oversight due to his failure to "acknowledge or incorporate the social relations of gender in his semiotic model" (63).

4. In this tradition, Bakhtin says, "woman is essentially related to the material bodily lower stratum; she is the incarnation of this stratum that degrades and regenerates simultaneously." He qualifies this by arguing that this dynamic "is in no way hostile to woman and does not approach her negatively. . . . She is ambivalent" (240). Bakhtin argues that this comic tradition is neither "hostile" nor "negative" toward women because it celebrates and privileges the reviled lower stratum as a rich, life-affirming opposition to authority and the status quo. However, his characterization of the female body as "ambivalent" glosses over the long-standing philosophical disdain toward women precisely because they "incarnate" the lower body stratum. Pinpointing Bakhtin's claim that women are the very incarnation of the lower-body mix of the repugnant and the generative, Rowe notes the echo of "the most enduring and misogynist of philosophical traditions," identifying women as material—the lower body—and men as spirit and soul—the upper body (34).

5. This episode lampoons little-girl beauty pageants that are considered appropriate in some strands of popular culture, as seen in the controversial reality-television series *Toddlers and Tiaras* (2009–). A Kathy Griffin *D List* episode satirized this phenomenon as well ("Toddlers and Re-modelers"). Child beauty pageants came to national attention with the 1996 murder of six-year-old JonBenet Ramsey, who had been a frequent contestant in such contests. Photographs of the child in glamourous clothing and makeup prompted criticism of the sexualization of children in these pageants.

6. *Not Without My Daughter* was a 1991 film about an American woman es-

caping with her daughter from her husband in Iran, giving a political twist to the subgenre of the mother-daughter melodrama.

7. In musicals, pausing the narrative for a song marks a privileged moment in several ways. The song delivers emotional intensity, signals key information or a turning point, sets a mood, and reinforces the status of the text as entertainment—that is, as fictional and fabricated. Postmodern pop culture, always self-conscious of itself as fictive, has brought the musical back into popularity after a late-twentieth-century decline, as seen in *High School Musical* (2006), which appeared just as *The Sarah Silverman Program* was being planned and written, and later in the hit television show *Glee* (2009–). For the status and functions of songs in musicals, see Rick Altman, 65–67, as well as Richard Dyer's widely cited essay "Entertainment and Utopia" in *Only Entertainment*, 17–34.

8. See Davies for a summary of these theories and Limon for the development of the theory of abjection. Also see Billig's discussion and dispute of Davies's conclusions, 268–269. While Davies distinguishes between serious anti-Semitism and the "playfulness" of jokes, Billig calls attention to the danger of dismissing self-deprecating humor as "just a joke."

9. The case for the effeminacy of the Jewish male body and for the bracketing of Jews and women as morally and physically inferior was made in Otto Weininger's influential 1903 book *Sex and Character*, the treatise that influenced German theories of Aryanism. See Gilman's discussion of Weininger, 133–137.

10. In the "Hot Voodoo" musical number set in a nightclub, Dietrich in a gorilla suit follows black-skinned "African" showgirls onstage and slowly stripteases from the animal costume down to her own showgirl clothes, adding a large, blond wig. For the genealogy of this image in relationship to European theories of race, see Petro, 136–156.

11. Gilman emphasizes how the "darkness" of the Jew's skin color was conflated with filth, which was ascribed to the Jew's unsanitary living conditions, and with congenital diseases (99–100, 171–174). The iconography of the Jew as ape in nineteenth-century Europe has been documented by Marc A. Weiner's study of the traditions informing Richard Wagner's anti-Semitism. See especially his chapter "Smells," 195–259. In American popular culture the best-known usage of the ape as anti-Semitic image may be in the musical number "If You Could See Her" in the Broadway play *Cabaret*. Set in Berlin during the rise of the Third Reich, *Cabaret* darkly lampoons the seductiveness of fascism and the insidious nature of bigotry. In "If You Could See Her," the emcee dances with and sings to someone in a gorilla costume who wears a dress and feminine accessories. The punch line of the song is "If you could see her as I do, she doesn't look Jewish at all."

12. Stormfront.org, with its emblem "White Pride World Wide," posts an unflattering photo of Silverman as "the most obnoxious jew of all, Sarah Silverfish," and her photos can be found on sites like *First Light*, where she's described as foremost in a long line of Jewish comics who are part of the "evil, antichristian global takeover agenda."

13. John Limon contends that by 1960, stand-up comedy in the United States

was primarily performed by and identified with Jewish men whose influence—the performance of abjection and abject bodies—extends into late-night television comedy and the women comics who emerged at the end of the twentieth century. Also see James D. Bloom on the influence of Jewish comedy in even more pervasive forms, from popular music to fiction. For a history of African American humor and its growing influence in American culture, see Watkins.

14. During the first half of 2010 the tea party movement was accused of racism by the NAACP, precipitating the movement's distancing of itself from conservative bloggers and writers like Andrew Breitbart, who circulated the video clip of Sherrod in July.

CHAPTER FOUR

1. This is a reference to the popular musical *Miss Saigon*, famous for its staging of a helicopter descending to and rising from the stage in a reenactment of the U.S. forces pulling out of Vietnam in 1972. The heroine is a Vietnamese bar girl abandoned by an American soldier in a retelling of the *Madame Butterfly* narrative. The female prototype of the abandoned Asian woman fits into Cho's list of standard stereotypical roles for Asian actors.

2. Lowe argues that in the designation "Asian American" the "American" element of citizenship "has been defined over against the Asian immigrant, legally, economically, and culturally" (4). In her chapter "Immigration, Citizenship, Racialization" Lowe analyzes the immigration history that has produced and complicated notions of the Asian American and that continues to imply that this identity points to the "foreigner within" even for those born in the United States (5).

3. Lee makes a case for the strategic use of space in Cho's performances, the literal space of the stage and the spaces of family and American life in which Cho has experienced uneasiness. The experience of "intense public scrutiny" of her body, says Lee, has led Cho to "seize" public space as a primary strategy of her comedy, which literally "repositions" her body through her elaborate mimicries and physical performances (109).

4. See Cho's essay "Crush Crash," in *Feminisms and Womanisms*, ed. Althea Prince and Susan Silva Wayne (Toronto: Woman's Press, 2004), 219–221; her foreword to *Yes Means Yes! Visions of Female Sexual Power and a World without Rape*, ed. Jaclyn Friedman and Jessica Valenti (Berkeley, CA: Seal, 2008), 1–4; and her essay "Grab the Brass Ring of Equality," in *50 Ways to Support Lesbian and Gay Equality*, ed. Meredith Maran and Angela Watrous (San Francisco: Inner Ocean, 2005), 145–146.

5. Sidonie Smith and Julia Watson include both recovery narratives and consciousness-raising narratives in the category of "conversion" autobiographies.

6. Sarah Moon Cassinelli, in an analysis of ethnic representation on television, comments that the Asian American family on *All-American Girl* "became a vehicle to perpetuate a stereotypical vision of immigration, race identity, and ethnicity in

American culture" (141–142). The problem, Cassinelli finds, is evident in the title of the series itself, which seems to insist—in a politically correct way—that the native-born, second-generation daughter is as American as the clichéd and iconic girl next door. By glossing over all the racial issues of the second generation of Asian descent, the title instead "enacts a double-erasing" by eliminating both the "Asian" and the "Asian American" elements of the show and its main character (135).

7. Warhol and Michie discuss the reasoning behind the anonymity aspect of Alcoholics Anonymous as a form of protection for members as well as a way "to keep any one person from embodying the A.A. identity in the public eye" (341).

8. Speaking of her renewed energy on stage after sobriety, Cho writes that "when the crowd is right, the night is relatively young, and God is there, nobody does it better" (204). Likewise, in her early description of coming back "from the dead" after sobriety, she writes that "someone or something or Jesus rolled the rock away [from the tomb]" (11).

9. The collective protagonist of the recovery narrative does not have a discrete, stable identity. The alcoholic in AA remains in process—never recovered, always in recovery. For Warhol and Michie the in-process nature of the protagonist is linked to the radically social nature of the entire recovery process. The "'self' is a process, not an entity" because "it exists in social interaction," they write. "The acquisition and continual retelling of the story becomes the very process that constitutes the alcoholic's self" (340). The recovery story works in contradictory ways, they point out, because it enacts a new identity, one of being in recovery, but also works against individualized identity so that within the program people are known only by their first names. Indeed, individual difference, the claim that one's story is unique, is anathema: "The discourse of the master narrative not only erases difference but pathologizes it," they write (339), because it typically indicates a subject who resists identification as an alcoholic, usually through the insistence that his or her story is different and therefore that the recovery narrative is not relevant.

10. My thanks to Robyn Warhol for pointing this out to me.

11. Warhol and Michie note that twelve-step programs are radically social in nature: "The focus is a communal one, the story collective, rather than individualized," and the self is constituted as "resembling and relating to others" (334). The point of recovery is to find the resemblance with others so that individual traits matter less than the commonality of addiction. Thus the book version of *I'm the One That I Want* concludes with a generalization about self-acceptance, while the film concludes with an aggressive demand to be heard as a very specific voice: "I'm gonna succeed as myself . . . Korean American, fag hag, shit starter, girl comic, trash talker." The tone is one of triumph rather than of the gratitude or humility that usually characterizes recovery stories, as in Cho's generous comments in the book about the remarkable people who taught her the power of love.

12. Bacalzo observes that the film showcases Cho's ability to take charge of her own story through "her theatrical presence, creating a direct relationship between her live performing body and the audience." As a comic she controls the audience's

laughter through her timing and pauses, "repeating bits and phrases that she knows will garner an enthusiastic response" (48).

13. Commenting on this routine, Lee emphasizes how Cho exposes white pleasure in the "reification of the live Asian body," so that "Cho's performance troubles whiteness by dramatizing the ill effects" of this "gimmick (118–119).

14. Cho's impersonations of her mother have prompted several critical commentaries. See Cassinelli's argument about "imposture" versus "impersonation," 137–138, as well as Brian Lewis's argument about Cho's impersonations of her mother's reactions to gay culture and gay pornography. Her mother's naive honesty, he says, works as a critique of the tawdry, hypersexualized images of the gay porn industry. Martínez also links the maternal impersonation to queer politics, specifically to camp comedy, emphasizing how this mimicry "functions to denaturalize the association of immigrant communities with homophobia" (157).

15. Cho makes this announcement by way of a comic fantasy about what would happen if Karl Lagerfeld, a well-known fashion designer, ended up in prison. Cho spins out an imaginary scenario of Lagerfeld as a murderer because opponents of his use of animal fur brand him that way. Lee notes that antisodomy laws would allow the incarceration of people like Lagerfeld for being gay, so when Cho says she loves "fags" she aligns herself with criminality, foreshadowing her self-description as outcast and as target of groups such as the Ku Klux Klan that persecute Asians and homosexuals (116–117, 112).

16. See Martínez's reading of this opening, which he interprets as key to Cho's use of camp and disidentification with heterosexuality, 142–151.

17. Also see Martínez's use of Muñoz in relation to Cho, 140–141.

18. *The Cho Show* was widely acknowledged as Cho's chance to remake the disastrous *All-American Girl* on her own terms. Reviews were mixed. Some reviewers were charmed by the interactions with Cho's parents and the campy scenarios. Among favorable reviews, Danny Hooley called it "the most fun reality series about a star's family since season one of MTV's *The Osbournes*," and Robert Lloyd admired its upbeat tone. Others panned it. Matthew Gilbert found it self-aggrandizing and an obvious "infomercial about the Cho brand"; the Everett, Washington, *Herald* said it duplicated Griffin's *D List*; and Mark Perigard faulted it for rehashing Cho's bitterness about *All-American Girl*.

CHAPTER FIVE

1. My thanks to Kimberly Springer for pointing out these connections.

2. In reception studies of black and ethnic humor, Cooper and Banjo come to very different conclusions about the ways comic stereotypes and culturally intimate humor are read by white audiences. Banjo, in a quantitative study published in 2011, concludes that interpretations of racial humor ultimately depend on "social identity," but she finds growing evidence of "cultural competence" among

white audiences who are able to discern that the stereotype rather than the ethnic or racial group is the butt of the humor, suggesting that "audiences may be maturing into more sophisticated and competent media consumers" (156). In contrast, Cooper, who uses qualitative methods to gauge the reception of Richard Pryor's comedy in racially mixed groups, finds a more problematic set of responses in that both black and nonblack participants tended to read Pryor's comedy "through the lens of dominant stereotypes" (244–245).

3. The discourse about Michelle Obama as an angry black woman emerged again in 2012 with the publication of the book *The Obamas* by Jodi Kantor, a former White House correspondent. The book implies that the First Lady, though careful not to make direct policy interventions or assertions, was nonetheless influential in her husband's thinking and decisions. Critics and pundits have said the book fuels the stereotype of the furious, domineering Sapphire. Analyzing the extensive discussions of the stereotype in the wake of the book's appearance, journalist Kathleen Parker reported that "65 million" links showed up when she Googled "angry black woman"; she noted that few commentators were willing to specify Ms. Obama's anger as "black," even though the racial implications of their charges were clear.

4. For a different take on Goldberg's stardom, see Mia Mask, who debates some of the criticisms most often made of Goldberg's persona and film choices, 105–140.

5. My thanks to Kimberly Springer for this insight.

6. Also see Andrew Ross's history of black hipness, originally framed in terms of black music, especially the importance of insider/outsider status regarding cultural knowledge, 82–83. Concerning the appropriations of black culture by whites, James Snead introduced the term "exclusionary emulation" to describe how "the power and trappings of black culture are initiated while at the same time their black originators are segregated away and kept at a distance" (60).

7. See Springer, "Policing," paragraphs 9–10, 13; Spillers, 86–90; Hammonds, 175–180.

8. Patricia Hill Collins uses Smith's insight to discuss the black lesbian as the "outsider within" who experiences the intersection of multiple oppressions to the point that there are no "pure" victims or perpetrators (*Black Feminist Thought*, 125–126). Sykes herself made a wry joke about her position in these multiple conflicts when she announced in late 2011 that she had a double mastectomy after a diagnosis of breast cancer. "How many things could I have?" she asked during her interview on *The Ellen Show*. "I'm black, then lesbian. I can't be the poster child for everything!" (in Finn).

9. Marlon Ross illustrates how the closet paradigm, the textual history of hidden desire before the coming out into visibility, eliminates entire populations not participating in this textual history and "progress" toward visibility and a new identity (173, 180). Likewise, the "invention of heterosexuality," rendering the binary category of the norm as opposed to the homosexual, erases the differences of the sexed black body that made it likewise "abnormal" (168). Also see Patricia Hill Collins on the issues of visibility and the black female body as deviant (*Black Feminist Thought*, 129–131).

10. In addition to her appearances on *Ellen* in the year following her outing as a married lesbian, Sykes made several appearances on *The Tonight Show with Jay Leno* and *The Late Late Show with Craig Ferguson* and appeared on *Jimmy Kimmel Live, Chelsea Lately, The Rosie Show, Piers Morgan Tonight,* and *The Mo'Nique Show.*

CHAPTER SIX

1. Anna McCarthy finds that the post-1960s development toward seriality in sitcoms, narratives developed over entire seasons, privileges heterosexuality because "seriality seems to revolve around romance plots and couples." Reflecting Freudian ideas of sexual development, "queer desire gets left behind as the genre 'matures'" (598–599).

2. See McCarthy's summary of these debates about the relative success and failure of *Ellen* in terms of queer politics as well as her own analysis of what the series suggested about the possibilities of queer discourse on network television, 594–596. Also see Candace Moore's discussion of the controversy, 21–22.

3. Jim Paratore, president of the company that would produce her talk show, said DeGeneres's Emmy performance was the turning point after her previous network failures: "Ellen came out there and made people proud. People began to step back and remember how talented she was" (in Fonseca, "New Queen").

4. DeGeneres's talk show began as a morning show and moved to the 4 p.m. Eastern time slot that was vacated when Winfrey's show went off the air in 2011. Up to that point, DeGeneres's show had not achieved the high ratings of Winfrey's. When Oprah announced the end of her show, DeGeneres began her monologue with a big grin and the announcement "Oprah quit!"

5. DeGeneres herself has identified the comedy of her persona as "skirting"—evading issues, glossing over the topic at hand, pointing to distractions to avoid a direct statement. In her book *My Point . . . and I Do Have One,* she writes that someone asked why she always wears "pants and never skirts," and her reply is that "if they mean the *verb* skirt, well, they're dead wrong. I'm always skirting" (93). John Limon and Candace Moore have cited this pun as a rich entry into DeGeneres's comic style for very different reasons, and they both make elegant arguments about its significance. Limon pinpoints the joke as DeGeneres's constant evasion of the status of her body (116–117), while for Moore, skirting is the performance of queerness. Moore's focus is "the multiple queer appearances and disappearances of Ellen DeGeneres" on her sitcoms and her talk show (18). Moore argues that the verbal skirting, "distancing her comedy from the bodily, from her body and the material consequences of the world," ends up nevertheless "leaking other meanings." For Moore, this leakiness complements the physical displays that "convey and rely on utter embodiment" (30). In short, Moore comes down on the side of the body precisely because visibility, no matter how playful and ambiguous, is central to LGBQT politics.

6. Lisa Duggan has introduced and defined the term "homonormative" as "a politics that does not contest dominant heteronormative assumptions and institutions but upholds and sustains them while promising the possibility of a demobilized gay constituency and a privatized, depoliticized gay culture anchored in domesticity and consumption" (50).

7. See, for example, David Martin-Jones, *Deleuze and World Cinema* (2011); Barbara M. Kennedy's *Deleuze and Cinema: The Aesthetics of Sensation* (2003); Laura U. Marks, *The Skin of the Film: Intercultural Cinema, Embodiment, and the Senses* (1999); and Patricia Pisters, *The Matrix of Visual Culture: Working with Deleuze in Film Theory* (2003). Also see the work of Carol Siegel, founder of the journal *Rhizomes*, which features scholarship influenced by Deleuze. For an extended Deleuzian study of stardom, see Marcia Landy's *Stardom, Italian Style* (2008), which draws on Deleuze's concepts of "movement image" and "time image" in order to account for the shift in the treatment of Italian stars and star bodies following World War II.

8. The feminist implications of this approach in film studies are spelled out by Elena del Rio, who speaks of the importance of the body as process for feminism and of feminism itself as a becoming that plays out in popular culture. Del Rio finds that feminism consistently has resisted concepts of the body as autonomous and posited the body in relationship to other bodies, that is, as a dynamic rather than a closed, bounded entity (116). Generally, feminist interest in Deleuze focuses on transformation, mutability, and becoming as the forces that can be tapped for desired social change. Feminists who draw on Deleuze also focus on the body, or "corporeal feminism," as Elizabeth Grosz phrases it, rejecting binary divisions between the body and what it signifies; bodies are instead sites of struggle and production; identity is not a stable entity but rather involves "a whole range of forces" within the categories of sex, class, race, and so on that are always in play (181). The payoff is a politics of creativity that resists binary, phallocentric thinking.

9. When the celebrity body is dis-organ-ized in this way, it can be thought of as the "body without organs," unlimited by systems of representation and categorization but instead circulating in multiple ways (Deleuze and Guattari, *Thousand Plateaus*, 30).

10. Braidotti specifies "a healthy disregard for the distinction between high and low culture" as a key element of Deleuzian feminism (*Metamorphoses*, 111). See her discussion of Princess Diana (107–109). In "Cyberfeminism with a Difference," see her discussion of Michael Jackson, Dolly Parson, and Elizabeth Taylor.

Bibliography

The Advocate. "Wanda Sykes: Comedian." Jan. 13, 2009, 72.

Allen, Robert C. *Horrible Prettiness: Burlesque and American Culture*. Chapel Hill: Univ. of North Carolina Press, 1991.

Altman, Rick. *The American Film Musical*. Bloomington: Indiana Univ. Press, 1987.

Anderson, Sam. "Irony Maiden: How Sarah Silverman Is Raping American Comedy." *Slate*, Nov. 10, 2005.

Anderson-Minshall, Diane. "She's a Brick House: Wanda Sykes Thinks She Isn't a Sex Symbol." *Curve*, Nov.–Dec. 2010, 44+.

Armstrong, Jennifer. "No. 2 Tina Fey." *Entertainment Weekly*, Nov. 21, 2008, 34–36.

———. "ShePop: What Do the Super Bowl, 'Burn Notice,' and Will Ferrell Have in Common? Fun with Postfeminism!" *Popwatch* (blog). *Entertainment Weekly*, Feb. 3, 2009.

Armstrong, Stephen. "Tina Fey; Funny Woman; Giving It Some Wellie." *Sunday Times* (London), Feb. 22, 2009.

Around the Sphere. "Life Hands You Lemons, You Cast Tina Fey." March 29, 2010.

Arthurs, Jane. "Sex and the City and Consumer Culture: Remediating Postfeminist Drama." *Feminist Media Studies* 3.1 (2003): 83–98.

Babuscio, Jack. "Camp and the Gay Sensibility." In *Gays and Film*. Ed. Richard Dyer, 40–57. London: BFI, 1977.

Bacalzo, Dan. "The One That She Wants: Margaret Cho, Mediatization, and Autobiographical Performance." In *Embodying Asian/American Sexualities*. Ed. Gina Masequesmay and Sean Metzger, 43–49. Lanham, MD: Rowman and Littlefield, 2009.

Bakhtin, Mikhail. *Rabelais and His World*. 1965. Trans. Hélène Iswolsky. Bloomington: Indiana Univ. Press, 1984.

Baldwin, Kristen. "Tina Fey." *Entertainment Weekly*, Dec. 21, 2001, 40–41.

Ballard, Scotty. "Wanda Sykes: Comedian, Writer, and Performer Takes Charge on TV Series 'Wanda at Large.'" *Jet*, Oct. 13, 2003, 58–62.

Banjo, Omotayo. "What Are You Laughing At? Examining White Identity and Enjoyment of Black Entertainment." *Journal of Broadcasting and Electronic Media* 55.2 (2011): 137–159.

Banks, Morwenna, and Amanda Swift. *The Joke's on Us: Women in Comedy from Music Hall to the Present Day.* London: Pandora, 1987.

Barreca, Regina, ed. *Last Laughs: Perspectives on Women and Comedy.* New York: Gordon and Breach, 1988.

———. *They Used to Call Me Snow White . . . but I Drifted: Women's Strategic Use of Humor.* New York: Viking, 1991.

Barth, Belle. *If I Embarrass You, Tell Your Friends.* LP record. After Hours Records, 1960.

Baumgardner, Jennifer, and Amy Richards. *Manifesta: Young Women, Feminism, and the Future.* New York: Farrar, Straus, Giroux, 2000.

Berg, Allison. "Trauma and Testimony in Black Women's Civil Rights Memoirs: *The Montgomery Bus Boycott and the Women Who Started It, Warriors Don't Cry,* and *From the Mississippi Delta.*" *Journal of Women's History* 21.3 (2009): 84–107.

Berger, John. *Ways of Seeing.* London: BBC Press, 1972.

Berman, Marc. "Dancing Queen." *Mediawatch* 16.44 (2006): 30.

Bersani, Leo. "Is the Rectum a Grave?" *October* 43 (1987): 197–222.

Billig, Michael. "Humour and Hatred: The Racist Jokes of the Ku Klux Klan." *Discourse and Society* 12.3 (2001): 267–289.

BlogHer. "Sarah Palin at the RNC." Sept. 9, 2008.

Bloom, James D. *Gravity Fails: The Comic Jewish Shaping of Modern America.* Westport, CT: Praeger, 2003.

Bociurkiw, Marusya. "It's Not about the Sex: Racialization and Queerness in *Ellen* and *The Ellen DeGeneres Show.*" *Canadian Woman Studies* 24.2/3 (2005): 176–181.

Bogle, Donald. *Toms, Coons, Mulattoes, Mammies, and Bucks: An Interpretive History of Blacks in American Films.* New York: Viking, 1973.

Bordo, Susan. *Twilight Zones: The Hidden Life of Cultural Images from Plato to O. J.* Berkeley: Univ. of California Press, 1997.

Boris, Eileen. "Feminist Currents." *Frontiers* 33.1 (2012): 101–105.

Boskin, Joseph. "Beyond Kvetching and Jiving: The Thrust of Jewish and Black Folkhumor." In *Jewish Wry: Essays on Jewish Humor.* Ed. Sarah Blacher Cohen, 53–79. Bloomington: Indiana Univ. Press, 1987.

Braidotti, Rosi. "Cyberfemininity with a Difference." In *Futures of Critical Theory: Dreams of Difference.* Ed. Michael Peters, Mark Olssen, and Colin Lankshear, 239–259. Lanham, MD: Rowman and Littlefield, 2003.

———. *Metamorphoses: Towards a Materialist Theory of Becoming.* Malden, MA: Polity, 2002.

Braidotti, Rosi, with Judith Butler. "Feminism by Any Other Name." In *Feminism Meets Queer Theory.* Ed. Naomi Schor and Elizabeth Weed, 31–67. Bloomington: Indiana Univ. Press, 1997.

Braziel, Jana Evans. "Sex and Fat Chics: Deterritorializing the Fat Female Body." In *Bodies out of Bounds: Fatness and Transgression*. Ed. Jana Evans Braziel and Kathleen LeBesco, 231–254. Berkeley: Univ. of California Press, 2001.

Brown, Edward. "We Wear the Mask: African American Contemporary Gay Male Identities." *Journal of African American Studies* 9.2 (2005): 29–38.

Buchanan, Mike. *Feminism: The Ugly Truth*. LPS Publishing, Amazon Digital Service, 2012.

Butler, Judith. "Against Proper Objects." In *Feminism Meets Queer Theory*. Ed. Naomi Schor and Elizabeth Weed, 1–30. Bloomington: Indiana Univ. Press, 1997.

———. *Gender Trouble: Feminism and the Subversion of Identity*. New York: Routledge, 1990.

Calhoun, Ada. "43 Minutes with Margaret Cho." *New York Magazine*, Nov. 15, 2010.

Carby, Hazel V. "Policing the Black Woman's Body in an Urban Context." *Critical Inquiry* 18.4 (1992): 738–755.

Carmon, Irin. "The Daily Show's Woman Problem." *Jezebel*, June 23, 2010.

Carpio, Glenda. "Black Women, Black Humor." *Bulletin of the American Academy of Arts and Sciences* (Summer 2010): 33–36.

Carroll, Jeffrey. "Margaret Cho, Jake Shimabukuro, and Rhetorics in a Minor Key." In *Representations: Doing Asian American Rhetoric*. Ed. Luming Mao and Morris Young, 266–278. Logan: Utah State Univ. Press, 2008.

Carter, Kelley L. "For Wanda Sykes, Life's an Adventure." *USA Today*, Nov. 6, 2009.

Cassinelli, Sarah Moon. "'If We Are Asian, Then Are We Funny?': Margaret Cho's All-American Girl as the First (and Last?) Asian American Sitcom." *Studies in American Humor* 17 (2008): 131–144.

Cho, Margaret. "Crush Crash." In *Feminisms and Womanisms*. Ed. Althea Prince and Susan Silva Wayne, 219–221. Toronto: Woman's Press, 2004.

———. Foreword to *Yes Means Yes! Visions of Female Sexual Power and a World without Rape*. Ed. Jaclyn Friedman and Jessica Valenti, 1–4. Berkeley, CA: Seal, 2008.

———. "Grab the Brass Ring of Equality." In *50 Ways to Support Lesbian and Gay Equality*. Ed. Meredith Maran and Angela Watrous, 145–46. San Francisco: Inner Ocean, 2005.

———. *I Have Chosen to Stay and Fight*. New York: Penguin, 2005.

———. *I'm the One That I Want*. New York: Ballantine, 2001.

Ciasullo, Ann M. "Making Her (In)Visible: Cultural Representations of Lesbianism and the Lesbian Body in the 1990s." *Feminist Studies* 27.3 (2001): 577–608.

Clarke, Gerald. "Barbs for the Queen (and Others)." *Time*, April 11, 1983, 85–88.

Clements, Marcelle. "Speaking Softly while Tromping on Taboos." *New York Times*, Nov. 9, 2005.

Cleto, Fabio. *Camp: Queer Aesthetics and the Performing Subject*. Ann Arbor: Univ. of Michigan Press, 1999.

Coates, Ta-Nehisi. "American Girl." *The Atlantic*, Jan./Feb. 2009.

Cohan, Steven. *Incongruous Entertainment: Camp, Cultural Value, and the MGM Musical*. Durham, NC: Duke Univ. Press, 2005.

Coleman, Jenny. "An Introduction to Feminisms in a Postfeminist Age." *Women's Studies Journal* 23.2 (2009): 3–13.

Collins, Kathleen. "The Sarah Silverman Program." *Bitch Magazine: Feminist Response to Pop Culture* 36 (Summer 2007): 73.

Collins, Patricia Hill. *Black Feminist Thought: Knowledge, Consciousness, and the Politics of Empowerment*. New York: Routledge, 2000.

———. *Black Sexual Politics: African Americans, Gender, and the New Racism*. New York: Routledge, 2004.

Cooper, Evan. "Is It Something He Said: The Mass Consumption of Richard Pryor's Culturally Intimate Humor." *Communication Review* 10.3 (2007): 223–247.

Cragin, Becca. "Lesbians and Serial TV: Ellen Finds Her Inner Adult." In *The New Queer Aesthetic on Television: Essays on Recent Programming*. Ed. James R. Keller and Leslie Stratyner, 193–208. Jefferson, NC: McFarland, 2006.

Crimp, Douglas. "Right On, Girlfriend!" *Social Text* 33 (1992): 2–18.

Crimp, Douglas, and Michael Warner. "No Sex in *Sex*." In *Madonnarama: Essays on Sex and Popular Culture*. Ed. Lisa Frank and Paul Smith, 93–110. Pittsburgh: Cleis Press, 1993.

Cuomo, Chris J. "Thoughts on Lesbian Differences." *Hypatia* 13.1 (1998): 198–205.

Dailey, Kate. "Leslie Knope, Liz Lemon, and the Feminist Lessons of NBC's 'Parks and Recreation.'" *Newsweek*, April 8, 2010.

Davies, Christie. "Exploring the Thesis of the Self-Deprecating Jewish Sense of Humor." In *Semites and Stereotypes: Characteristics of Jewish Humor*. Ed. Avner Ziv and Anat Zajdman, 29–46. Westport, CT: Greenwood Press, 1993.

DeGeneres, Ellen. *My Point . . . and I Do Have One*. New York: Bantam, 1995.

Deleuze, Gilles, and Felix Guattari. *Anti-Oedipus: Capitalism and Schizophrenia*. Trans. Robert Hurley, Mark Seem, and Helen R. Lane. Minneapolis: Univ. of Minnesota Press, 1983.

———. *A Thousand Plateaus: Capitalism and Schizophrenia*. Trans. Brian Massumi. Minneapolis: Univ. of Minnesota Press, 1987.

del Rio, Elena. *Deleuze and the Cinemas of Performance: Powers of Affection*. Edinburgh, Scotland: Edinburgh Univ. Press, 2008.

Donnelly, Matt. "Funny Girl Tina Fey Lands the March Cover of Vogue." *Los Angeles Times*, Feb. 12, 2010.

Douglas, Mary. *Purity and Danger: An Analysis of Pollution and Taboo*. London: Routledge and Kegan Paul, 1966.

Dow, Bonnie J. "Ellen, Television, and the Politics of Gay and Lesbian Visibility." *Critical Studies in Mass Communication* 18.2 (2001): 123–140.

———. *Prime Time Feminism: Television, Media Culture, and the Women's Movement since 1970*. Philadelphia: Univ. of Pennsylvania Press, 1996.

Dowd, Maureen. "What Tina Wants." *Vanity Fair*, Jan. 2009.

Doyle, Sady. "13 Ways of Looking at Liz Lemon." *Tiger Beatdown* (blog), March 24, 2010.

Du Bois, W. E. B. "The Souls of Black Folk." In *Literary Theory: An Anthology*. Ed. Julie Rivkin and Michael Ryan, 868–872. Malden, MA: Blackwell, 1998.

Duggan, Lisa. *The Twilight of Equality?: Neoliberalism, Cultural Politics, and the Attack on Democracy*. Boston: Beacon, 2003.

Dyer, Richard. *Heavenly Bodies: Film Stars and Society*. 2nd edition. New York: Routledge, 2004. Originally published 1986.

———. *Only Entertainment*. New York: Routledge, 1992.

———. *Stars*. 2nd edition. London: BFI, 2002. Originally published 1979.

———. *White*. New York: Routledge, 1997.

Early, Gerald. "A Brief History of African American Humor." *Bulletin of the American Academy of Arts and Sciences* (Summer 2010): 29–33.

Falcone, Lauren Beckham. "Comedy Heavyweight Tina Fey Shed Pounds, Gained Success." *Boston Herald*, Dec. 4, 2008.

Farley, Christopher John, and Simon Robinson. "Dave Speaks." *Time*, May 23, 2005.

Feuer, Jane, Paul Kerr, and Tise Vahimagi, eds. *MTM "Quality Television."* London: BFI, 1984.

Fey, Tina. *Bossypants*. New York: Little, Brown, 2011.

———. "Confessions of a Juggler." Excerpt from *Bossypants. New Yorker*, Feb. 14, 2011, 64–67.

———. "Oprah Talks to Tina Fey." Interview by Oprah Winfrey. *O: The Oprah Magazine*, Feb. 1, 2009.

———. "Tina Fey Reveals All (and Then Some) in *Bossypants*." Interview by Terry Gross, *Fresh Air*, WHYY, National Public Radio, April 13, 2011.

Fienberg, Daniel. "HitFix Interview: Wanda Sykes of 'The Wanda Sykes Show.'" *Fein Print* (blog). *HitFix*, Nov. 7, 2009.

Finn, Natalie. "Wanda Sykes Reveals Breast Cancer Diagnosis, Double Mastectomy." *E! Online*, Sept. 22, 2011.

firstlightforum.wordpress.com. "Sarah Silverman: Comic or Just Another Jew Cot Case?" March 17, 2009.

Fischer, Lucy. "Sometimes I Feel Like a Motherless Child: Comedy and Matricide." In *Comedy/Cinema/Theory*. Ed. Andrew S. Horton, 60–78. Berkeley: Univ. of California Press, 1991.

Fisher, Carrie. *Wishful Drinking*. New York: Simon and Schuster, 2008.

Flinn, Caryl. "The Deaths of Camp." In *Camp: Queer Aesthetics and the Performing Subject*. Ed. Fabio Cleto, 433–457. Ann Arbor: Univ. of Michigan Press, 1999.

Foley, Bridget. "Ellen." W, March 2007: 496+.

Fonseca, Nicholas. "The Most Annoying, Riotous, Irritating, Honest, Shameless, Savvy, Polarizing Woman in Hollywood." *Entertainment Weekly*, June 6, 2008, 34.

———. "The New Queen of Nice." *Entertainment Weekly*, Sept. 12, 2003.

Foucault, Michel. *Discipline and Punish: The Birth of the Prison*. Trans. Alan Sheridan. New York: Vintage Books, 1995.

Fox, Margalit. "Jean Carroll, 98, Is Dead; Blended Wit and Beauty." *New York Times*, Jan. 3, 2010.

Fraiberg, Allison. "Between the Laughter: Bridging Feminist Studies through Women's Stand-Up Comedy." In *Look Who's Laughing: Gender and Comedy*. Ed. Gail Finney, 315–334. London: Gordon and Breach, 1994.

Franke-Ruta, Garance. "Creating a Lie: Sylvia Ann Hewlett and the Myth of the Baby Bust." *American Prospect*, July 1, 2002, 30–33.

Franklin, Nancy. "Watching Wanda." *New Yorker*, May 5, 2003, 102.

Freud, Sigmund. *Civilization and Its Discontents*. Trans. James Strachey. New York: Norton, 1961.

———. *Jokes and Their Relation to the Unconscious*. Trans. James Strachey. New York: Norton, 1963.

Freydkin, Donna. "The Inimitable Tina Fey." *USA Today*, Oct. 24, 2008.

Friedman, Jaclyn, and Jessica Valenti. Introduction to *Yes Means Yes! Visions of Female Sexual Power and a World without Rape*. Ed. Jaclyn Friedman and Jessica Valenti, 5–11. Berkeley, CA: Seal, 2008.

Friend, Tad. "Hostile Acts: On Television." *New Yorker*, Feb. 5, 2007, 76.

Frye, Northrup. *Anatomy of Criticism*. Princeton, NJ: Princeton Univ. Press, 1957.

Gay, Lesbian, and Straight Education Network (GLSEN). "GLSEN Proud to Work with Wanda Sykes on Ad Council." Press release, Nov. 17, 2008.

Gilbert, Joanne R. *Performing Marginality: Humor, Gender, and Cultural Critique*. Detroit: Wayne State, 2004.

Gilbert, Matthew. "'Cho Show' Is All about the Drama Queen." *Boston Globe*, Aug. 21, 2008.

Gillooly, Eileen. "Women and Humor." *Feminist Studies* 17 (3): 273–292.

Gilman, Sander. *The Jew's Body*. New York: Routledge, 1991.

Glover, Karen S. "Citizenship, Hyper-Surveillance, and Double Consciousness: Racial Profiling as Panoptic Governance." In *Surveillance and Governance: Crime Control and Beyond*. Ed. Mathieu Deflem, 241–256. Bingley, England: Emerald, 2008.

Glover, Terry. "The Top 20 Comedians of All Time." *Ebony*, April 2011, 82–85.

Goodyear, Dana. "Quiet Depravity." *New Yorker*, Oct. 24, 2005, 50+.

Gordon, Dexter B. "Humor in African American Discourse: Speaking of Oppression." *Journal of Black Studies* 29.2 (1998): 254–276.

Gray, Frances. *Women and Laughter*. Charlottesville: Univ. Press of Virginia, 1994.

Griffin, Kathy. *Official Book Club Selection: A Memoir According to Kathy Griffin*. New York: Ballantine, 2009.

———. "When to Try Harder and When to Walk Away." In *Thirty Things Every Woman Should Have and Should Know by the Time She's 30*. Ed. editors of *Glamour* and Pamela Redmond Satran, 107–110. New York: Hyperion, 2012.

Grigoriadis, Vanessa. "Dirty Rotten Princess." *Rolling Stone*, Nov. 17, 2005, 66–70.

Grosz, Elizabeth. *Volatile Bodies: Toward a Corporeal Feminism*. Bloomington: Indiana Univ. Press, 1994.

Haggins, Bambi. *Laughing Mad: The Black Comic Persona in Post-Soul America*. New Brunswick, NJ: Rutgers Univ. Press, 2007.

Halberstam, J. Jack. *Gaga Feminism: Sex, Gender, and the End of Normal*. Boston: Beacon, 2012.

Hall, Stuart. "The Whites of Their Eyes: Racist Ideology and Media." In *Silver Linings: Some Strategies for the Eighties*. Ed. George Bridges and Rosalind Brunt, 28–52. London: Lawrence and Wishart, 1981.

Hamilton, Marybeth. *"When I'm Bad, I'm Better": Mae West, Sex, and American Entertainment*. Berkeley: Univ. of California Press, 1997.

Hammonds, Evelynn M. "Toward a Genealogy of Black Female Sexuality: The Problematic of Silence." In *Feminist Genealogies, Colonial Legacies, Democratic Futures*. Ed. M. Jacqui Alexander and Chandra Talpade Mohanty, 170–182. Routledge: New York, 1997.

Hannaham, James. "Beyond the Pale." *New York Magazine*, June 28, 2005.

Haramis, Nick. "How Do Glossies Solve a Problem Like Tina Fey?" *BlackBook .com*, March 2010.

Harris, Anita. "Mind the Gap: Attitudes and Emergent Feminist Politics since the Third Wave." *Australian Feminist Studies* 25.66 (2010): 475–484.

Hart, Hugh. "Kathy Griffin Just Can't Shut Up." *New York Times*, June 15, 2008.

Hartmann, Margaret. "Joan of Snark: 30 *Rock* Parodies Jezebel." *Jezebel*, Feb. 25, 2011.

———. "Olivia Munn's Groin Spurs Maxim Cover Controversy." *Jezebel*, Jan. 12, 2011.

Havrilesky, Heather. "I Like to Watch." *Salon*, Feb. 4, 2007.

Hayward, Susan. "Stardom: Beyond Desire?" In *History of Stardom Reconsidered*. Ed. Kari Kallioniemi, Kimi Kärki, Janne Mäkelä, and Hannu Salmi, 47–55. Turku, Finland: International Institute for Popular Culture, 2007.

Heffernan, Virginia. "Anchor Woman." *New Yorker*, Nov. 3, 2003.

Hensley, Dennis. "Somewhere over the Rainbow." *The Advocate*, Aug. 26, 2008.

Herald (Everett, WA). "Margaret Cho Gets Her Griffin on in VH1 Series." Aug. 18, 2008.

Hermes, Joke. "Reading Gossip Magazines: The Imagined Communities of 'Gossip' and 'Camp.'" In *The Celebrity Culture Reader*. Ed. P. David Marshall, 291–310. New York: Routledge, 2006.

Higginbotham, Evelyn Brooks. "African-American Women's History and the Metalanguage of Race." *Signs: Journal of Women in Culture and Society* 17.2 (1992): 251–274.

Hitchens, Christopher. "Why Women Aren't Funny." *Vanity Fair*, Jan. 2007.

Holloway, Lynette R. "Wanda." *Ebony*, Aug. 2007, 71.

Holmlund, Chris. "Postfeminism from A to G." *Cinema Journal* 44.2 (2005): 116–121.

hooks, bell. *Black Looks: Race and Representation*. Boston: South End, 1992.

Hooley, Danny. "'Cho Show' Shocks by Being Sweet." *News Tribune*, Aug. 21, 2008.

Hope, Randy. "Wanda Sykes Has a Seat at the Table." *Gay and Lesbian Times*, Feb. 26, 2009, 26.

Horowitz, Susan. *Queens of Comedy: Lucille Ball, Phyllis Diller, Carol Burnett, Joan Rivers, and the New Generation of Funny Women*. London: Routledge, 1997.

Horton, Donald, and R. Richard Wohl. "Mass Communication and Para-Social Interaction: Observations on Intimacy at a Distance." *Psychiatry* 19.3 (1956): 215–230.

Huffington Post. "Sarah Silverman Calls Fox News a '24-Hour-a-Day Racism Engine,' Fox News Hits Back." June 2, 2010.

Isherwood, Charles. "Look Out, Celebrities: Her Aim Is True." *New York Times*, March 14, 2011.

Itzkoff, Dave. "I'm Not a French Maid, I Just Play One on TV." *New York Times*, June 27, 2010.

Jacobs, A. J. "Ellen (The Knife) DeGeneres: Soft Power Comes to American Idol." *Esquire*, Feb. 2010.

———. "The Real Tina Fey." *Esquire*, April 2010, 80–87.

Jenkins, Henry. *What Made Pistachio Nuts? Early Sound Comedy and the Vaudeville Aesthetic*. New York: Columbia Univ. Press, 1992.

Jewell, K. Sue. *From Mammy to Miss America and Beyond: Cultural Images and the Shaping of U.S. Social Policy*. London: Routledge, 1993.

Johnson, Lakesia D. *Iconic: Decoding Images of the Revolutionary Black Woman*. Waco, TX: Baylor Univ. Press, 2012.

Jones, Oliver. "Talking Trash with . . . Kathy Griffin." *People*, June 16, 2008, 116.

Kantor, Jodi. "Elite Women Put a New Spin on an Old Debate." *New York Times*, June 22, 2012.

———. *The Obamas*. New York: Little Brown, 2012.

Kaplan, Erin Aubry. "Who's Afraid of Michelle Obama?" *Salon*, June 24, 2008.

Karger, Dave. "The Real American Idol." *Entertainment Weekly*, Feb. 26, 2010.

Karlyn, Kathleen Rowe. *Unruly Girls, Unrepentant Mothers: Redefining Feminism on Screen*. Austin: Univ. of Texas Press, 2011.

Karpel, Ari. "Black and Gay Like Me." *The Advocate*, March 2009, 54+.

Kennedy, Barbara M. *Deleuze and Cinema: The Aesthetics of Sensation*. Edinburgh: Edinburgh Univ. Press, 2000.

Kibler, M. Alison. *Rank Ladies: Gender and Cultural Hierarchy in American Vaudeville*. Chapel Hill: Univ. of North Carolina Press, 1999.

King, Geoff. *Film Comedy*. London: Wallflower, 2002.

Kohen, Yael. *We Killed: The Rise of Women in American Comedy*. New York: Farrar, Straus, Giroux, 2012.

Kort, Michele. "As Ellen Goes, So Goes the Nation." *The Advocate*, Oct. 7, 2008, 46+.

Krakauer, Steve. "Sarah Silverman: Fox News." *Mediaite.com*, June 2, 2010.

Kristeva, Julia. *Powers of Horror: An Essay on Abjection*. New York: Columbia Univ. Press, 1982.

Krutnik, Frank. "General Introduction." In *Hollywood Comedians: The Film Reader*. Ed. Frank Krutnik, 1–20. New York: Routledge, 2003.

Lander, Christian. *Stuff White People Like: The Definitive Guide to the Unique Taste of Millions*. New York: Random House, 2008.

Landy, Marcia. *Stardom, Italian Style: Screen Performance and Personality in Italian Cinema*. Bloomington: Indiana Univ. Press, 2008.

Lee, Hye Jin, and Huike Wen. "Where the Girls Are in the Age of New Sexism: An Interview with Susan Douglas." *Journal of Communication Inquiry* 33.2 (2009): 93–103.

Lee, Rachel. "'Where's My Parade?' Margaret Cho and the Asian American Body in Space." *Drama Review* 48.2 (2004): 108–132.

Lee, Shayne. *Erotic Revolutionaries: Black Women, Sexuality, and Popular Culture*. Lanham, MD: Hamilton, 2010.

Leitch, Will. "Animal Magnetism: You May Never Understand Sarah Silverman." *New York Magazine*, April 19, 2010.

Lewis, Brian. "Redefining 'Queer' through Blue Humor: Margaret Cho's Performances of Queer Sexualities." *Philament: An Online Journal of the Arts and Culture*, June 9, 2010.

Lewis, Paul. "Beyond Empathy: Sarah Silverman and the Limits of Comedy." *Tikkun*, Sept./Oct. 2007, 88–89.

Limon, John. *Stand-Up Comedy in Theory, or, Abjection in America*. Durham, NC: Duke Univ. Press, 2000.

Lloyd, Robert. "Margaret Cho, on Her Own Terms." *Los Angeles Times*, Aug. 21, 2008.

Lott, Eric. *Love and Theft: Blackface Minstrelsy and the American Working Class*. New York: Oxford Univ. Press, 1993.

Lotz, Amanda. "Postfeminist Television Criticism: Rehabilitating Critical Terms and Identifying Postfeminist Attributes." *Feminist Media Studies* 1.1 (2001): 105–121.

Lowe, Lisa. *Immigrant Acts: On Asian American Cultural Politics*. London: Duke Univ. Press, 1996.

Madison, D. Soyini. "Crazy Patriotism and Angry (Post)Black Women." *Communication and Critical/Cultural Studies* 6.3 (2009): 321–326.

Maerz, Melissa. "'New Girl' Gets a New Attitude." *Entertainment Weekly*, March 23, 2012.

Marie Claire. "Tina on Top." May 2008.

Marks, Laura. *The Skin of the Film: Intercultural Cinema, Embodiment, and the Senses*. Durham, NC: Duke Univ. Press, 2000.

Martel, Ned. "Please, Please Watch Me, I Have Myself to Give." *New York Times*, Aug. 29, 2005.

Martin, Linda, and Kerry Segrave. *Women in Comedy*. Secaucus, NJ: Citadel, 1986.

Martínez, Ernesto Javier. *On Making Sense: Queer Race Narratives of Intelligibility*. Stanford, CA: Stanford Univ. Press, 2012.

Martin-Jones, David. *Deleuze and World Cinemas*. London: Continuum, 2011.

Mask, Mia. *Divas on Screen: Black Women in American Film*. Urbana: Univ. of Illinois Press, 2009.

Masugi, Ken. "Viewing Russia from Your Window." *National Review*, Sept. 29, 2008.

Maynard, John. "Comedian Wanda Sykes, Pulling No Punch Lines." *Washington Post*, Oct. 14, 2006.

Mayne, Judith. *Cinema and Spectatorship*. London: Routledge, 1993.

Mazey, Steven. "Cho Beautiful: Margaret Cho." *Ottawa Citizen*, Oct. 18, 2008.

McCarthy, Anna. "Ellen: Making Queer Television History." *GLQ: A Journal of Lesbian and Gay Studies* 7.4 (2001): 593–620.

McEwan, Melissa. "Tina Fey." *Shakesville* (blog), Feb. 12, 2010.

McRobbie, Angela. "Postfeminism and Popular Culture: Bridget Jones and the New Gender Regime." In *Interrogating Postfeminism*. Ed. Tasker and Negra, 27–39.

Medhurst, Andy. "Camp." In *Lesbian and Gay Studies: A Critical Introduction*. Ed. Andy Medhurst and Sally R. Munt, 274–293. London: Cassell, 1997.

Mellencamp, Patricia. "Situation Comedy, Feminism, and Freud: Discourses of Gracie and Lucy." In *Studies in Entertainment: Critical Approaches to Mass Culture*. Ed. Tania Modleski, 80–95. Bloomington: Indiana Univ. Press, 1986.

Merrill, Lisa. "Feminist Humor: Rebellious and Self Affirming." In *Last Laughs: Perspectives on Women and Comedy*. Ed. Regina Barrecca, 271–280. New York: Gordon and Breach, 1988.

Merritt, Layla J. "Wanda Sykes: 'Sick and Tired.'" *New York Amsterdam News*, Oct. 12, 2006, 23.

Meyer, Michaela D. E. "'Maybe I Could Play a Hooker in Something!': Asian American Identity, Gender, and Comedy in the Rhetoric of Margaret Cho." In *Representations: Doing Asian American Rhetoric*. Ed. Luming Mao and Morris Young, 279–292. Logan: Utah State Univ. Press, 2008.

Meyer, Moe. "Under the Sign of Wilde: An Archaeology of Posing." In *The Politics and Poetics of Camp*. Ed. Moe Meyer, 75–109. London: Routledge, 1994.

Mitchell, Heidi. "Tina's Way." *Town and Country*, Feb. 2009, 88+.

Mizejewski, Linda. "Dressed to Kill: Postfeminist Noir." *Cinema Journal* 44.2 (2005): 121–127.

———. "Feminism, Postfeminism, Liz Lemonism: Comedy and Gender Politics on *30 Rock*." *Genders: An Online Journal* 55 (2012).

———. "Queen Latifah, Unruly Women, and the Bodies of Romantic Comedy." *Genders: An Online Journal* 46 (2007).

———. *Ziegfeld Girl: Image and Icon in Culture and Cinema*. Durham, NC: Duke Univ. Press, 1999.

Mock, Roberta. "Heteroqueer Ladies: Some Performative Transactions between Gay Men and Heterosexual Women." *Feminist Review* 75 (2003): 20–37.

Monson, Ingrid. "The Problem with White Hipness: Race, Gender, and Cultural Conceptions in Jazz Historical Discourse." *Journal of the American Musicological Society* 48.3 (1995): 396–422.

Moore, Candace. "Resisting, Reiterating, and Dancing Through: The Swinging Closet Doors of Ellen DeGeneres's Televised Personalities." In *Televising Queer Women: A Reader.* Ed. Rebecca Beirne, 17–31. New York: Palgrave Macmillan, 2008.

Moore, Suzanne. "Television: Ellen Degeneres Comes Out." *New Statesman*, Nov. 14, 1997, 47.

Morreale, Joanne. "Do Bitches Get Stuff Done?" *Feminist Media Studies* 10.4 (2010): 485–487.

Moseley, Rachel, and Jacinda Read. "'Having It Ally': Popular Television (Post-) Feminism." *Feminist Media Studies* 2.2 (2002): 231–249.

Mulvey, Laura. "Visual Pleasure and Narrative Cinema." *Screen* 16.3 (1975): 6–18.

Muñoz, José Esteban. *Disidentifications: Queers of Color and the Performance of Politics.* Minneapolis: Univ. of Minnesota Press, 1999.

Munt, Sally. *Heroic Desire: Lesbian Identity and Cultural Space.* New York: NYU Press, 1998.

Nashawaty, Chris. "Ball Buster: Sarah Silverman Is Biting and Crass and Actually Has Something to Say." *Entertainment Weekly*, Nov. 11, 2005.

Nason, David. "'Are We Ready to See Hillary Age?'" *News.com.au*, Dec. 19, 2007.

Negra, Diane. *What a Girl Wants? Fantasizing the Reclamation of Self in Postfeminism.* London: Routledge, 2009.

Negra, Diane, and Su Holmes. Introduction to *Going Cheap? Female Celebrity in Reality, Tabloid, and Scandal Genres*, special issue of *Genders: An Online Journal* 48 (2008).

New York Times. "Ellen and 'Ellen' Come Out." May 1, 1997.

Newman, Judith. "Ellen Enchanted." *Ladies Home Journal*, March 2009, 118–121.

———. "From Sarah Silverman, an Adorable Look, Followed by a Sucker Punch." *New York Times*, May 9, 2010.

Nussbaum, Emily. "It's the Revenge of the Ignorant Sluts." *New York Times*, May 11, 2003.

———. "The Meta Follies: From Monty Python to 30 Rock." *New York Magazine*, Oct. 18, 2009.

O'Keefe, Alice. "Queen of Outrage." *New Statesman*, Oct. 27, 2008, 46.

Osborne-Thompson, Heather. "The Comedic Treatment of Reality: *Kathy Griffin: My Life on the D List, Fat Actress*, and *The Comeback*." In *Reality TV: Remaking Television.* Ed. Susan Murray and Laurie Ouellette, 278–298. 2nd edition. New York: NYU Press, 2009.

Ovalle, Priscilla Peña. *Dance and the Hollywood Latina: Race, Sex, and Stardom.* New Brunswick, NJ: Rutgers Univ. Press, 2011.

Palin, Sarah. "Charles Gibson Interviews Sarah Palin." Interview. *ABC World News with Charles Gibson*, Sept. 11, 2008.

Palmer, Gareth. "The Un-dead: Life on the D-List." *Westminster Papers in Communication and Culture* 2.2 (2005): 37–53.

Parker, Kathleen. "Denigrating Michelle Obama with the 'Angry Black Woman' Slur." *Washington Post*, Jan. 13, 2012.

Pearson, Kyra. "'Words Should Do the Work of Bombs': Margaret Cho as Symbolic Assassin." *Women and Language* 32.1:36–43.

Perigard, Mark A. "'Cho Show' Has More Yuck than Yuks." *Boston Herald*, Aug. 21, 2008.

Petro, Patrice. *Aftershocks of the New: Feminism and Film History*. New Brunswick, NJ: Rutgers Univ. Press, 2002.

Pisters, Patricia. *The Matrix of Visual Culture: Working with Deleuze in Film Theory*. Stanford, CA: Stanford Univ. Press, 2003.

Porter, Laraine. "Tarts, Tampons, and Tyrants: Women and Representation in British Comedy." In *Because I Tell a Joke or Two: Comedy, Politics, and Social Difference*. Ed. Stephen Wagg, 65–93. New York: Routledge, 1998.

Powell, Michael, and Jodi Kantor. "After Attacks, Michelle Obama Looks for a New Introduction." *New York Times*, June 18, 2008.

Projansky, Sarah. "Mass Magazine Cover Girls: Some Reflections on Postfeminist Girls and Postfeminism's Daughters." In *Interrogating Postfeminism*. Ed. Tasker and Negra, 40–72.

———. *Watching Rape: Film and Television in Postfeminist Culture*. New York: NYU Press, 2001.

Quinn, Erin. "Margaret Cho's Painful Secret." *Us Weekly*, Sept. 8, 2008, 62+.

Radner, Hilary. *Neo-Feminist Cinema: Girly Films, Chick Flicks, and Consumer Culture*. New York: Routledge, 2011.

Raskin, Richard. "The Origins and Evolution of a Classic Jewish Joke." In *Semites and Stereotypes: Characteristics of Jewish Humor*. Ed. Avner Ziv and Anat Zajdman, 87–104. Westport, CT: Greenwood, 1993.

Reed, Jennifer. "Ellen DeGeneres: Public Lesbian Number One." *Feminist Media Studies* 5.1 (2005): 23–36.

———. "Lesbian Television Personalities—A Queer New Subject." *Journal of American Culture* 32.4 (2009): 307–317.

———. "Sexual Outlaws: Queer in a Funny Way." *Women's Studies* 40 (2011): 762–777.

Rice, Lynette. "Hollywood Insider: The Next Oprah Winfrey." *Entertainment Weekly*, Aug. 13, 2010.

Rich, Frank. "There's a Battle Outside and It's Still Ragin'." *New York Times*, July 25, 2010.

Richardson, Niall. "As Kamp as Bree: The Politics of Camp Reconsidered." *Feminist Media Studies* 6.2 (2006): 157–174.

Robertson, Pamela. *Guilty Pleasures: Feminist Camp from Mae West to Madonna*. Durham, NC: Duke, 1996.

Roof, Judith. *All about Thelma and Eve: Sidekicks and Third Wheels*. Urbana: Univ. of Illinois Press, 2002.

Ross, Andrew. *No Respect: Intellectuals and Popular Culture*. London: Routledge, 1989.

Ross, Marlon B. "Beyond the Closet as Raceless Paradigm." In *Black Queer Studies: A Critical Anthology*. Ed. E. Patrick Johnson and Mae G. Henderson, 161–189. Durham, NC: Duke Univ. Press, 2005.

Rowe, Kathleen. *The Unruly Woman: Gender and the Genres of Laughter*. Austin: Univ. of Texas Press, 1995.

Rubinoff, Joel. "What Makes Tina So Darn Funny." *Toronto Star*, Nov. 28, 2008.

Russell, Danielle. "Self-Deprecatory Humour and the Female Comic: Self-Destruction or Comic Construction?" *Thirdspace* 2.1 (2002).

Russo, Mary. *The Female Grotesque: Risk, Excess, and Modernity*. New York: Routledge, 1995.

Sager, Mike. "Sarah Silverman and Jimmy Kimmel." *Esquire*, Jan. 2007, 86+.

Schwarz, Margaret. "The Horror of Something to See: Celebrity 'Vaginas' as Prostheses." *Genders: An Online Journal* 48 (2008).

Scott, A. O. "A Comic in Search of the Discomfort Zone." *New York Times*, Nov. 11, 2005.

———. "The Lady or the Teddy?" *New York Times*, June 29, 2012.

Seidman, Robert. "Why Bringing 30 Rock Back Isn't Crazy." *TV by the Numbers*, April 3, 2008.

Selke, Lori. "Reasons We Love Sarah Silverman." *Curve*, Nov. 2008, 80.

Shales, Tom, and James Andrew Miller. *Live from New York: An Uncensored History of "Saturday Night Live."* Boston: Little Brown, 2002.

Shapiro, Fred R. *The Yale Book of Quotations*. New Haven, CT: Yale Univ. Press, 2006.

Sharkey, Betsy. "Critic's Notebook." *Los Angeles Times*, April 18, 2010.

Shea, Danny. "Sarah Silverman Calls Fox News 'a 24-Hour-a-Day Racism Machine.'" *Huffington Post*, June 2, 2010.

Showden, Carisa R. "What's Political about the New Feminisms?" *Frontiers: A Journal of Women Studies* 30.2 (2009): 166–198.

Shugart, Helene A. "Performing Ambiguity: The Passing of Ellen DeGeneres." *Text and Performance Quarterly* 23.1 (2003): 30–54.

Silverman, Sarah. *The Bedwetter: Stories of Courage, Redemption, and Pee*. New York: Harper Collins, 2010.

Smith, Barbara. "Toward a Black Feminist Criticism." In *Black Feminist Cultural Criticism*. Ed. Jacqueline Bobo, 7–23. Malden, MA: Blackwell, 2001.

Smith, Kristin. "Saving Silverman: How the Gays Rescued Our Favorite Straight Comic." *Curve*, May 2010, 44–47.

Smith, Sean. "The Girl Can't Help It: Celeb-Baiting Comedian Kathy Griffin." *Newsweek*, June 12, 2006, 70.

Smith, Sidonie. *Subjectivity, Identity, and the Body: Women's Autobiographical Practices in the Twentieth Century*. Bloomington: Indiana Univ. Press, 1993.

Snead, James. *White Screens, Black Images: Hollywood from the Dark Side*. New York: Routledge, 1994.

Sochen, June. "Slapsticks, Screwballs, and Bawds: The Long Road to the Performing Talents of Lucy and Bette." In *Women's Comic Visions*. Ed. June Sochen, 141–157. Detroit: Wayne State Univ. Press, 1991.

Solomon, Deborah. "Funny Girl: Questions for Sarah Silverman." *New York Times*, Jan. 21, 2007.

Southgate, Martha. "A Funny Thing Happened on the Way to Prime Time." *New York Times*, Oct. 30, 1994.

Spacks, Patricia Meyer. *Gossip*. New York: Knopf, 1985.

Spillers, Hortense. "Interstices: A Small Drama of Words." In *Pleasure and Danger: Exploring Female Sexuality*. Ed. Carole D. Vance, 73–99. Boston: Routledge and Kegan Paul, 1984.

Spitznagel, Eric. "The Daily Show's Olivia Munn on Sex, Comedy, and the Holocaust." *Vanity Fair*, July 2, 2010.

———. "Sarah Silverman: The New Kong of Comedy." *Maxim*, June 2007, 94+.

Springer, Kimberly. "Divas, Evil Black Bitches, and Bitter Black Women: African American Women in Postfeminist and Post-Civil-Rights Popular Culture." In *Interrogating Postfeminism*. Ed. Tasker and Negra, 249–276.

———. "Policing Black Women's Sexual Expression: The Cases of Sarah Jones and Renee Cox." *Genders: An Online Journal* 54 (Summer 2011).

———. "Waiting to Set It Off: African American Women and the Sapphire Fixation." In *Reel Knockouts: Violent Women in the Movies*. Ed. Martha McCaughey and Neal King, 172–199. Austin: Univ. of Texas Press, 2001.

Stacey, Jackie. *Star Gazing: Hollywood Cinema and Female Spectatorship*. New York: Routledge, 1994.

Stadtmiller, Mandy. "Life on the Me-List." *New York Post*, Feb. 19, 2009, 39.

Stallybrass, Peter, and Allon White. *The Politics and Poetics of Transgression*. Ithaca, NY: Cornell Univ. Press, 1986.

Stanley, Alessandra. "Cruel, Clueless and, for a Change, Female." *New York Times*, Feb. 1, 2007.

———. "Ellen, 'Idol,' and the Power of Niceness." *New York Times*, April 4, 2010.

———. "Still Biting the Hand that Feeds." *New York Times*, Oct. 15, 2009.

———. "Who Says Women Aren't Funny?" *Vanity Fair*, April 2008.

Stein, Joel. "Wanda Sykes Wants It All." *Time*, Nov. 8, 2004.

Stein, Ruthe. "Sarah Silverman—So Not PC, So Very Funny." *San Francisco Chronicle*, Nov. 18, 2005.

Steinberg, Jacques. "Miss Congeniality Wants the Oscars to Be Fun." *New York Times*, Oct. 5, 2006.

Sturtevant, Victoria. *A Great Big Girl Like Me: The Films of Marie Dressler*. Urbana: Univ. of Illinois Press, 2009.

Sykes, Wanda. *Yeah, I Said It*. New York: Atria, 2004.

Tasker, Yvonne. *Working Girls: Gender and Sexuality in Popular Cinema*. London: Routledge, 1998.

Tasker, Yvonne, and Diane Negra. "In Focus: Postfeminism and Contemporary Media Studies." *Cinema Journal* 44.2 (2005): 107–110.

———, eds. *Interrogating Postfeminism: Gender and the Politics of Popular Culture.* Durham, NC: Duke Univ. Press, 2007.

———. "Introduction: Feminist Politics and Postfeminist Culture." In *Interrogating Postfeminism.* Ed. Tasker and Negra, 1–25.

Taylor, Ella. *Prime-Time Families: Television Culture in Postwar America.* Berkeley: Univ. of California Press, 1989.

Teinowitz, Ira. "'SNL' Playing a Role." *Television Week*, Oct. 27–Nov. 3, 2008, 3–4.

Theweleit, Klaus. *Male Fantasies. Vol. One: Women, Floods, Histories, Bodies.* Trans. Stephen Conway. Minneapolis: Univ. of Minnesota Press, 1987.

Thompson, Deborah. "Calling All Fag Hags: From Identity Politics to Identification Politics." *Social Semiotics* 14.1 (2004): 37–48.

Tillman, Aaron. "'Through the Rube Goldberg Crazy Straw': Ethnic Mobility and Narcissistic Fantasy in *Sarah Silverman: Jesus Is Magic.*" *Studies in American Humor* 3.20 (2009): 58–84.

Traister, Rebecca. "'30 Rock' Takes on Feminist Hypocrisy—and Its Own." *Salon*, Feb. 25, 2011.

———. "The End of the Hairy, Joyless Feminist." *Washington Post*, May 16, 2012.

———. "The Tina Fey Backlash." *Salon*, April 14, 2010.

Turner, Victor. *The Ritual Process: Structure and Anti-Structure.* Ithaca, NY: Cornell Univ. Press, 1969.

Van Meter, Jonathan. "Miss Tina Regrets." *Vogue*, March 2010, 458+.

Vavrus, Mary Douglas. "Putting Ally on Trial: Contesting Postfeminism in Popular Culture." *Women's Studies in Communication* 23.3 (2000): 413–429.

Wakeman, Jessica. "Exclusive Q&A: Diablo Cody Talks Megan Fox, Therapy, and Doing 'The View' with Courtney Love." *The Frisky*, Sept. 8, 2009.

Walker, Lisa M. "How to Recognize a Lesbian: The Cultural Politics of Looking Like What You Are." *Signs: Journal of Women in Culture and Society* 18.4 (1993): 866–891.

Walker, Nancy. "Toward Solidarity: Women's Humor and Group Identity." In *Women's Comic Visions.* Ed. June Sochen, 57–81. Detroit: Wayne State Univ. Press, 1991.

Walker, Rebecca. "Becoming the Third Wave." *Ms.*, Jan./Feb. 1992, 39–41.

Wallace, Kelsey. "Bridesmaids Revisited." *Bitchmedia* (blog), *Bitch Magazine*, May 13, 2011.

Ward, Elijah G. "Homophobia, Hypermasculinity, and the US Black Church." *Culture, Health, and Sexuality* 7.5 (2005): 493–504.

Warhol, Robyn R. *Having a Good Cry: Effeminate Feelings and Pop-Culture Forms.* Columbus: Ohio State Univ. Press, 2003.

Warhol, Robyn R., and Helena Michie. "Twelve-Step Teleology: Narratives of Recovery/Recovery as Narrative." In *Getting a Life: Everyday Uses of Autobiography.* Ed. Sidonie Smith and Julia Watson, 327–350. Minneapolis: Univ. of Minnesota Press, 1996.

Warner, Michael. *Fear of a Queer Planet: Queer Politics and Social Theory*. Minneapolis: Univ. of Minnesota Press, 1993.

Watkins, Mel. *On the Real Side: Laughing, Lying, and Signifying—The Underground Tradition of African-American Humor that Transformed American Culture*. New York: Simon and Schuster, 1994.

Weber, Brenda. *Makeover TV: Selfhood, Citizenship, and Celebrity*. Durham, NC: Duke Univ. Press, 2009.

Weiner, Jennifer. "'How I Stay Strong and Centered': The Real Reason Ellen DeGeneres Looks So Amazing at Age 52." *Shape*, May 2010, 59+.

Weiner, Marc A. *Richard Wagner and the Anti-Semitic Imagination*. Lincoln: Univ. of Nebraska Press, 1995.

Weiss, Andrea. *Vampires and Violets: Lesbians in Film*. New York: Penguin, 1993.

White, Rosie. "Funny Women." *Feminist Media Studies* 10.3 (2010): 355–358.

Williams, Mary Elizabeth. "Is Olivia Munn Too Sexy for 'The Daily Show'?" *Salon*, June 25, 2010.

Wiltz, Teresa. "Coming up in the World: D-List Brings Her A-Game." *Washington Post*, Sept. 25, 2008.

Witchel, Alex. "Low-Key Writer Brings Bite to 'SNL': Tina Fey Adds Fresh Comedy." *Houston Chronicle*, Dec. 9, 2001.

Wojcik, Pamela Robertson. "Mae West's Maids: Race, 'Authenticity,' and the Discourse of Camp." In *Hop on Pop: The Politics and Pleasures of Cultural Studies*. Ed. Henry Jenkins, Tara McPherson, and Jane Shattuc, 287–299. Durham, NC: Duke Univ. Press, 2002.

Wong, Curtis M. "Ellen DeGeneres' JC Penney Partnership Slammed By Anti-Gay Group One Million Moms." *Gay Voices* (blog), *Huffington Post*, Feb. 1, 2012.

Wright, Pike. "Essay of Borat and Sarah Silverman for Make Benefit of Cultural Learnings about Racism." *This Magazine*, Jan.–Feb. 2007, 42–43.

Zacharek, Stephanie. "Baby Mama." *Salon*, April 23, 2008.

———. "Sarah Silverman: Jesus Is Magic." *Salon*, Nov. 15, 2005.

Index

Italic page numbers indicate photographs.

251

16, 18; and stand-up, 111–112, 228–
229n13. *See also* Jewish identity
Jewish identity, 43, 44, 199; abjection of,
and comedy, 111, 222n7; compared/
contrasted with African American
identity, 113; and Sarah Silverman, 11,
97, 98, 99, 109, 110–116, 117, 161, 184.
See also anti-Semitism
The Jew's Body (Gilman), 113, 228n11
Jezebel.com, 86, 87
Jezebel stereotype. *See* African Ameri-
can female stereotypes
Johnson, Lakesia, 169
Johnston, Jay, 99
Jolie, Angelina, 211
Jones, Jenny, 14, 201
Judging Amy (1999–2005), 79
Juno (2007), 11–12, 80

Kaling, Mindy, 11, 20
Kantor, Jodi, 232n3
Kaplan, Erin Aubry, 170
Karlyn, Kathleen Rowe. *See* Rowe,
Kathleen
Karpel, Ari, 185
Kathy Griffin: My Life on the D List
(2005–2010), 2, 31, 32–35, 36, 37, 39,
40, 41, 42, 44, 45, 46, 47, 48, 58, 153,
231n18
Keaton, Buster, 21, 22
Keaton, Diane, 21
Kibler, M. Alison, 18–19
Kidman, Nicole, 26, 32, 52, 55, 56
King, Geoff, 104
Klausner, Julie, 12
Knocked Up (2007), 20
Krakowski, Jane, 27, 62, 69, 79
Kristeva, Julia, 31, 223n2
Krutnik, Frank, 21
Ku Klux Klan, 113, 118, 231n15
Kunis, Mila, 18

Ladies Home Journal, 191, 202, 218
Lady Gaga, 8, 9. *See also* Gaga feminism

Lagerfeld, Karl, 231n15
Lampanelli, Lisa, 2, 17
Lander, Christian, 51
Late Night with Conan O'Brien (1993–
2009), 93, 117
Lathan, Sanaa, 23
Latifah, Queen, 201
Lauper, Cyndi, 144
Laurel and Hardy, 20
Lear, Norman, 118
Lebowitz, Fran, 12
Lee, Rachel, 129, 133, 142, 229n3,
231nn13,15
Lee, Shayne, 161, 163, 181, 182, 185, 187
Lee, Spike, 115
Leibovitz, Annie, 3, 5, 10, 70–71
Leitch, Will, 117
Lemon, Liz, 62–63, 66–70, 72–90.
See also Liz Lemonism
Leno, Jay, 42, 54, 55, 189, 190
lesbians and lesbian identity: black, 20,
180, 185–186, 232n8; butch, 16, 209;
and children, 46; and Ellen De-
Generes, 28, 51, 188, 191, 192, 194,
195–200, 202–204, 206, 207, 210, 211,
212–213, 215–216; femme, 16, 52, 146,
195, 206, 209; humor of, characterized as "masculine," 1, 16; and Kathy
Griffin, 46–47, 55, 57, 145, 223n5;
and Sarah Silverman, 96–97; and
Wanda Sykes, 28, 158, 163, 164–165,
182–183, 185–188
Lewis, Jerry, 20, 29, 103
Lewis, Paul, 92
Limbaugh, Rush, 7, 12, 165, 177
liminality, 218, 224n8; and comedy,
24, 40; of Ellen DeGeneres's celebrity, 206; and Kathy Griffin, 26, 34,
38–41, 51, 58, 223n1; and Margaret
Cho, 144; of the outsider or misfit,
21, 26, 38, 77; of sidekicks, 21, 38, 40;
and Tina Fey/Liz Lemon, 71, 77; of
the unruly woman, 23; vaudeville and
burlesque as, 18